PROFESSIONAL INTERIOR PLANTSCAPING

By
Barbara L. Collins, M.S.

ISBN 1-58874-141-9

Published by

Stipes Publishing L.L.C
204 W. University Ave.
Champaign Illinois 61820

Dedication

This book is dedicated to the hard working, often little recognized, professional interior plantscapers and their educators.

Acknowledgments

I would like to thank the College of DuPage and all the businesses that allowed me to take pictures of the plants. Thanks goes to the nurseries and greenhouses for their helpful assistance. My deep gratitude to Professor Floyd A. Giles for his guidance (as well as for his illustration on subirrigation in this book). I especially wish to thank my husband, Chuck, who was my unofficial editor and organizer. Without his help, this book would still be in my dreams.

Table of Contents

Introduction

This book is designed to develop, clarify and enrich the useful knowledge a professional interior plantscaper needs to achieve sucessful plant care and selection in commercial, governmental and leisure environments. The content comes from my years working in the industry and reflects ten years of teaching interior plantscaping at the College of DuPage; Glen Ellyn, Illinois. Needless to say, I encourage professors of ornamental horticulture to consider this book as a text or supplemental material for their plant interiorscape program.

After a brief history of indoor plant use, the key plant physiological factors are discussed in Chapter 2. Next, plant care maintenance needs and the technology to successfully satisfy those needs is presented in Chapter 3.

Chapter 4 reveals the key features of the major plant families and plant groups that dominate the interior plantscape market, while Chapter 5 addresses the range of effective plants on an individual basis.

My hope is that this book will help you more efficiently maintain your interior plant habitat and to choose with greater precision replacement plants that are esthetically pleasing, easier to maintain and long-lived.

Aechmea fasciata
silver vase plant   p. 29

Aeschynanthus lobbianus
lipstick plant   p. 30

Aglaonema spp. 'Stripes'
p. 32

Aglaonema spp. 'Jewel
of India'   p.33

Alocasia x amazonica
'Argentea'   p. 34

Alpinia zerumbet 'Variegata'
variegated shell ginger   p. 35

Anthurium x cultorum 'Paula'
p. 36

Aphelandra squarrosa 'Dania'
zebra plant   p. 38

Araucaria heterophylla
Norfolk Island pine p. 77

Asparagus densiflorus 'Meyersii'
Myers fern   p. 40

Aspidistra elatior 'Variegata' &
(background) 'Milky Way'   p. 41

Aucuba japonica 'Variegata'
gold dust plant   p. 41

Bambusa vulgaris 'Striata'
feathery bamboo   p. 42

Bamboo canes & *Hedera canariensis*
Algerian ivy   p. 42, 93

Beaucarnea recurvata
ponytail palm   p. 42

Begonia x *hiemalis*
Rieger begonia   p. 43

Begonia x *rex-cultorum* 'Escargot'
rex begonia   p. 44

Bougainvillea spp. 'Harrisii'
p. 45

Bucida buceras
black olive   p. 46

Caladium x *hortulanum* 'Carolyn
Whorton' fancy-leaf caladium p. 47

Plate 2

Calathea spp. 'Medallion' p. 48

Caryota mitis fishtail palm p. 49

Chamaedorea elegans parlor palm p. 50

Chamaedorea seifrizii reed palm p. 50

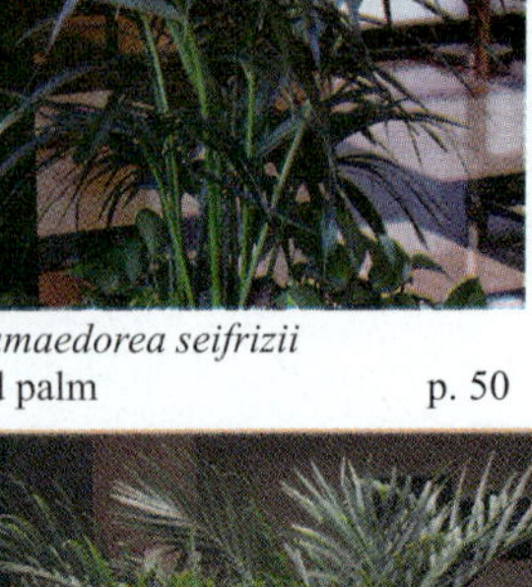

Chamaedorea erumpons bamboo palm p. 51

Chlorophytum comosum 'Vittatum' spider plant p. 52

Spider plant, African violet, & kalanchoe p. 52, 134, 103

Chrysalidocarpus lutescens areca palm p. 53

Chrysanthemum x *morifolium* decorative mum p. 54

Chrysanthemum x *morifolium* daisy mum p. 54

Chrysanthemum x *morifolium* & *Neoregelia carolinae* p. 54, 111

Chrysanthemum x *morifolium* spoon mum p. 54

Cissus rhombifolia 'Ellen Danica' oak-leaf ivy p. 57

x *Citrofortunella mitis* 'Variegata' variegated calamondin orange p. 58

Codiaeum variegatum var. *pictum* 'Mammy' p.59

Cordyline terminalis 'Xerox' & *Alpinia zerumbet* 'Variegata' p. 60, 35

Crassula ovata & *C. ovata* 'Variegata' jade plants p. 61

Cryptanthus bivittatus 'Pink Starlight' & *Tillandsia* spp. p. 62, 150

Cycas revoluta sago palm p. 63

Cyclamen persicum 'Deep Rose Improved' p. 65

Dianthus spp. 'Whisper'
mini carnations   p. 66

Dieffenbachia spp.
'Camouflage'   p. 67

Dieffenbachia spp.
'Sparkles'   p. 67

Dizygotheca elegantissima
false aralia   p. 68

Dracaena deremensis
'Lisa'   p. 69

Dracaena deremensis
'Warneckii'   p. 70

Dracaena deremensis
'Lemon Lime'   p. 70

Dracaena deremensis
'Rikki'   p. 70

Dracaena fragrans 'Massangeana' corn plant p. 71

Dracaena fragrans 'Santa Rosa' corn plant   p. 71

Dracaena marginata
marginata   p. 72

Dracaena reflexa
'Song of India'   p. 74

Epipremnum aureum
'Marble Queen'   p. 75

Epipremnum aureum 'Neon'
pothos   p. 75

Erica persoluta 'Sachi'
heather   p. 76

Eucharis x grandiflora
Amazon lily   p. 76

Eugenia myrtifolia
eugenia   p. 77

Euphorbia milii 'Salmon'
crown of thorns   p. 78

Euphorbia pulcherrima
'Carousel' poinsettia   p. 80
Courtesy of Fischer USA

Euphorbia pulcherrima
'Jingle Bells 3' poinsettia   p. 82

Exacum affine
Persian violet   p.83

x Fatshedera lizei
aralia ivy   p. 84

Fatsia japonica
Japanese fatsia   p. 84

Ficus benjamina 'Jacqueline'
weeping fig   p. 85

Ficus benjamina
'Spire'   p.86

Ficus benjamina 'Indigo'   p. 86

Ficus benjamina 'Midnight'   p. 86

Ficus maclellandii 'Alii'   p. 86

Ficus binnendijkii
'Amstel King'   p. 86

Ficus pumila
creeping fig   p. 86

Ficus elastica 'Altissima'
rubber tree   p. 88

Ficus elastica 'Green Gem'   p. 88

Ficus elastica 'Tricolor'   p. 88

Ficus elastica
'Decora Burgundy'   p. 88

Ficus lyrata 'Compacta'
fiddle leaf ficus   p.89

Fittonia verschaffeltii
var. *argyroneura*   p. 90

Guzmania spp. 'Cherry'
p. 92

Guzmania spp. 'Puna Gold'
p. 92

Guzmania spp. 'Symphony Encore'
p. 92

Guzmania dissitiflora 'Major'
p. 92

Hedera helix 'Ann Ganie'
English ivy   p. 93

Hedera canariensis
Algerian ivy   p. 93

Heliconia illustris 'Golden Torch'
                                p. 94

Heliconia psittacorum 'Andromeda' parrot's beak   p. 94

Hemigraphis alternata 'Exotica'
waffle plant   p. 95

Hibiscus rosa-sinensis 'Jim Hendry'
                                p. 96

Hippeastrum spp. 'Rose Marie'
amaryllis   p. 98

Homalomena 'Emerald Gem'
                                p. 99

Homalomena 'Purple Sword'   p. 99

Howea forsteriana 'Keeline'
Kentia palm   p.100

Hoya carnosa 'Exotica'
variegated wax plant   p. 101

Hydrangea macrophylla, big-leaf hydrangia &
Begonia x *hiemalis,* Rieger begonia p. 102, 43

Kalanchoe blossfeldiana 'Tenflame'
                                p. 104

Ledebouria socialis
silver squill   p. 104

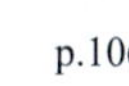

Leucospermum cordifolium
pincushion flower   p. 105

Lilium longiflorum
Easter lily   p.106

Liriope muscari &
Phalaenopsis hybrids   p. 107, 118

Livistonia chinensis
Chinese fan palm   p. 107

Maranta leuconeura var. *kerchoviana*
rabbit's tracks   p. 108

Maranta leuconeura var.
erythroneura   p. 108

Plate 6

Monstera deliciosa
Swiss cheese plant   p. 108

Monstera adansonii
Swiss cheese plant   p.109

Musa acuminata 'Dwarf Cav-
endish' banana plant   p. 109

Neoregelia carolinae 'Flandria'
                         p. 110

Neoregelia carolinae 'Ultima'
                         p. 111

Nephrolepis exaltata 'Dallasii'
Dallas fern   p. 112

Nephrolepis cordifolia 'Duffii'
lemon button fern   p. 112

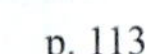
Adiantum raddianum
delta maidenhair fern   p. 113

Davallia mariesii var. *stenolepis*
squirrel's foot fern   p. 113

Platycerium bifurcatum
staghorn fern   p. 114

Pteris ensiformis 'Victoria'
Victoria brake fern   p. 114

Oxalis rubra
red-leaf oxalis   p. 115

Pandanus utilis
screw pine   p. 115

Pelargonium x *domesticum* 'Tiara'
Martha Washington geranium p. 116

Peperomia caperata
emerald-ripple peperomia   p. 117

Peperomia obtusifolia
baby rubber plant   p.117

Phalaenopsis 'Angel's Touch'
moth orchid   p. 118

Phalaenopsis 'The Queen'
moth orchid   p. 118

Sophrolaeliocattleya 'Dark Waters'
mini-cattleya   p. 119

Cymbidium 'Pink Diamond'
Cymbidium orchid   p. 119

Ludisia discolor
jewel orchid   p. 119

Miltonia 'Red Sky'
pansy orchid   p.119

Oncidium altissimum
butterfly orchid   p. 119

Paphiopedilum 'Green Goddess'
lady's-slipper orchid   p. 120

Philodendron spp. 'Autumn'
                                p. 121

Philodendron spp. 'Black Cardinal'
                                p. 121

Philodendron spp. 'Imperial Green'
                                p. 121

Philodendron spp. 'Moonlight'
                                p. 121

Philodendron spp. 'Prince of Orange'
                                p. 121

Philodendron scandens
susp. *oxycardium*   p. 122

Philodendron selloum 'Hope'
dwarf tree philodendron   p. 122

Philodendron selloum 'Xanadu'
dwarf tree philodendron   p. 122

Philodendron selloum
tree philodendron   p. 123

Phoenix roebelenii
pygmy date palm   p. 124

Pilea cadierei
aluminum plant   p. 125

Pilea involucrata
'Moon Valley'   p. 125

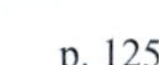

Plectranthus coleoides 'Marginatus'
white-edged Swedish ivy   p. 126

Podocarpus gracilior
weeping podocarpus   p. 127

Podocarpus gracilior
'Pyramid' & *Dieffenbachia*
'Camille'   p. 127, 67

Polyscias balfouriana 'Marginata'
variegated balfour aralia   p. 128

Polyscias guilfoylei
black aralia p. 128

Polyscias scutellaria
fabian or plum aralia p. 128

Polyscias fruticosa
Ming aralia p.129

Primula vulgaris 'Dana Mix'
English primrose p. 130

Radermachera sinica
China Doll p. 131

Rhapis excelsa
lady palm p. 132

Rhododendron simsii
magenta single azalea p. 132

Rhododendron simsii
pink double azalea p. 132

Rhododendron simsii
white double azalea p. 132

Rosa chinensis var. *minima*
miniature rose p. 133

Saintpaulia ionantha
African violet p. 134

Sansevieria trifasciata 'Laurentii' snake plant p. 135

Sansevieria trifasciata
'Silver Queen' p. 135

Schefflera actinophylla 'Amate'
Austrialian umbrella plant p. 136

Schefflera actinophylla
'Renegade' p. 136

Schefflera arboricola
Hawaiian schefflera p. 137

Schefflera arboricola 'Trinette'
variegated Hawaiian schefflera p.137

Schlumbergera truncata
crab or Thanksgiving cactus p. 139

Sedum pachyphyllum
jelly beans p. 139

Senecio cruentus
cineraria p. 140

Senecio rowleyanus
string of beads   p. 140

Sinningia speciosa 'Plum'
gloxinia   p. 141

Spathiphyllum spp. 'Domino'
peace lily   p.143

Spathiphyllum spp. 'Starlight'
peace lily   p. 143

Spathiphyllum spp.'Sensation'
peace lily   p. 143

Strelitzia nicolai, white
bird-of-paradise   p. 144

Strelitzia reginae
bird-of-paradise flower   p. 144

Streptocarpus saxorum
false African violet   p. 145

Syngonium podophyllum 'Exotic
Cream' nephthytis   p.146

Tolmiea menziesii
piggyback plant   p. 147

Veitchia merrillii
adonidia palm   p. 148

Washingtonia robusta
Washington palm trunk   p. 145

Vriesea spp. 'Asahii'
painted feathers   p. 149

Vriesea spp. 'Ella'
painted feathers   p. 149

Vriesea spp. 'Splenriet' &
Liriope muscari   p 149, 107

Yucca elephantipes
spineless yucca   p. 151

Zamia furfuracea
cardboard palm   p. 152

Zamioculcas zamiifolia
ZZ Plant   p. 152

Zantedeschia spp.
calla lily   p. 153

Zebrina pendula
wandering Jew   p. 154

Chapter 1
The History of Plant Interiorscape

Early History

As far back as recorded history, humankind has had a close relationship with plants. Between 1500 and 1000 B.C., the Sumerians, the Egyptians, the Minoans of Crete and the Chinese were growing useful and decorative plants in stone containers.

By 605 B.C., the Hanging Gardens of Babylon were built by King Nebuchadnezzar for his Median wife. At this time, Babylon was the largest and one of the most important cities of the ancient world. These gardens were on the rooftop and terrace of his royal palace. They consisted of ornamental gardens including trees, flowers, fruits, fountains and plants in stone containers. Clearly, this shows a strong connection between man, plants, wealth and position.

The ancient Greeks held an annual celebration every spring honoring Adonis, the god of the growing world. They planted lettuce and barley seeds around his statue and believed that germination represented Adonis' return. This idea of the "Adonis Garden" spread throughout the Mediterranean region and is still practiced today.

The Romans cultivated fruits, forced roses and grew unusual plants in stone containers in their inner courtyards. Here was an unroofed open area where the chimney flue released warm air. Adding a roof enclosure of thin sheets of mica or talc and eventually glass created the idea of a greenhouse.

During the Dark Ages (476 - 1000 A.D.), the monks in monasteries of Europe were the keepers of plants grown mainly for culinary and medicinal use. When castles were built in the Middle Ages, containerized plants were used for decoration. The Renaissance period of the fifteenth and sixteenth centuries brought plants to the forefront as an art form. This increased interest in learning about plants, especially exotic ones.

Wealthy merchants sailed the seas from the days of Christopher Columbus throughout the eighteenth century in search of exotic plants. By the 1670s, the Dutch built orangeries originally used to grow oranges and other tropical citrus trees but included exotic plants. These orangeries were masonry structures with many windows and were heated by stoves.

In England, the first attached orangery was constructed in 1710 designed by Talman and built for William Blaythwayt, a politician and ambassador. It had a flat, slate roof with glass windows. Inside grew trees in large tubs and ornamental plants.

A small scale portable terrarium, the Wardian case, was invented by a London surgeon, Dr. Nathaniel Ward in 1842. This was a sealed glass case, impervious to the elements yet allowed light to enter. Wardian cases allowed seafarers improved success in collecting plants. It soon became the rage in Victorian England and the United States.

Until 1845, England imposed a glass tax, restricting its use. After the repeal, gardeners were allowed to substitute glass for walls and winter gardens, greenhouses and conservatories began their ascent to popularity. Winter gardens were often public areas, greenhouses were strictly for growing and conservatories were rooms attached to county estates for leisure activities of the family, with the common purpose of housing tender plants.

In 1851, Sir Joseph Paxton designed the Crystal Palace, the Great Exhibition Building in Hyde Park, England. It was four thousand feet long and one hundred feet tall, all enclosed with glass. It was a celebration of the machine age which introduced improved techniques and new materials including the widespread use of metal framing material and large segments of glass. Inside, a row of lime trees complete with fruit grew. The Crystal Palace inspired local governments to create conservatories as a focal point in public parks. Soon, countries such as France and Germany built public winter gardens, usually financed by a commercial company, used as an educational and recreational exhibit. The influence of such great growing structures was felt throughout the world.

The United States also was caught up in the same rage. Conservatories, whether built in public parks or attached to wealthy estates, popped up everywhere. Architecture became most fanciful and decorative toward the end of the nineteenth century; Gothic, Moorish and Japanese styles were popular. Plants such as the Boston fern, the cast-iron plant and the parlor palm were found in many fashionable homes, hotels and other public areas. Window boxes and Wardian cases allowed more people to grow plants indoors.

Over the course of World War I and the Depression era, these great structures fell in disrepair; maintenance and fuel costs were exorbitant. Many were torn down. But the idea of capturing the energy of the sun to grow beautiful plants indoors, did not.

Modern History

Since World War II, women have entered the work force on a large scale. Correspondingly, plants have had an increasing presence in the work environment. Women especially (not to the exclusion of men) appreciate the positive benefits of bringing the plant world indoors.

By 1949, the interior plantscaping industry was just beginning with $13 million in wholesale value of foliage plants sold. Ten years later, the figure was doubled and increased steadily until 1976 when the value was $236 million.

In the mid-70s, the "plant boom" occurred in the United States. Why was the growth so spectacular then? Indoor malls and office atriums became popular. Office buildings had larger windows allowing higher light levels. Improvements in indoor climate control were developed. Women, again, entered the work force in record numbers and they demanded plants.

There also was a back to the earth movement which encouraged everyone to grow plants. Soilless mixes and new containers improved drainage and the ease of caring for plants indoors. Books, magazines, television as well as home decorators tout the value of beautiful, tropical plants even to this day.

By 1990, the industry had passed the half-billion mark and again, increased steadily.

In 1998, the interior plantscape industry installed $1.2 billion worth of plants used for the interior. This figure reflects about $503 million of foliage plants and $701 million of flowering containerized plants.

For 2000, the total sales were $1.4 billion. The division between foliage sales of $574 million and flowering plant sales of $781 million reflects the fact that using plants in the interior is more popular than ever. Foliage plants can be further divided into two groups: 1. Those in growing containers, sales total of $487 million, and 2. Those grown in hanging baskets, accounting for $87 million.

Flowering plants have steadily increased in use. The number of units sold of the top three are: 1. poinsettias (27%), 2. chrysanthemums (10%) and 3. azaleas (6%). Dollarwise, poinsettias account for 30% of total sales, mums for 13% and azaleas for 7%. Orchids accounted for 13% in the dollars spent; however; they account for only 4% of units sold. Other flowering plants such as *Kalanchoes, Cyclamen* and *Exacum* account for 53% of units sold and 37% of dollars spent.

Chapter 2
Important Physiological Factors for Successful Plant Management

Light

The most important factor in maintaining a successful and profitable interiorscape is matching the plant with the light available. Obviously, many interior locations have less than the desirable amount of light. Utilizing plants that tolerate lower light is the best way of handling those areas. The industry is always looking for new plants and cultivars to increase that market.

The law of limiting factors states that too much or too little of any one factor can limit the growth of a plant even if all other factors are at or near the optimum level required by that plant. And, light is the most important limiting factor in the interiorscape. It also is very difficult, short of installing supplemental lighting, to increase. So, the most important lesson is to match the plant to the proper environment. Too much light and the leaves will curl down, become pale and blister (often called sunburned) then turn brown at the leaf margins. Ultimately, the leaf will die and fall off. The condition is worsened when coupled with dry soil and high temperature. Not enough light, and the leaves may be smaller and thinner and the stems elongated due to the lengthening of the internodal spaces.

As the indoor climate is characterized by low light levels, careful adjustments must be made:

1. Gradually reduce watering. (Plants don't dry out as easily in low light.)
2. Reduce fertilizing or don't fertilize at all. (A lower rate of photosynthesis and growth occurs.)
3. If possible, reduce room temperature. (In general, low light plants prefer temperatures from 60-70° F. These lower temperatures also reduce the chances for spider mite infestation.)
4. If possible, increase humidity. (This also reduces the need for watering and prevents spider mites.)
5. Favor slow-growing plants as they require less light than fast-growing ones.
7. Plants with variegated leaves need higher light since they have less chlorophyll and need all the light they can get to photosynthesize. When placed in low light areas, the variegation tends to disappear (More chlorophyll must be manufactured.)

Next, we will take a deeper look at light as the most influential of plant health and maintenance factors.

Light Characteristics: intensity, quality and duration

Light Intensity refers to the amount of light per square-foot per hour. It is formally measured in foot-candles. We can categorize light intensity into three levels:

- **Low light intensity ranges from 50-100 foot-candles.**
- **Medium light intensity ranges from 101-300 foot-candles.**
- **High light intensity is greater than 300 foot-candles.**

An easy, practical way to determine light intensity:

1. Place a piece of white paper an inch or two under a leaf.
2. If you see a fuzzy but definite shadow, medium light levels are present.
3. If you don't see a shadow, then the area has low light levels.
4. A clearly outlined shadow indicates a high light level.

After some practice, interiorscapers will be able to judge the light level of an area accurately.

We may also use light meters to accurately measure intensity. When using a light meter, it's best to take several readings at various heights of the plant and then to calculate the average.

Another way to measure light intensity is to use a 35 mm camera with an aperture mode. Set the ASA to 100 and the aperture to f4. Check the camera's computer-determined shutter speed while focusing on a blank sheet of white paper placed a couple of feet in front of the camera. The light intensity is the reciprocal of the shutter speed (as an example, an exposure of 1/200 indicates 200 foot-candles).

When the sun is the main source of light intensity such as in an atrium, then it is affected by season (stronger in the summer), cloudiness and transparency of the glass. What if the overall intensity is too low? Then interiorscapers need to change plants frequently or use artificial plants.

Light Quality or Color. The blue spectrum is most efficient for photosynthesis; the red spectrum for chloroplast and hormone production. As all the necessary colors are included in sunlight, it is the most preferred light-source. Incandescent bulbs emit considerable red light and fluorescent bulbs are relatively deficient in red. An incandescent-fluorescent combination works well.

Light Duration. The duration of light or photoperiod for plants is twelve hours based upon their native habitat (usually near the equator). As total light equals intensity times duration, one can partially compensate for a decreased duration by a modest increase in intensity. In many typical professional situations the light duration is about eight hours a day and this chronic total light insufficiency creates a long-term stress. In the plant management industry, one tries not to have to replace plants more often than annually due to total light insufficiency.

Can I improve my plant by further increasing the intensity or duration of the light-source beyond the usual recommendations? First of all, most plants do not fare well if the client's light intensity is substantially different from the native habitat and some plants, for example poinsettias, need a full twelve-hour diurnal (daily) rest period in order to produce color. If we are so fortunate to have full total light sufficiency, will a slight increase be beneficial? It depends on whether we want to maintain the plant as it is or to encourage further growth. And this issue is addressed by the light compensation point.

Light Compensation Point. Photosynthesis is the process whereby plants use light or radiant energy from the sun to chemically convert water and CO_2 into glucose which the plant then uses as food with the release of oxygen. The reverse process whereby glucose and oxygen are used for energy is called respiration. When photosynthesis and respiration are equal, then the plant is existing at its light compensation point. When photosynthesis is greater than respiration, then the plant grows. When photosynthesis is less than respiration, then the plant declines. We try to keep the plant slightly above the light compensation point, in order to provide enough energy to replace yellowing foliage as it ages.

Light Acclimation or Shade Conditioning

A good interiorscaper understands the importance of proper light acclimation. This is a preventative health management program based on the knowledge that plants can adjust their internal structure and processes to maintain a healthy balance in various environments if given sufficient opportunity. Properly acclimated plants will be healthy plants.

A reputable grower will grow his plants in shade rather than in the open, sunny field. This is one reason why ficus trees that are "acclimated" or "shade-conditioned" are more expensive. A ficus tree grown under the bright sun with light intensities of over 10,000 foot-candles, will languish in an interiorscape as light intensities may be as low as 50 foot-candles. Unusually low-priced tropical plants are likely to be field grown.

Most plants are "shade-grown" or "shade-conditioned" under wood slatted lath roofs or sometimes loosely woven fabric. These provide from 30-90% shade and in the case of ficus plants 73% shade is used. After the plants achieve their optimal size in about three months, the plants are shipped to a holding facility where light is again reduced to 350-750 foot-candles for three or four weeks. During this time, the leaves actually undergo a physical change. Some leaves may drop which is normal. The new leaves that form will be thinner, longer and darker green. These are shade leaves, better adapted to low light. The old leaves will change, too.

Leaf thickness changes in low light for several reasons. The most important is the layer of cells in which photosynthesis occurs thins out. This palisades layer consists of tall, narrow cells which shorten and spread out creating the thin, long leaf. Other factors are a thinner epidermal or top layer of cells and thinner cell walls.

Within cells, chloroplasts increase in number resulting in a darker green leaf color. These chloroplasts have the ability to migrate and will disperse throughout the cell in order to capture more light energy. Within these chloroplasts, are grana structures where light energy reacts with chlorophyll. The grana resemble stacks of plates When exposed to high intensity light, the grana are upright and vertical along the outer wall of the chloroplasts. Under low intensity light, the grana have the ability to disperse throughout the entire chloroplast thus becoming more efficient. Finally, chlorophyll actually increases and may double as light levels decrease. These changes take from two weeks to two months, depending upon the plant species.

The internodal spaces between leaves on the branches also is increased. This contributes to an open, airy feeling, especially in ficus trees. So, look for this feature rather than tightly grown with small, thick leaves.

Final acclimation occurs at your chosen interiorscape. Start by placing the plant in a slightly higher light than its ultimate location to further acclimate it. Complete light acclimation is an ongoing process until every leaf has been changed or renewed.

Characteristics of Shade Leaves	**Characteristics of Sun Leaves**
Dark green color	Light green color
Large and thin	Small and thick
Few new leaves	Many new leaves
Leaves widely spaced	Leaves close together
Leaves held horizontally	Leaf held upright
Thin leaf petioles	Thick leaf petioles

Reverse Acclimation. Once foliage is acclimated to its final low light location, moving it to higher intensity light may result in leaf burn.

Plants for High Light Levels.

Cacti and many succulents such as *Crassula ovata*, jade plant and *Sedum* spp.
Beaucarnea recurvata, ponytail palm.
Yucca elephantipes, yucca plant.
Some palms such as *Caryota mitis*, fishtail palm; *Chrysalidocarpus lutescens*, areca palm and *Veitchia merrillu*, adonidia palm and other tall palms.
Alocasia x *amazonica*, alocasia.
Alpinia spp., ginger plants.
Bambusa spp., bamboo.
Bucida buceras, black olive.
x *Citrofortunella mitis*, calamondin orange.
Some *Ficus* species.
Hedera helix, English ivy.
Heliconia spp., lobster claw.
Kalanchoe blossfeldiana, kalanchoe.
Musa spp., banana plant.
Pandanus spp., screw pine.
Phoenix roebelenii, pygmy date palm.
Polyscias fruticosa, ming aralia.
Strelitzia spp., bird-of-paradise.
Zamia furfuracea, cardboard palm.

Plants for Medium Light Levels. Most other plants grow well in varying degrees of medium light levels. Contrary to popular belief, most palms used in the interiorscape natively grow as understory plants and are best suited for a medium light level, not high.

Plants for Unusually Low Light Levels— less than 50 foot-candles.

Aspidistra elatior, cast-iron plant
Epipremnum aureum, golden pothos plant
Sansevieria trifasciata, snake plant

Plants for Low Light Levels of 50 foot-candles.

Some *Aglaonemas*, Chinese evergreen plant
Chamadorea elegans, parlor palm, for temporary placement.
Ficus 'Spire', *F. maclellandii* 'Alii' and *F. binnendijkii* 'Amstel King' survive better than expected.
Most *Dracaena* plants.
Ficus 'Indigo', 'Midnight' and 'Midnight Princess'.
Homalomena survives but tends to become leggy.
Howea forsteriana, kentia palm.
Tolmiea menziesii, piggyback plant.
Philodendron scandens subsp. *oxycardium*, heart-leaf philodendron.
Spathiphyllum, peace lily.

Artificial Plants

We often laugh at the term, but there are times when artificial plants are very advantageous. Ideally, that dark location under a stairway or the high ledge in an atrium are not only hard to see but they are hard to reach for watering and grooming. In this case, artificial ivy or pothos plants work well.

In one situation, a boardroom that was located in a lower level without windows was used only once a month at the very most. The rest of the time, it was dark. The ficus trees were frequently replaced. The solution was to install high quality silk plants with preserved trunks.

There are several companies that sell botanically-correct and excellent quality fabricated and preserved trees and palms, silk or fiberglass plants[1]. So, rather than thinking of these non-living plants as our competitors, we should embrace them for special situations.

Temperature

Most interiorscapes are maintained at a temperature obviously comfortable for its human inhabitants, from 65 to 80° F. Night temperatures are often five to ten degrees lower. The majority of interior plants adapt well to those temperatures. Temperature is seldom a problem if changes are gradual and not far beyond the recommended range.

But, sometimes temperatures fluctuate more than is realized. Generally, temperatures lower than 50° F. and higher than 90° F. cause plant damage. When I worked in the interior industry, a row of *Aglaonema* 'Silver Queen' was placed near the sliding doors leading to an unheated parking garage. During an unusually cold snap in winter when the temperatures went below zero, the doors got stuck in the open position overnight. When I found the doors open the next morning, I knew those plants were damaged, even though they looked fine. I documented the incident and sure enough, within a week, the leaves turned pale green with the margins curling downward—due to damage of the top epidermal layer of cells— typical symptoms of chilling injury. Mature foliage on older plants are most often damaged. *Dracaenas* and *Dieffenbachias* are also very susceptible. This injury may also occur in the summer from air conditioning vents.

Heat injury occurs when temperatures are greater than 90° F. The plants wilt, lower leaves turn yellow and develop brown edges or tips and the older leaves may fall off. I remember talking with an interior plantscaper in Florida who said that heat injury can be a serious problem in buildings where the air conditioning is turned off for the weekend and the indoor temperatures soar. Palms seem to be best suited for these types of

---

[1]   Many of these artificial plants are available to twenty or more feet tall. The larger ones are easily installed in sections. The leaves are treated with ultraviolet stabilizers to prevent brittleness and color fading. Many plants are fire-retardant.

conditions and have minimum damage. It is important to water plants well if you anticipate heat injury problems. Transpiration helps cool plants off. Also, be careful of temperature conditions near heating vents and windows.

Cold-tolerant Plants—to at least 45° F.

Aglaonema 'Maria Christina', 'Rachel', 'Stripes'; Bay, Elite and Star of India Series

Araucaria heterophylla, Norfolk Island pine

Aucuba japonica, gold dust plant

Blechnum 'Silver Lady' fern

Chlorophytum comosum, spider plant

Cordyline terminalis, Hawaiian ti plant

Crassula ovata, jade plant

Cycas revoluta, sago palm

Dracaena deremensis 'Warneckii', striped dracaena, and 'Costarricana'.

Erica spp., heather

Euphorbia, with the exception of the poinsettia

x *Fatshedera lizei*, aralia ivy

Fatsia japonica, Japanese fatsia

Ficus 'Spire'

Ficus elastica, rubber tree

Hedera helix, English ivy

Howea forsteriana, kentia palm

Liriope muscari, liriope

Nephrolepis cordifolia 'Kimberly Queen' and 'Western Queen' fern

Platycerium bifurcatum, staghorn fern

Oxalis rubra, red-leaf oxalis

Phoenix roebelenii, pygmy date palm

Plectranthus australis, Swedish ivy

Podocarpus macrophyllus, podocarpus

Polyscias balfouriana, balfour aralia

Primula vulgaris, English primrose

Rhapis excelsa, lady palm

Schefflera spp.

Schlumbergera, holiday cactus and other cacti

Senecio cruentus, cineraria

Spathiphyllum 'Sensation', 'Sensation Jr.', peace lily

Tolmiea menziesii, piggyback plant

Yucca elephantipes, spineless yucca

Zamia furfuracea, cardboard palm

Zamioculcas zamiifolia, ZZ Plant

Heat-tolerant Plants— to at least 95° F.

Most of the true palms (in the Arecaceae family)

The tree ferns

Many cacti

Many of the *Alpinias*, ginger plants

Beaucarnea recurvata, ponytail palm

Cordyline terminalis, Hawaiian ti plant

Cycas revoluta, sago palm

Dracaena fragrans 'Massangeana', corn plant

Epipremnum aureum, golden pothos

Euphorbia, with the exception of the poinsettia

Ficus elastica, rubber tree

Nephrolepis spp., and other ferns

Phoenix roebelenii, pygmy date palm

Radermachera sinica, radermachera

Schefflera spp.

Sedum morganianum, burro's tail

Spathiphyllum 'Sensation', 'Sensation Jr.', peace lily

Syngonium podophyllum, nephthytis

Yucca elephantipes, spineless yucca

Zamia furfuracea, cardboard palm

Zamioculcas zamiifolia, ZZ Plant

Air Quality

Humidity. Relative humidity is the amount of moisture held in the air at a specific temperature. Interiors are often 25-50%, (20% or less in winter) but most plants can tolerate 25 % except for ferns and some thin leafed plants. Symptoms include brittle leaves or leaves with brown tips (tipburn). This is a difficult situation to change and in most instances, adequate soil watering will compensate for low humidity. Another effective method is to place plants close together in groups (mass plantings). Other ways to increase humidity are to add moisture through humidifiers, to employ water gardens and to place plants in trays filled with pebbles and water.

Hand misting increases humidity only while the moisture remains on the foliage, usually not more than thirty minutes. At that rate, it would need to be done every hour or two to be effective. Therefore, hand misting is not practiced by interiorscapers.

Gases. Without oxygen plant cells would die, but if light is adequate photosynthesis yields enough for their own needs. We breathe out carbon dioxide as one of our waste products and if our plants are growing, they are a net absorbers of carbon dioxide (and grow more vigorously when these carbon dioxide levels are higher than present in outside air).

Energy efficient office buildings as well as homes have been designed in recent years. These structures often have airtight construction, sealed windows and increased insulation. Because the air exchange with the outdoors is so often seriously diminished the number of indoor air pollutants is increased. Some of the most common are formaldehyde, benzene and carbon monoxide. Formaldehyde is very commonly used in insulation, pressed wood products and as a sizing agent for carpeting. Benzene is a solvent present in cleaning supplies, paint and plastics. Carbon monoxide gas results from faulty heating systems. Fumes from all of these may cause headaches, nausea, skin rashes, eye irritation and congestion. When health problems result from increased indoor air pollutants in these modern buildings, the situation is called sick building syndrome.

NASA under the guidance of Dr. B. C. Wolverton had conducted closed chamber tests since the 1970s whereby plant leaves, roots and soil have been proven to remove air pollutants. Some of the effective plants are aglaonemas, philodendrons, golden pothos and spider plants for removing formaldehyde. Bamboo palm, striped and red-edged dracaena, English ivy, peace lily, snake plant, chrysanthenum and gerber daisy best remove formaldehyde, benzene and carbon monoxide. Two large floor plants for every 100 square feet have been recommended. Further studies are ongoing.

Chapter 3
Plant Maintenance

Watering Requirements

The most common reason why plants die is overwatering. When in doubt, underwater. Roots require proper aeration in addition to proper moisture.

When to Water. When is the best time to water a plant? Just prior to the wilting[1] point when the color of the foliage might pale slightly or when the foliage looks like it may be starting to droop. These are the hardest signs to identify, but both are good indicators. Keeping records helps interiorscapers learn the watering requirements of each plant.

Soil probes are useful tools for checking the moisture level of the soil[2]. Probes have four or five notched openings placed an inch apart along the plastic or metal shaft. Just insert the soil probe as far into the growing container as possible, give it a ¼ turn and pull it out. Each notch brings a soil sample up with it. Examine the soil starting with the top notch and proceed downward. Most plants require a moderate moisture at the lowest levels.

1. If the soil is dry, it will be loose and will fall apart easily.
2. If it is moderate, the soil will be damp.
3. If it is moist, then the soil mass will drip water when squeezed.

My advice is to examine the soil using this soil probe tool. What you see is what you get! It is the closest simulation to the old "finger stick" method which is hard on the hands when servicing hundreds of plants. With table top gardens and small plants, the weight of the container can be used to indicate when to water.

An alternate tool is the moisture meter with a needle that measures from dry to wet soil. They are not always accurate because soluble salts can raise the reading significantly.

All plants have varying water needs, but basically, it's a matter of the amount of water and the frequency of watering. Watering depends upon the light intensity and how fast the plant grows. Other factors are: the size of the plant and the proportion of foliage, the amount and thickness of the roots, the size of the container, room temperature, and humidity.

The terminology used in this book is:

Dry: Water the soil thoroughly and allow it to fully dry between waterings.

Moderately dry: Water the soil thoroughly and allow it to dry out ¾ of the way down; the bottom ¼ should be slightly moist.

Moderately moist: Water the soil thoroughly and allow it to dry out ⅓ to ½ of the way down; the bottom ½ should be slightly moist.

---

[1]   Wilting may also be caused by high temperatures and low humidity, cold soil, and root necrosis.

[2]   While soiless mixes or other media are used for planting, for the sake of simplicity, the term "Soil" is used throughout this book. Soilless mixes are usually composed of 55-65% Canadian sphagnum peat moss. The rest of the components are composted softwood bark, coarse perlite, a wetting agent, limestone and nutrients.

Moist: Keep the entire soil mass slightly moist at all times.

How Much to Water. Water the entire soil mass until it percolates throughout the soil. Make sure water is not just running down the perimeter of the container. Listen for the sound of water trickling out of the bottom of the growing container. If interiorscapers are using an open decorative container, then the excess water drains out into a saucer. Be especially careful when watering a closed decorative container, one without drainage holes.

Signs of Overwatering. Wilting of leaves is the first sign. Check the moisture level of the soil. Look for older foliage that turns bright yellow. The new foliage is soft and pale yellow. Stem, root and crown rot represents advanced problems and the plants will not recover. If no improvement is made, then assume that the soluble salt buildup is high and treat accordingly.

Signs of Underwatering. Wilting of leaves is the first sign. Check the moisture level of the soil. The most common sign of serious underwatering is brown leaf tips (tipburn) most commonly occurring in the monocots (plants with long strappy foliage and parallel leaf venation). Dicots (plants with netted venation and round or elliptical shaped foliage) most often have evenly dried foliage with dry leaf margins, resulting in leaf drop. New growth dries up and is brown.

How to Water

For large areas, watering machines are used. These are pressurized so the water comes out easily. They come in different sizes from small which holds about eight gallons to the large size that holds about fifty gallons. Useful attachments such as watering wands with easy turn on/shut off valves and flexible spray heads are available.

In atriums and shopping malls, hoses with watering wands are the easiest to use. Try to use hoses during off hours when traffic is light. Any spills must be immediately wiped up and "Caution, Wet Floor" signs are useful.

For smaller areas, two-gallon watering cans are used.

Watering Hard to Reach Areas. Hanging baskets must be watered very carefully, especially if they are placed in offices above computers. Try using ice cubes or DriWater[3] in these and other hard to reach areas.

DriWater is a time release water product composed of 98% water and 2% food grade ingredients to form a semisolid clear gel. The flexible, sausage shaped, plastic enclosed tube is simply slit lengthwise and placed with the opening touching well watered soil. Soil bacteria break down the food grade ingredients that bind the water. Slowly, the gel returns to its liquid water state. The 9 oz. gel pack will provide water for three or four weeks in a six inch diameter growing container. DriWater is also a timesaver around the holidays when poinsettias are everywhere and for flowering plants such as hydrangeas which require constantly moist soils. Cover DriWater with moss, if necessary.

Subirrigation Systems. Although top-watering plants is most widely practiced in the industry, there is another method using subirrigation. Water is added to a reservoir located in the base of the container via a fill tube that extends from just inside the container at the soil level down to the reservoir.

All of these systems work in a similar fashion by using the soil's natural tendency to draw up water from the wet lower level to the dry upper level of soil. With interiorscapers checking and adding water every two to four weeks, time spent watering is decreased. More time is available for detecting problems and keeping foliage clean.

The plants benefit in many ways. As long as the reservoir has water in it, the soil moisture at any given level is constant, leading to a less stressed plant. Less stressed plants are healthy plants, thus reducing replacements which costs money, manpower and time.

Water soluble fertilizer may be added to the reservoir. Excessive soluble salts collect at the

---

[3]   The address is 50 Old Courthouse Square, Suite 606; Santa Rosa, CA 95404.

surface, where few roots grow. This top layer of soil may be replaced if necessary. With top-watering, salts are washed down to the roots.

The advantages of this efficient water delivery system seem overwhelming, but its adoption has been slow in the United States. The change-over period requires either (1) continuing to top-water the existing plants while replacing or adding new plants with subirrigation or (2) retrofitting the existing plant containers. The effect of this transition period is either (1) the benefit of decreased watering visits is precluded or (2) retrofitting requires "on-site" expertise and extra hours.

Another recurrent difficulty with the subirrigation systems, is the potential for overwatering. As will be evident after reading the following "Subirrigation Procedures" section, as long as there is any water in the reservoir, the plant will be correctly watered. But in many subirrigation systems it is possible to overfill the reservoir and flood the plant's soil. Safeguards that are completely practical, economic and free from water spillage or leakage have not been perfected.

Subirrigation Procedures.   When the subirrigated plant arrives, check the water level of the reservoir. (The immediate impulse is to top-water as the soil on the surface is dry. Don't water yet.) The amount left in the reservoir is monitored with an clear plastic tube with markings indicating how much water is left. This tube is placed in the fill tube and lowered into the bottom of the reservoir. Place your thumb over the open top of this straw-like tube, pull it out and note the water level.

One doesn't need to add water until the reservoir is empty, as the soil will draw up water just as well whether the tank is ¼ or ¾ filled. When refilling, knowing the total capacity of the particular reservoir helps to avoid overfilling.

Clients must also be educated when they notice scheduled visits occurring less often. They must be reassured that plants are healthy and quality is improved.

There are three basic systems[4] in use, fabric wick systems, the media wick systems and vacuum sensor systems.

Fabric Wick Systems. A simple fabric wick system is demonstrated by the Water Tech system. In this case, the unit consists of a plastic shell with a water reservoir at the base and a fabric wick which draws the water up to an absorbant pad in contact with the bottom of the growing container. A fill tube extends along the side.

This plastic shell is then placed into a decorative container. There is no retrofitting necessary and on an average, the water reservoir requires filling every two weeks.

Media Wick Systems. In this system, water is drawn up through a specific medium (such as perlite), then up through the soil. An example is the Mona Plant System which consists of a water reservoir with cups that extend from within the reservoir upward into the soil of the growing container. The cups are filled with a highly absorbent medium. A fill tube is attached to the reservoir. On an average, the water reservoir requires filling every three to four weeks.

---

[4]   The three examples are offered by Primescape Products, P.O. Box 710, Deerfield, IL 60015.

Vacuum Sensor Systems. An example of this system is the Controlled Watering Systems. When the soil begins to dry, a sensor notes this and opens the valve allowing water to be drawn upward from the reservoir. When the soil is sufficiently moist, the sensor closes the valve. On an average, the water reservoir requires filling every three to four weeks. Decorative containers with built in systems are also available.

Foliage Care

Our goal is to provide clients with attractive, good quality plants. Keeping the plants looking their best is both a business objective and reflects upon the professionalism of the interiorscape industry.

The Yellow Leaf. Frequently, one is urgently called about "a yellow leaf" from someone with a Chicken Little voice: "My plant is dying! My plant is dying!" Frankly, one yellow leaf is not a death knell, but once a leaf starts to turn yellow, it will never turn green again. So, with each visit, remove all leaves that have begun to turn yellow.

Leaves turn yellow for any number of reasons:
1. Insufficient light,
2. As a natural process of aging as new growth appears.
3. As a sign of overwatering.
4. Insufficient nitrogen, especially seen in high light areas.
5. Insects or disease.
6. Heat or chilling injury.

A good interiorscaper will be able to spot that leaf that is beginning to decline. Anticipating problems before they become evident is a skill that is learned through experience.

Cleaning Foliage. Cleaning the foliage is an ongoing task. Not only does a clean plant look its best, it also uses the light energy more efficiently. Cleaning also helps interiorscapers spot pests and disease at an early stage. A useful cleaning solution that is frequently recommended is:

1. Use a quart spray bottle.
2. Add ¼ tsp. of a mild dishwashing soap such as Dove or Ivory.
3. Then add 1 tbsp. of 70% isopropyl alcohol —rubbing alcohol.
4. Fill the container with water, mixing the ingredients.

For plants with large foliage, spray on the top and bottom sides. Use two sponges or Mini-Paws[5] (Each consists of a tube of polyester fabric with an open top and bottom designed to slide up over the wrist when not in use.)—one on the top and one on the underside of the leaf to clean. Gently pull the leaf through. For plants with small foliage, place the plant on a sheet of plastic larger than the width of the plant and spray well. Allow the solution to drip off the leaves, then shake the plant to remove any excess solution and let it dry. Place the plant back in its original spot.

While not an "approved pesticide," I have found the cleaning solution listed above to be quite effective at controlling plant pests and disease. It is thought the alcohol dries out the problem while the soap smothers it. When I used this alcohol and soap solution, I could clean off small populations of pests right under the noses of finicky office workers. They would even comment about how nice and clean the plants smelled!

Leaf Shine Products. Many leaves have a natural glossy leaf due to a waxy substance, cutin, in the top cuticle layer and using a leaf shine product is unnecessary. However, some clients prefer a slightly higher glossy appearance and then, it may be added to the above cleaning solution at ¼ the recommended strength. This adds enough of a shine without an artificial look. Always read the label; there are some plants that do not tolerate these products.

Feather Dusters. To use or not to—that is the question. Feather dusters do a thorough and speedy job removing loose dirt and dust from leaves, especially useful for plants with numerous, small ones. But for plants that are prone to pests and disease, they may spread these from

---

[5]   Plant Mini-Paws manufactured by Evergreen Interiors, 13027 Lakeview Granada Dr., Lakeside, Ca. 92040.

plant to plant. Disinfect feather dusters with a 10% bleach solution or the above alcohol and soap solution after every use, especially if problems are encountered.

Retractable ostrich feather dusters are considered to be the best. They collect and hold dust the best, and maintain their shape after disinfection.

Tipburn. Monocots, a classification of plants that have parallel veins and long, strappy leaves, frequently develop tipburn on mature foliage. It is characterized by brown or gray leaf tips inwardly followed by an area of yellow. It occurs less frequently with dicots (plants with netted venation and round or elliptical shaped foliage) and is characterized by similar leaf margins.

There may be several causes:

1. Allowing the soil to become too dry.
2. Low humidity.
3. Excessive soluble salts.
4. Toxic levels of fluoride. (See fluoride toxicity.)
5. Chloride toxicity, particularly noted in a swimming pool area.
6. Boron toxicity, if fertilized liberally with a fertilizer containing boron.

Note: Tipburn tends to get worse over time because of the accumulations of causes #3 through #6.

Plants Less Prone to Tipburn.

1. Monocots with leathery, fibrous foliage are less inclined to having damage occur to their leaves. *Beaucarnea recurvata*, ponytail palm and *Yucca elephantipes*, yucca plant are two examples.
2. Dicots, in general, and improved cultivars such as the 'Amate' umbrella plant and many cultivars of *Ficus*, weeping fig.
3. Those plants with thick, succulent foliage such as *Crassula ovata*, jade plant and *Sansevieria trifasciata*, snake plant.
4. Many of the euphorbias—plants with thick foliage well adapted for arid areas. They contain a milky sap and the flowers are surrounded by colorful bracts. Examples are *Codiaeum variegatum* var. *pictum*, croton plant and most members of the *Euphorbia* genus.

5. The cycads, *Cycas revoluta*, sago palm and *Zamioculcas zamiifolia*, ZZ Plant.
6. Most succulents.

Trimming and Removing Foliage. There are two ways to remove dried leaf tips. For plants with wide, strappy foliage such as the corn plant, gently fold the leaf in half at the tip along the midrib. Using scissors, cut the brown tip off on an acute angle, creating a new leaf tip. A disadvantage is that you are creating a new area of necrosis with that cut and ultimately, you'll need to recut the tip.

The other solution is to remove the entire leaf at its base. This method must be done with discretion or you may end up with a leafless cane. Sometimes, a combination of both methods is best. Always disinfect scissors after use.

Pruning Stems and Branches. Succulent stems are easy to remove with a good pair of plant scissors. These scissors should have a notch at the base in order to hold the stem in place.

Ficus trees and other woody plants require the use of high quality pruners to remove branches. Small foldable saws are also available for larger branches. Always disinfect tools after use.

Phototropism. Plants are phototropic (will grow toward peak light), and uneven growth occurs on those plants that are close to a window or such a light source. Give the container a quarter turn clockwise every week.

Soil Care

The Container Effect. Because of the force of gravity, the bottom soil is wetter than that near the surface; often too wet for roots to live (root cells need oxygen, too). This situation is called the container effect and contributes to plant demise. We can counter this effect by increasing the holding power of the upper layers of soil relative to the lower layers of soil. Particles of smaller size have more surface area relative to their volume and thus have more surface tension, or water holding power, than the equivalent volume of larger size soil particles.

Using soil constituents in the upper soil levels that because of either their smaller particle size or stronger surface adherence can balance the downward force of gravity and yield a more evenly moist soil.

We can ascertain if we have a problem by checking the moisture level at various depths of the container soil. Placing coarser texture medium amendments such as perlite or vermiculite near the bottom of the container will decrease the pull on the container's water relative to the upper soil layers and restore the water balance that, on Earth, gravity has upset.

An additional advantage of the aforementioned lower container soil amendments is increased pore space facilitating excellent root areation and total container drainage. Purchasing plants from reputable and skilled establishments where issues of water balance and depth-dependent soil constituents have been accounted for will save us the heartache and the time to remedy the container effect.

Fertilizers—How much and how often? The second leading cause of plant death is overfertilization. Many people feel if a little bit is good, a lot is better. Not so in the interiorscape. First of all, consider the location of the plant. We know that most interior plants are placed in low light areas. Low light means less water and less fertilization.

Next, look at the purpose of the plant. It probably fits perfectly in its given location. Therefore, we don't want it to grow and limiting fertilizer facilitates this goal.

From approximately October through March, most plants are not actively growing, so don't ever fertilize during those months. When new growth begins in the spring, then it's time to consider fertilizing. If a plant looks healthy, then don't fertilize. On the other hand, some plants actively growing and in bright light may need a second fertilizer treatment in summer. Use ¼ of the recommended amount of fertilizer. While most fertilizers come in a 1-1-1 balance, I personally recommend a 3-1-2 balance such as Peter's 24-8-16 Tropical Foliage Fertilizer[6]. This product is also essentially fluoride-free and very low in boron which helps prevent tipburn.

Types of Fertilizers. With the water-soluble type fertilizer, nutrients are immediately available to the plant. Make sure plants are well watered. Measure the liquid or granules and add to the water. Mix well. Application amounts are only approximate and judgment is based on experience (sometimes painfully earned).

Slow release pellets coated with plastic or sulfur are another delivery system. They gradually release fertilizer over a six to eight month period. One disadvantage is that a substantial rapid release of nutrients is not available for immediate deficiencies or growth needs.

Helpful hints: As a plant matures, its fertilizer needs decrease. For long-lived trees such as *Ficus*, after many years fertilizers tend to acidify the soil requiring the addition of an amendment such as lime.

Soluble Salts. Conservative use of fertilizer minimizes soluble salt buildup. The reactions of the fertilizer with the soil generate sodium chloride, calcium carbonate (calcite) and iron sulfides. These byproducts (salts) burn the feeder roots and root hairs. They prevent the plant from absorbing water, so the symptoms are the same as those of underwatering. These include: wilting of leaves, tipburn, dry leaf margins, leaf drop, and eventual plant death.

Softened water also contributes to soluble salt buildup. Check with the building's engineering department as to whether the water is softened. Oftentimes, just the hot water is softened so use the cold water.

Another indication of salt buildup is when the salt is visible on the mulch. The treatment for excessive soluble salt buildup is leach irrigation. After leaching, replace the mulch (while the excessive salt is gone, the mulch is forever stained).

Leach Irrigation. Certainly, there are times when this chore must be done. I recommend to team up with someone on a nice day in the early fall. Take the plants outdoors. Use a garden hose and spray the soil gently until the water draining out is clear.

---

[6]   The address is: The Scotts Company; Marysville, Ohio; 43041.

If done indoors, allow the water to drain through the soil and collect in the saucer, if an open decorative container is used. Use a turkey baster to remove the leachate collected in the saucer. For closed decorative containers, the leached water must be pumped from the bottom.

Fluoride Damage. Fluoride damage is similar to soluble salt damage. The foliage of monocots (plants with parallel venation on long, strappy leaves) develops unsightly tipburn. Dicots (plants with netted venation and round or elliptical shaped foliage) most often have evenly dried foliage with dry leaf margins. Toxic levels of fluoride (F⁻) develop in time from watering with water with levels above one to two parts per million unless the fluoride is removed by leach irrigation. Also, the fluoride in fertilizers contribute to the buildup.

Normal Soil Compaction. After a plant is on an account for awhile, the top inch of soil seems to disappear and more soil should be added. Carefully, cut open the plastic bag of soil and add some. Sometimes, a bit of soil ends up on the carpeting or floor. An easy way to pick it up is to use your plastic ID card. Place the long end on an angle and scrape up the soil. It's so easy and quick—no one will ever know you spilled!

Easy to Maintain Plants. Interiorscapers are always looks for interesting easy-care plants. Easy-care plants are durable and tough plants that are able to stand up to a certain amount of abuse. They usually have thick, leathery or succulent foliage. Temperature fluctuations, low humidity, ability to tolerate being bumped into by carts or luggage, as well as being moved most often by housekeeping or the setup crew, are factors that make these favorites.

1. Many plants in the araceae or arum family, including *Aglaonema*, *Dracaena* and *Epiprumnum*, golden pothos.
2. The improved *Ficus* cultivars.
3. The improved *Schefflera* cultivars.
4. *Kentia forsteriana* 'Keyline' and other palms.
5. The cycads, *Cycas revoluta*, sago palm and *Zamioculcas zamiifolia*, ZZ Plant.
6. Succulents in the crassulaceae family such as *Crassula ovata*, jade plant.

7. Typical hanging basket plants such as: *Plectranthus australis*, Swedish ivy; *Tolmiea menziesii*, piggyback plant; and *Zebrina pendula*, wandering Jew.
8. *Aspidistra elatior*, cast-iron plant; *Beaucarnea recurvata*, ponytail palm; *Hoya carnosa*; *Podocarpus* spp.; *Sansevieria trifasciata*, snake plant and *Yucca elephantipes*, yucca plant.
9. All of the bromeliads.
10. Flowers include *Chrysanthemum* x *morifolium* and *Kalanchoe blossfeldiana*.

Replacement. Replacing plants is an ongoing responsibility. The time to order a replacement is when a plant begins to decline. If the same kind of plant keeps on being replaced without success, suggest a different kind of plant. Creative input is often welcomed. As always, consider the light level as most important.

Plants for Narrow Spaces.

1. Plants grown on totems, columns and pyramids.
2. *Ficus* 'Midnight' and 'Spire'; *Ficus lyrata* 'Suncoast' and 'Suncoast Compacta', fiddle-leaf fig.
3. *Dracaenas* such as *D. fragrans*, corn plant; *D. deremensis* 'Compacta' and 'Lisa'; *D. reflexa*.
4. *Podocarpus macrophyllus* 'Maki' and *P. gracilior* 'Pyramid'.
5. *Polyscias fruticosa*, parsley aralia and *P. guilfoylei*, black aralia.
6. *Sansevieria trifasciata*, snake plant.
7. *Schefflera* 'Renegade'.
8. *Spathiphyllum*, those which are upright growers including 'Sensation Jr.'.

Foliage vs. Flowering Plants. Foliage plants typically last a year while flowering plants last from two to four weeks. Foliage come in a variety of size, color and texture variation, while flowering plants have dramatic and colorful blossoms. Therefore, a mainstay of foliage plants with a focal point of flowers is a good objective. (Usage of cut flower arrangements is limited by their expense, short-life, and high maintenance needs. Normally, cut flowers are replaced every five to seven days and the water should be changed every three to five days.)

Choosing Foliage Plants. Foliage plants are sold by the diameter of the growing container. The 8, 10, 14, 17-inch sizes are quite standard. The 12-inch size is less common as is 21-inches. Typical hanging baskets are 8, 10 and 12-inch sizes. The 2 ½, 4 and 6-inch sizes are suited for underplantings, small area groundcover and as table top plants. Larger than 21-inches are sometimes available or able to be ordered. Bare root and balled-and-burlapped trees are also special order items.

When choosing tall plants, measure the height to make sure they will fit. Comparing the height of plants in different container sizes occasionally reveals similar heights. The difference is in the plants per pot (ppp).

Consider plants with unusual shapes, colors, trunk forms, patterned and textured foliage. Exciting new plants are coming to the market all the time. Good wholesalers also enjoy seeking out new offerings and honoring requests for special plants. Keep your eyes opened and be choosy.

Choosing Flowering Plants. Flowering plants are sold by the diameter of the growing container, also. The 6, 6 ½ and 8-inch sizes are standard. The 4 and 4 ½-inch sizes are also available. The difference in the half inch means that more plants are in each container. While available in the 10 and 12-inch sizes, hanging basket are used less frequently. Miniature flowering plants are in the 2 ½ to 3-inch sizes.

Many flowering plants are now available year-round. Some are seasonally available such as poinsettias. Growers that allot more bench space per plant have plants with more flowers because the plant's foliage is fuller. Upright plants indicate that those were grown too close together, probably to save costs.

For many plants, select those with many individual stems. Chrysanthemums have twenty or more "sticks" as they are called. Other plants are single stemmed but have many branches such as the azalea. The grower was responsible to pinch off early growth forcing the azalea to branch well. Look for many blooms and buds showing color. It's not a bad idea to order a couple of extra flowering plants. Use the best looking plants and then you'll have replacements, if necessary.

Most flowering plants are simply discarded after use. However, the rebloomers such as cyclamen are often sent to nursing homes.

Flower Rotation Programs. Flowering plants are replaced according to the contract between the client and the interior plantscaping company. Intervals are:

1. A two-week program with twenty-six rotational replacements per year.
2. A three-week program with seventeen rotational replacements per year.
3. A four-week program with thirteen rotational replacements per year.
4. A three to six month program with four to two rotational replacements per year. (See Bromeliads in Chapter 4.)
5. Only for specific events.
6. Combinations of the above.

Foliage Plants with Colorful Foliage. As an economical replacement for flowering plants, foliage plants with colorful foliage may be substituted.

Aglaonema cultivars, Chinese evergreen.
All bromeliads.
Caladium x *hortulanum*, caladium.
Codiaeum variegatum var. *pictum*, croton.
Cordyline terminalis cultivars, Hawaiian ti plant.
Dieffenbachia spp.
Philodendron spp.

Others to consider are those plants with variegated or other colored foliage:

Alocasia spp.
Alpinia zerumbet 'Variegata', variegated shell ginger, other gingers and gingerlike plants.
Aucuba japonica 'Variegata', gold dust plant
Blechnum 'Silver Lady' fern
Calathea, *Maranta* and *Stromanthe*
Chlorophytum comosum, spider plant
Variegated *Dracaena* cultivars, such as *D. reflexa* 'Song of Jamaica'
Epipremnum aureum cultivars
Eucharis grandiflorum, Amazon lily
Variegated *Ficus* cultivars
Variegated *Heliconia* spp.
Ledebouria socialis, silver squill

Oxalis rubra, red-leaf oxalis
Plectranthus spp., variegated Swedish ivy
Sansevieria trifasciata, snake plant
Variegated *Schefflera actinophylla*, Hawaiian
   schefflera
Spathiphyllum, peace lily
Syngonium podophyllum, nephthytis
Zebrina pendula, wandering Jew
Smaller plants such as: *Begonia rex-cultorum*,
   rex begonia; *Dracaena surculosa*, gold
   dust dracaena; *Fittonia* spp., red-nerve
   plant; *Hoya* cultivars, wax plant;
   Hemigraphis alternata 'Exotica', waffle
   plant; *Hypoestes phyllostachya*, polka dot
   plant; *Peperomia* spp.; *Pilea cadierei*, aluminum plant; *Pteris* spp., brake fern.

Care of New Arrivals. After plants are ordered, check with the wholesaler when the delivery will take place. Ask their driver to page you upon arrival or try to meet at the loading dock.

1. Check the invoice for correct plants.
2. If plants are boxed, check that the boxes are intact.
3. If plants are sleeved, remove the funnel shaped paper sleeves.
4. Check the plant for proper size, both in height and diameter of container.
5 . Quickly, inspect the plants for damage or unacceptable conditions including crushed or bruised foliage, broken stems, or loose *Dracaena* canes.
6. Approve the order by signing the invoice.

Preparation for Installation. Once the plants are in the building, there usually is a designated workroom where plants can be cleaned and prepared for installation.

1. Check the plant carefully. Remove damaged leaves.
2. Check for signs of insects and disease.
3. Clean foliage.
4. Make sure the soil level is adequate.
5. Sometimes, an handful of slow release fertilizer is added to the top of the soil before delivery. Remove excess.

Ideally, new plant arrivals should be isolated for a couple of weeks in order to discover possible pest problems. Frankly, when plant replace-ments arrive, they are installed immediately because of time, space and lighting realities. So, check for problems extra carefully for the first few weeks.

Decorative Containers. There are two types of containers: open and closed. Open containers have drainage holes with a saucer underneath and are often made of terra cotta clay. The saucer should be plastic in the same color. Because clay saucers are porous and can leak, use them only on a cement floor such as in a swimming pool area.

Most decorative containers are closed—without drainage holes—and extra care must be taken when watering. They are most often made of ceramic and are elegant, expensive and heavy. Check the underside. If it is porous, a protective, waterproof liner or disk must be placed inside or underneath to prevent damage.

The two ceramic finishes are glossy and satin (matte). The color range is wide including navy blue and sage green to iridescent copper-green and marbled colors. Imported ceramics, pottery, and stoneware are available as specialty items that match specific decors. Lightweight fiberglass resembling ceramic also comes in all colors and finishes to reflect decorating trends.

Terra cotta containers range from low-cost and casual to expensive and elegant. A particular disadvantage of terra cotta is weight. Fiberglass/resin containers and polyurethane foam containers can be made to look like terra cotta. They also can simulate gray stone or granite.

Attractive metal containers are expensive and heavy to move. Plastic containers with metal finishes provide an effective alternative.

As far as shape is concerned, the obvious round shape, with its many variations, is most common in free standing containers. Square, rectangular, half round, flat bottom bowls and pedestal planters are also used. Some decorative combinations complete with wooden or metal stands are another option.

Hanging basket shapes come with rounded bases or as cylinders. Rectangular shelf planters used in many offices and wall mounted rectangular containers are also available.

Double Potting. Double potting is the most common method used for final installation. Plants remain in their growing container and are inserted into a decorative container. All signs of the growing container are covered.

Other Staging Materials. When double potting, the rim of the growing container should be one inch below the rim of the decorative container. It usually is not too high, but if it is, trim the excess. It's often too low, so place the growing container on top of a styrofoam block and disk. These disks are available in different diameters and thickness. This will also elevate the growing container out of any potential standing water.

A gap is created between the two containers. It is easily filled with a flexible foam spacer. This spacer is available in various lengths and has tape on one edge covered with a protective paper. For most cases, leave the tape covered. It's much easier to replace the plant when the collar is not stuck onto the side.

The last step is to cover the soil surface with decorative mulch. Mulches are aesthetically pleasing and hold in some moisture. The most popular is Spanish moss and pine bark mulch available in three sizes—small, medium and large—is also widely used. Others are sheetmoss, reindeer moss, or cocoa hulls.

Final Destination. Use a dolly to move the plant to its final destination. Wait until the plant is in place before watering; it makes for a lighter and drip-free transport. As the entire plant may be somewhat dry initially, recheck the water status on the next visit.

Planting Bed Installation. If a plant is to replace one in a planting bed, take it to the site after preparation, remove the old plant and growing container and install the new one.

Direct Planting. Large palms and trees that arrive bare-rooted are direct planted in the soil whether they are large containers or planting beds. A special maintenance team with proper equipment is necessary to facilitate installation.

New Designs. Once it is realized that interiorscapers know about the best plants for certain locations and can provide better replacements, then they may be given an opportunity to design. It may begin with a simple "We're thinking of redesigning the lobby. Do you have anything in mind?". Draw a neat sketch of the area, go home, do research, and create. Always consider the budget. Keep track of the time spent. If the plan is accepted, then bill for those extra hours. This is an easy way to enhance one's job and the success of your company.

Pest and Disease Control

Pest Control. Pests (insects and spider mites) are much more prevalent than disease. So, if leaves are suspect, first look for signs of a pest. Early detection is important for effective control.

Always carry a 10x magnifying lens to look for eggs, larvae and adults on both sides of the foliage, in the axils (the junction between the leaf petiole and stem), along the leaf petioles and the stem.

The University of Illinois Cooperative Extension Service and the Vocational Agriculture Service, as well as other universities, have prepared excellent guides complete with photographs and descriptions of pests and their biological controls. Reference books and websites also have good photographs and descriptions.

Plant researchers are continually working on developing cultivars that are more resistant to pests. Take advantage of these plants.

Pests. The most common pest in the interiorscape is the two-spotted spider mite, *Tetranychus uricae*. It is very small—from one-sixtieth to one-eightieth of an inch long and has eight legs, thus related to arachnids (spiders). It may be red, pale green or yellow with two dark markings towards the head.

Spider mites congregate in clusters on the undersides of the leaves, pierce the foliage and feed on the sap. The damage is characterized by yellow stippling at first, then becoming bronze or gray. Purple stippling occurs on new foliage. In severe infestations, they spin feathery webs. Eggs appear as clusters of tiny white dots. Eventually leaf drop occurs.

An easy way to prove an infestation is to shake a leaf over a piece of white paper. The little specks that fall are the mites. Hot, dry conditions encourage the development of mites.

Using a cleaning spray (see p. 12) is the safest and easiest way of control. In severe infestations use horticultural oil or a systemic miticide, although some resistance has been seen to the miticide. Replacing the plant may be cost effective. Moving the plant to where the humidity is higher and temperatures are lower is another method of dealing with spider mites.

Susceptible plants: *Dracaena marginata*, palms, English and Algerian ivy.

Mealybugs[7] are encountered far less often. They are easier to spot and harder to eradicate. They are oval, soft-bodied insects—body size is one-quarter to one-eighth of an inch in length—that form white waxy masses resembling cotton. They are in the same order of insects as scale; they all operate with piercing, sucking mouthparts. They excrete a clear, shiny and sticky substance called honeydew, found on the foliage and sometimes on the floor or furniture at hand.

Mealybugs often occur in hard to reach places such as in narrow leaf axils (the junction between the leaf petiole and stem). They also appear along the midrib on the undersides of leaves and on underground stems. The damage is similar to that of the scale insect—distorted, stunted, and yellow foliage. Cleaning with cotton swabs dipped in alcohol is an effective cure for a small infestation. Replacing the plant is cost effective in severe infestations.

Susceptible plants: *Aglonema*; *Alocasia*; *Eucharis grandiflora*, Amazon lily.

The third most important pest is the scale insect. The damage is similar to that of the mealybug—distorted, stunted, and yellow foliage. Honeydew, a sticky substance appearing on the leaf surface, is produced by the soft scale insects. Less common is the armored scale. Both scale types are composed of numerous genera.

Both are most easily spotted in the adult female stage as immobile, rounded[8], shellike structures (exoskeletons)— along the trunk and on the undersides of leaf midveins. Under each one-eighth of an inch exoskeleton, may be two thousand eggs. These eggs hatch into microscopic size slightly mobile crawlers, extremely difficult to detect. This is where a 10x hand lens becomes an important detection tool. Scale is most vulnerable at this time and a spray of cleaning solution should eliminate them.

If not, they choose a feeding site and use their piercing, sucking mouthparts to feed on plant sap. Once they become visible to the naked eye, they are mature and are very difficult to eradicate. For adult scale, remove the branches with heaviest infestation. Scrape off scales from other branches with a dull knife. Heavy infestations can kill the plant.

Susceptible plants: Palms; *Ficus benjamina*, weeping fig.

The greenhouse whitefly, *Trialeurodes vaporaiorum* has a wide body with wings held nearly parallel to leaf, and the sweet potato whitefly, *Bemisia tabaci*, has a narrow body with wings held at a 45° angle, are not commonly seen indoors unless present on new arrivals.

They are very bothersome because the adults easily fly when disturbed. The plants lack vigor while the foliage develops yellow stippling, leaf curling and wilt. Honeydew is often present.

The whitefly is a small—one-sixteenth of an inch—white, mothlike, winged insect with piercing, sucking mouthparts. It feeds on the top as well as the underside of leaves. Eggs are laid on the undersides of leaves attached to short stalks arranged in a circular or crescent shape. The immature insects are flat and almost colorless, difficult to detect. But this is the only time that they are vulnerable and can be eradicated. Use the 10x hand lens for detection.

Susceptible plants: The sweet potato whitefly is a problem for growers of poinsettias. Use hibiscus plants as isolated seasonals since they have built up a tolerance to insecticidal controls. Plants

---

[7]   The two main types of mealybug are the citrus mealybug, *Planococcus citri*, and the long-tailed mealybug, *Pseudoccus longispinus*.

[8]   The soft scale exoskeletons are rounded and are usually dark brown or black. The armored scale exoskeletons are oyster-shaped or flat and may be white, gray, dark red, purple, brown or black.

that have pubescent or hairy foliage are most likely to develop a whitefly problem. Luckily, the majority of foliage plants are glabrous (smooth).

Fungus gnats, *Bradysia coprophila*—with long legs and antennae—and shore flies, *Scatella stagnalis*—slightly smaller but with heavier bodies, short legs and antennae—are bothersome when they fly around plants. They both prefer constantly moist, highly organic soils and are treated similarly. A real culprit is the dumping of leftover coffee in plants. This provides an ideal medium.

The adults lay eggs in the soil which hatch into larvae. The larvae feed on roots in the top two inches of soil and vector both fungal and viral diseases.

If either are discovered, keep the soil as dry as possible. Other cures include working some diatomaceous earth into the top layer of soil, replacing the top two inches of soil, adding slices of potatoes and replacing every week (time consuming and only acceptable if a moss mulch hides the potatoes). Insecticide drenches may also be used.

Western flower thrips, *Frankliniella occidentalis* are occasionally brought in on new arrivals of chrysanthemum, lily and gloxinia flowers. They are one-eighth of an inch long and have fringed wings. They have rasping-sucking mouthparts and damage includes silvering, flecking, and distortion of flowers and sometimes on the undersides of new growth. Thrips vector tomato spotted wilt virus (TSWV). Replace any plants on which they are found.

Green peach aphids, *Myzus persicae* are uncommon but are occasionally brought in with new arrivals. They are pear-shaped and clearly visible in assorted colors of pale green, yellow and pink. They are wingless in small infestations. Winged aphids indicate a severe problem. They feed in colonies on tender new shoots and flower buds causing wilting, stunting, yellowing, curling of the foliage and distortion. Honeydew is present. Washing the foliage with a strong stream of water is a safe method of eradication.

Environmentally Friendly Solutions. Reasonably close attention to signs of pest infestation will catch the problem while it is still at a low level. Of course, we would like to start with the least toxic product. I have found the cleaning solution discussed under "Foliage" is effective at controlling low-level infestations. Another environmentally friendly choice is Safer brand insecticidal soap, made from fatty acids. Hot pepper spray is said to work well also.

Pesticide Use. An applicator's license is necessary for most interior pesticide usage. Obtaining the license involves passing a rigorous written test after extensive home study and some classroom instruction.

Spraying should take place during off-hours. One needs to suit up in a rubber overall outfit with hood, protective goggles, gloves and boots. Even with specialized hydrostatic sprayer systems, particles of the spray land on furniture or carpeting, so those items must be covered with plastic sheeting.

Applying a systemic insecticide to the soil is another chemical option. Systemics are less effective on trees with woody trunks and for treating armored scale. For expensive plants known to be susceptible to certain pests, systemics are applied prophylactically.

Resistance to pesticides, often requiring repeated applications, has become a real problem. After all this, shouldn't we consider alternative methods?

Biological Controls. Using beneficial insects is a safe way to control pests, not only for the environment but for the human health safety. Do your homework and learn about what beneficials are best. For those clients who are doubtful, inform them about what you will be doing. Tell them that the predatory and parasitic insects are often very tiny and will probably not even be noticed. Remind clients that beneficials are harmless to people. They attack and destroy only pests.

For best results, release beneficials in low to medium infestations. In severe infestations, first clean the foliage well, then use beneficials. Realize that it takes two to three weeks for results. Often, multiple releases are necessary, so refrigerate any extras. And remember that once the pest is eliminated, the beneficial insects will also die.

Beneficials are available from supply houses and are delivered by an express mail service. They arrive in containers filled with vermiculite, rice hulls or a similar material. Ladybeetles usually cling to white strips of paper in the containers. Always read the enclosed directions and follow carefully.

General predators. Green lacewings, *Chryoperia* spp. are effective for most pests. They arrive as first instar larvae—lacewings have three instar stages of development—which immediately consume spider mites, immature mealybugs, scale insects, and whitefly. Green lacewings have cannibalistic tendencies which help rid the area when the pests are gone. They are also available as eggs which hatch in three days. One precautionary word, if the lacewings reach maturity, they are one-half to three-quarters of an inch long and fly.

Ladybeetles (ladybugs), *Hippodamia convergens*, consume spider mites. Both larvae and adult stages consume all soft bodied pests, larvae and any eggs. Purchase the lady beetle in the larval stage; they are ravenous and can't fly. Whether releasing larvae or adults, spray the foliage with water. This will encourage these beneficials to remain on the plant. Adults tend not to fly and proceed to die when the pest is gone.

Australian ladybird beetles, *Cryptolaemus montrouzieri*, easily control mealybug, especially the citrus mealybug, Cryptos, as they are called, are also effective against soft scale.

Purchase these in the larval stage; they are ravenous and can't fly. Whether releasing larvae or adults, spray the foliage with water. This will encourage this beneficial to remain on the plant. Adults don't fly very much and proceed to die when the pest is gone.

Specific predators. Predatory mites, *Phytoseiulus persimilis* and *Mesosciulus longipes*, immediately search for spider mites upon release.

Other types of lady beetles include *Stethorus picipes* and *S. punctillum*. Each beetle is so small that it can fit on the head of a pin, and love to eat spider mites, too.

A tiny predatory wasp, *Leptomastix dactylopii*, controls mealybugs.

The purple scale predator, *Rhyzobius lophanthae*, controls soft scale.

A tiny black and yellow predatory wasp, *Metaphycus helvolus* , controls black and other soft scales with the exception of brown soft scale.

A tiny parasitic wasp, *Encarsia formosa*, controls the greenhouse whitefly. It is most effective with small populations and over a period of time since it needs to breed and lay eggs inside the pest.

Eretmocerus eremicus controls whitefly, better for control of the sweet potato whitefly rather than the greenhouse whitefly.

Another predator, *Delphastis pusillus*, consumes all stages of whitefly: eggs, nymphs, and adults.

The convergent ladybeetle, *Hippodamia convergens* and the pink-spotted ladybeetle, *Coleomegilla maculata*, control aphids.

A beneficial nematode, *Steinernema carpocapsae*, applied to the soil, controls large infestations of fungus gnat and shorefly larvae. A predatory mite, *Hypoaspis miles*, controls the adults.

Two phytoseid mites, Ozzie 1 and Ozzie 2, derived from *Neoseiulus cucumeris*, control the western flower thrip. Pirate bugs, *Orius* spp. are also used.

Disease Control. Placing the right plant for the location's light level and conscientious watering practices will facilitate a plant's natural health. Stressed, weakened plants are especially susceptible to disease. Also, avoid splashing water on the foliage (which engender fungal problems). Remember to regularly disinfect all cleaning tools and materials after use.

The University of Illinois Cooperative Extension Service and the Vocational Agriculture Service, as well as other university departments, have prepared excellent guides complete with photographs and descriptions of interior plant diseases and physiologic disorders (cold and heat injury, mineral excesses and deficiencies). Reference books and websites also have good information.

Plant tissue analysis may be a useful tool for an expensive showcase plant, but, in general, by the time the analysis is made, the plant looks terrible or has died.

Fungal Diseases. Fungal diseases are the most common and easily treated. The most common sign is a grouping of spots on various leaves. They start out as brown or gray pinhole-sized spots. If left untreated, they grow and fuse, ultimately causing the leaf to fall off. Sometimes these spots appear as concentric circles, surrounded by the newly infected area, a bright yellow. Under a 10x hand lens, look for raised black or brown dots (fruiting bodies) or thin white hairs (mycelia). Fungicide application is very effective in the early stages.

If the fungus infects the root or stem, leaves first wilt, then yellow and fall off. But, by the time these symptoms are seen, the plant is beyond recovery. This problem is most prevalent in warm, moist soil. Susceptible plants may be treated prophylactically with a systemic fungicide.

Bacterial Diseases. Bacterial diseases are less frequently encountered. They may be localized or spread throughout the plant. As leaf spots, they appear angular, stopping at the veins. They are often purple-black, oily or water-soaked looking surrounded by a bright yellow halo area. The spots become holes and eventually the leaf falls off.

The symptoms of bacterial root and stem rot are the same as fungal root and stem rot with the addition that usually the bacterial kind is very malodorous. Bacteriocides are often ineffective so the plant needs to be replaced. In most cases, *Erwinia* bacterial disease is the culprit.

Most **susceptible plants:** 'Janet Craig' *Dracaena* and English ivy.

Viral Diseases. Viral diseases are hardly ever seen. Viruses are tiny bodies of DNA that enter the plant cells and then take control. They may be vectored by whitefly, aphids and thrips. Smokers should thoroughly wash their hands to prevent transmission through tobacco products.

Symptoms include: general stunting of the plant, curled or stunted foliage, abnormal yellow and green coloration patterns in leaves or patches of yellow and green areas (mosaics) in normally green leaves. Dispose of the plant; there is no current treatment program.

Chapter 4
Major Plant Families And Groups

The Agavaceae or Agave Family

Members of this family are durable plants with thick, tough foliage. They are "no brainers" to maintain since keeping the soil fairly dry agrees well with them. The *Dracaena* genus which comprises most of the family grow well in low light. The rest of the family, the ponytail palm, the snake plant and the yucca plant grow best in medium high light. They all tolerate low humidity.

These plants are sensitive to fluoride tipburn appearing on the older foliage. Check with the local water commission about the amount of fluoride in the water. If no more than one part per million is present, then fluoride tipburn is less likely.

In general, this family is not bothered by pests; however, spider mites frequently appear on *Dracaena marginata*.

Originally from Africa and other tropical regions, these understory plants are propagated by sticking sections of cane into soil. The root system of these giants is sparse and fragile, especially when young. That's why it's important to obtain plants from a reputable grower whose concern is selling dracaenas with fully developed root systems. For shipping, the canes are separated with styrofoam and secured with tape. It's best to remove these mechanics after the plant is at its final location.

In order to achieve a staggered and uniformly full look to the plant, many canes are arranged in a growing container. If a 5-4-3-2 is ordered, the numbers refer to how many feet tall each cane is.

Technicians have been known to kill the dracaenas with kindness by overwatering. Use a soil probe to remove sections of soil and if the lowest level is moist, skip the watering on this service visit. This is the easiest way to prevent root and stem rot.

The first sign of overwatering is yellowing of the lower leaves. If overwatering continues, then the canes rot out. This really is a fooler because the bark looks intact, but the minute you squeeze that cane, you know. It squishes! The inside of the cane becomes malodorous mush. This is a result of the *Erwinia* stem rot.

To remove the diseased cane, grab it higher up, where the stem may still be intact. Twist the entire cane and dispose of it immediately. Ordering a replacement plant is the other option if the missing cane creates an obvious gap. Throw away all staging materials and disinfect the inside of the decorative container.

Fortunately, the industry favors us with ever new cultivars of these familiar plants. Colorful variegation and dramatic shapes continue to corner the market.

The Arecaceae or Palm Family

It's hard to imagine a tropical setting without thinking of palm trees. The majestic palms are distinctly different in appearance and growth from other plants. They evoke a feeling of a playful vacation getaway. Palms are single stemmed evergreen monocots that vary in size from many stories tall to table top garden size. The single trunks vary in thickness, color and texture. Some are very thin and suckering with many plants in a container so the appearance is shrubby. Others are thick and tall with foliage only appearing at the very top.

The palms are often confused with the cycads or some large ferns. The only thing that they have in common, besides a similar general look, is that all three are very ancient with palm fossils existing from the late Cretaceous period, approximately 70 million years ago.

The foliage has the typical parallel leaf venation of monocots but varies greatly in size and shape. The leaf arrangement falls into two relatively distinct categories: The feather palms have pinnately compound leaflets (resembling a feather). The fan palms have palmately compound leaflets (resembling an opened fan). New leaves are tightly closed and emerge vertically from the center of the plant. They are aptly called spear leaves.

Palms prefer from medium to high light although some species tolerate low light levels. Because of the fibrous and shallow root systems of palms, they perform well with crowded and root bound conditions.

Palms also require more watering than many other plants. The trick is to keep the soil moderately moist at all times. Too much water quickly causes yellowing of the foliage and eventually root rot. Underwatering causes the usual tipburn and causes new growth to dry up and die.

Palms require more fertilization than other plants. If prominent yellow spots on the foliage appear, add some fertilizer to correct this sign of potassium deficiency.

Palms are notorious for being very susceptible to two-spotted spider mites, mealybugs and soft scale insects. Any palm worth keeping should be treated prophylactically with a miticide and insecticide.

Helpful hints: Use the soap and alcohol solution for cleaning foliage—skip the use of a feather duster. When unwrapping a newly delivered palm, beware of creatures such as jumping frogs! The new spear leaves are tightly closed. In nature, strong winds cause them to open exposing the leaflets. Indoors, we must help nature along by manually pulling the leaflets apart.

Important fact: The very top of the trunk contains the apical meristemmatic tissue from where all growth originates. This is called the "heart". It is often protected by protective foliage or sometimes spines. If this terminal growing point or "heart" is damaged or destroyed, the entire plant dies.

The Araceae or Arum Family

Like most plants used in the interiorscape, this family consists of plants that naturally grow in the under story of tropical vegetation. Therefore, many are able to endure low light. The *Aglaonemas*, *Epipremnums* or pothos plants and *Zamioculcas* or ZZ plant thrive with infrequent watering. The *Spathiphyllums* also are great for low light but moist soil. Others utilize medium light levels and moderately moist soil, such as *Monstera deliciosa*, Swiss cheese plant; *Philodendrons* and *Syngoniums*. *Alocasias* and *Anthuriums* prefer high light but acclimate to less. Coupled with the families preference for warm temperatures and tolerance for low humidity, they are invaluable in many interiorscapes.

Many members of this family are stemless; the very long and fleshy, sheathed leaf petioles arise in a rosette pattern right from the soil (actually they are growing from an underground rhizome which is a thickened storage stem). The tough and leathery foliage adds to the plant's durability indoors. The foliage usually contains a milky sap. Other genera such as *Monstera* have long vines with aerial roots at the leaf nodes.

In some plants such as *Philodendron* spp., dumbcane, calcium oxalate crystals are present. These crystals cause swelling if ingested.

The inflorescence[1] consists of two parts: a large, colorful, cuplike spathe which is botanically a bract or modified leaf encircling a spadix which is a cylindrical, fleshy spike with minute, true flowers at its base. *Anthurium* and *Spathiphyllum* have dramatic and desirable inflorescence. In all others, remove it.

An interesting fact: Although plants in the arum family are monocots, many lack the typical parallel leaf venation. Therefore, they are subject to tipburn.

The Araliaceae or Aralia Family

Members of the aralia family consist of trees, shrubs and vines related to plants in the parsley family. Most of these plants originate in tropical area but some are also found in the temperate regions.

These are elegant and expensive interior plants. These plants have some of the most interesting foliage of any plant. The foliage is often palmately compound or palmately lobed and arranged alternately along the stem. Small cuttings are often placed in a table top garden but the main use is as trees.

Most of the aralias do best with light on the brighter side of medium and moderately moist soil. In some of these plants, such as false aralia, two types of leaves appear on the same plant: simply shaped juvenile leaves, and lobed mature leaves. Often in interior settings, only the juvenile leaves grow.

The *Scheffleras* are tough, durable, and easy to maintain plants. *Hedera* or English ivy is also good for cooler temperatures.

The *Polyscias* and the *Dizygothecas* genera are more difficult to maintain than other interiorscape plants. They are susceptible to pests such as spider mites and scale insects.

Helpful hint: Most aralias die because of uneven watering. Don't allow the soil to become too dry or too moist. Both cause severe leaf drop.

The Bromeliaceae or Pineapple Family

Bromeliads are striking plants with their prominent, brightly colored centers that resemble exotic, tropical flowers. The large, stiff foliage is unusual and very attractive, too. A wide range of inflorescence[2] and foliage styles are available. The myriad of unusual cultivars keeps increasing, all to our advantage.

Bromeliads are relatively new to the United States. They became wildly popular in the mid 1970s. They actually were discovered many years earlier in the mid-1860s by the Swedish botanist, Olaus Bromel and quickly became the rage in greenhouses throughout Europe.

These durable plants are excellent choices for flowering plant replacement. The blooms last a long time, from three to six months. Fewer replacements are necessary, thus lowering plant and labor costs.

And bromeliads are easy to maintain with their light watering schedule, pest and disease-free qualities and tolerance for extremes in temperature and humidity. The optimal temperature range is 55 to 85° F., which is very liberal as compared to other blooming plants.

Most of the various bromeliads require high light to maintain their full coloration. The more brightly colored the bromeliad, the more light required. It's that simple. Many of these make sensational underplantings in containers with large trees or add that splash of color to those plain looking ground covers.

Bromeliads naturally grow as either terrestrial or epiphytic plants—growing in tree crevices with aerial roots absorbing nutrients from water, air and dust particles. Most of the bromeliads commercially available are epiphytes but planted in a very lightweight soil, the point being that they often become top-heavy and must be anchored down.

Bromeliads include: *Aechmea fasciata*, silver urn plant; *Cryptanthus bivittatus*, earth star;

---

[1] Inflorescence refers to the true flowers combined with associated colorful parts (bracts and sepals) that we commonly refer to as the flower.

[2] This inflorescence consists of long-lasting, showy and colorful bracts (modified leaves) often referred to as the flower and short-lived, small true flowers located among the bracts.

Guzmania spp.; *Neoregelia carolinae*, striped blushing bromeliad; *Tillandsia cyanea*; and *Vriesea splendens,* sword plant.

Interesting facts: Once the inflorescence declines, the initial plant declines and dies. Nurserymen propagate bromeliads by offsets called "pups". High levels of ethylene are required to initiate blooming.

The pineapple, *Ananas comosus,* is a native of the tropical Americas and is used as a novelty item. The funny looking small green pineapple complete with top foliage sits at the top of a central stalk. More stiff, spiny-edged long, narrow gray to bronze-green leaves form a basal rosette. *A. bracteatus* 'Tricolor' is very ornamental with foliage striped and edged with cream. The fruit, attached bracts and leaf margins are pink.

The Moraceae or Mulberry Family

This is quite a diverse family that include many trees native to tropical rain forests such as *Ficus benjamina* which is, by far, the most widely-used plant in the interior plantscape industry. The family includes a wiry stemmed, tiny leafed creeping ground cover, *Ficus pumila.*

Improved cultivars are very tolerant of indoor conditions. They require from medium to medium high light and moist soils. *Ficus* tolerate a low humidity and a wide range of temperatures. These plants are less susceptible to scale insects and spider mites than their parent plants.

The glossy, leathery leaves have very pointy, but not sharp, leaf tips, well suited to naturally shed rainfall. This is an asset when cleaning these plants; make sure they are placed on a large sheet of plastic, spray with soapy water and shake the tree. The excess drips off.

Helpful hints: Those plants in higher light will need to be fertilized if the foliage begins to lose its dark green color. Because the *Ficus* genus has extensive root systems, subirrigation is not recommended.

The Orchidaceae or Orchid Family

The first orchids to reach Europe was brought from Latin American colonies by the Spaniards in 1510; it was vanilla. The Royal Botanic Gardens at Kew in London listed 15 tropical, decorative species in 1789. By the 1850s, hundreds more were widely available.

This is the largest family of blooming plants in the world. The orchid inflorescence[3] rises dramatically from the center of the plant. The foliage usually is not the most attractive, although some orchids have beautifully colored, delicate leaves. Most orchids have a specific pollinator: a bee, moth, ant or bird; others are self-pollinated.

Orchids have two types of growth—monopodial and sympodial. The growth of monopodial orchids is upon a single axis. *Phalaenopsis* with few leaves and one flower stalk is an example. Sympodial orchids have many pseudobulbs (thickened, storage stems called rhizomes that grow vertically or horizontally along the soil surface) and many leaves growing in several directions as in the *Cattleyas.*

In general, orchids are easy to maintain. They require medium light and high humidity. Tropical orchids are divided into three temperature ranges: cool growing (between 55 and 65° F.); intermediate growing (between 65 and 75° F.); and warm growing (between 75-90° F.)

Most indoor orchids are epiphytic—they have aerial roots absorbing nutrients from water, air and dust particles and are planted in fir bark, osmunda, or special formulations designed to drain well.

If keeping orchids year-round, fertilize half-strength with 30-10-10 during the growing season and use 20-10-10 from when the flower buds begin to emerge through flowering.

Helpful hint: The best way to detect an emerging flower stalk from a leaf stalk: The flower stalk has a slight bulge at the tip.

---

[3]   Orchid inflorescence consists of three petals and three sepals. Two petals are large, colorful and showy. The third petal is modified into a labellum or lip which contains the reproductive parts. The colorful sepals resemble the petals but are often slightly smaller.

The True Ferns

The ubiquitous Boston fern has been updated with a wide variety of improved, decorative cultivars many with better tolerances to indoor conditions. Table top ferns such as the *Pteris* genus have a desirable look atypical of ferns and are often planted in those table top gardens with flowering plants as the two have similar watering requirements. Another trend in ferns is to use the large tree ferns especially in atrium areas. They evoke a tropical feeling and resemble palm trees but have a greater proportion of foliage. Two of them are: *Blechnum gibbum*, Brazilian tree fern and *Cyathea cooperi*, Australian tree fern.

Although most ferns require moderate light, the high humidity required is the most limiting factor. They also require a consistently watered soil or they dry to a crisp within a matter of days. The ideal location is very close to running water such as a waterfall or fountain.

Many ferns are short-lived and are replaced on a regular basis. Ferns are usually grown in 4 to 6-inch diameter containers and 8 to12-inch hanging basket size.

For scale insects, use a one-half strength insecticidal soap solution to avoid frond damage. If a fern develops symptoms such as yellow fronds, stunted growth and leaf drop, then suspect root nematodes. Root swellings are a sure sign of the pest. In that case, discard the plant.

Ferns are members of many different families but they all have several things in common. The fronds are most often pinnately divided (featherlike). The leaflets are called pinnae (pinna, singular) and are arranged along the rachis (midrib). The rachis becomes the petiole towards the base. The rhizomes (thickened storage stems) are either just under the soil surface or exposed.

Interesting fact: Those dark spots on the undersides of the pinnae are sori (cases covering clusters of spore producing structures). They are a normal part of reproduction. Do not confuse these with scale insects.

Cacti and Other Succulents

Succulents are plants that have evolved enlarged stems or leaves which store water to help survive arid conditions. Cacti are, by far, the largest group of succulents. Cacti are further defined by having sharp spines, as most do. Spines are modified leaves that no longer photosynthesize but become a defense against predators. The spines are surrounded by an areole which is a small pad of tissue originating as a condensed lateral shoot.

Cacti are curiously almost exclusively a native of deserts of the Americas—so give them, and most succulents, desert conditions—high light, dry soil and low humidity. Needless to say, they are very durable in the interiorscape. Water thoroughly only twice a year, in early spring when growth begins and then again in early summer.

A small group of cacti are very different in appearance and habitat— the *Schlumberga* genus, holiday cactus— which grow in shady, moist areas. Their spines have been reduced to hairs.

The main storage structure of a cactus plant and some succulents is the thick and green photosynthesizing stem. Most cacti and other succulents die from rot diseases caused by overwatering. Mealybugs are the main insect problem.

Gardens or atriums with a southwest look are most appropriate for the hundreds of kinds of cacti and succulents available. Of course, care must be taken whether maintaining cacti or placing them out of the mainstream of traffic. Wrap a vertically folded column of newspaper around the cacti when removing or replacing.

Examples include:

Haworthia spp., from the lily family, are small succulents suited for table top gardens. There are many species but they all appear in attractive stemless rosettes with that are thick and fleshy with attractive white raised growths called tubercles.

Opuntia microdasys, rabbit ears cactus, looks more like mouse ears, with green flattened round sections called cladophylls (flattened branches that look like and photosynthesize as leaves). They are attached in sections, one on top of another, up to the top, where two or more sections appear. Typical of most cacti, it blooms in winter. The large flowers are bright yellow. *O. microdasys* var. *albispina* 'Polka Dots', dwarf rabbit ears, has distinguishing white glochids—spines with barbed tips—and remains small— up to one foot tall.

Mammilaria elongata, golden stars cactus, sometimes referred to as lady fingers, is upright, cylindrical and petite. This cactus multiplies by producing close growing offsets.

Parodia leninghausii, golden barrel cactus, is also upright and cylindrical but is large. The vertical patterning along the column with dense white hairs at the top creates an interesting look.

Chapter 5
Individual Plants

Aechmea fasciata
Silver Vase Plant
Bromeliaceae or Pineapple Family
**A native of Mexico to Argentina in
   the tropical regions**
**Light: On the brighter side of me-
   dium**
Soil: Moderately dry

The silver vase plant was discovered in Brazil in 1826 and it has been popular ever since.
It's easy to see why with the winning combination of long-lasting color, low maintenance and
wide range of tolerances. (See color plate 1.)

The spiny inflorescence is a rosette of colorful bracts (modified leaves) that appear in a soft
pink to peach. The tiny flowers look like blue
berries before they open to pale blue flowers.
They are densely packed along the central bracts.
The strappy, thick and serrated foliage is banded
alternately with silvery-green and dark green.

Length of bloom time: Purchase plants when
the bracts are low in the center of the plant and
barely showing color. Then, they last from three
to four months. Do not purchase with blue flowers present; the plant is past its prime.

Temperature: A wide range, 55 to 85° F., and
can tolerate short periods of cooler and warmer
temperatures.

Humidity: Adapts to low humidity although
moderate is preferred.

Overall shape: V-shape.

Texture: Bold.

Availability: The 6-inch diameter container size
is eighteen inches tall. Larger sizes are available.

Placement: En masse, anywhere color is desired.
As a substitute for flowering plants. Although
these plants may be more expensive initially, in
the long run they are economical because of the
long lasting color, durability and minimal upkeep.

Be aware that: The foliage typically has spiny
edges. Wear long sleeves when replacing them or
choose a spineless cultivar.

Helpful hint: Secure the plant well as the silver
vase plant tends to become top-heavy.

Cultivars include:

'Chantinii' has an orange and yellow inflorescence.

'Friederike' has a large red inflorescence and very
dark green foliage.

'Morgana' has mostly silvery foliage with a pink-
peach inflorescence upon an upright plant.

'Primera' has a bright pink inflorescence with
loosely arranged foliage.

'Romero' is dark red-purple.

'Spineless' has pink inflorescence but the foliage
is spineless and great for easy installation.

'Starbright' is peach-colored.

Aeschynanthus lobbianus
Lipstick Plant
Gesneriaceae or Gesneriad Family
**A native of the Indonesian rain
     forests**
Light: Medium
Soil: Moderately moist

The lipstick plant is known for its tubular three inch long flowers: a true reddest red lipstick color. (See color plate 1.) They look like they are emerging from a purple lipstick case. This part actually is the calyx (The collection of usually green sepals that surround the flower.) In this case they are modified and colorful. The pendant flowers appear in groups at the terminal ends of the plant.

This is also an easy to maintain foliage plant. It is often used particularly for its attractive and neat foliage. The oval and pointed, glossy dark green leaves have a depressed and prominent midrib visually dividing each leaf in half. The foliage is neatly arranged in opposite pairs along a tough and wiry stem creating the trailing and cascading effect.

Length of bloom time: This relative of the African violet usually blooms for a couple of months in summer.

Temperature: Warm, from 70 to 80° F. are preferred.

Humidity: Moderate; but higher, if possible, when blooming.

Overall shape: Vining with gracefully arched stems.

Texture: Medium.

Availability: Year-round as a foliage plant most often in hanging basket sizes.

Placement: Best used in hanging basket displays. It may also be an underplanting of a containerized tree. Or as a flowering plant where it can be viewed up close.

Be aware that: This is an epiphytic plant—it gets nutrition from water, air and dust particles, and is planted in a lightweight mixture.

Helpful hint: This plant will flower in low light. Keeping the soil moderately dry during the winter months encourages the plant to bloom.

Related species:

A. *marmoratus*, tiger vine, is known for its light green, diffuse, angled striping on the dark green leaf.

A. *speciosum* has yellow flowers.

Aglaonema spp.
Aglaonema, Aglao, Chinese Evergreen
Araceae or Arum Family
Bred from native plants of tropical Southeast Asia especially the Philippines, Malaysia and Thailand
Light: From medium to low
Soil: Moderately dry

Aglaonemas have long been a "workhorse of the industry" because they fill a real void of "what do I install in those poorly lit areas?" This is a good foliage plant that keeps its variegation under such conditions. Better yet, the lower the light, the more horizontal and visible the leaves become. The elliptical and arching foliage softly arises from a central rosette on fleshy leaf petioles. Adding to the soft touch is the contrast in coloration. Many plants per pot contribute to the full, wide feeling. The thick and durable foliage is great for withstanding harsh interior plantscapes. Easy maintenance plus many tolerances make this a versatile plant.

For many years, there had been just a few aglaonemas widely available: A. 'B.J. Freeman' with light green foliage, A. 'Emerald Beauty' with primarily dark foliage and A. 'Silver Queen' which is predominantly light green with dark green accents. They are quite elegant and fit the needs of the industry. The main drawback is that they are intolerant to cooler locations. Many new series have been developed to combat this issue. (See below.)

Temperature: Intermediate to warm, from 60 to 90° F. Some cultivars are able to tolerate lower temperatures without chilling injury

Humidity: Moderate.

Overall shape: A rounded, wide plant with strong horizontality as well as angularity and minor verticality. 'Silver Queen' is wider with arching foliage while many other improved cultivars are tall with upright foliage.

Texture: Bold.

Availability: From table top size through 17-inch diameter containers, but most common in 10 to 14-inch sizes.

Placement: From elegant specimen plants in hotel lobbies, to locations under dark stairways, this plant is surely a winner. The interesting color patterns are complimentary in combination with any other solid color foliage. The light colored aglaonemas will brighten up any dark corner.

Be aware that: Resist the urge to overwater. Stem rot caused by *Erwinia* bacteria or numerous fungi will be avoided. Soluble salt build up causes leaf tips to brown. Pests rarely are a problem, although, mealybugs may appear on the underside of the leaf along the midrib or in the folds of the leaf petiole.

Helpful hint: Choose the cultivars that are cold tolerant if any question of a draft is possible. Some cultivars are also more pest and disease resistant than others.

Three previously mentioned cultivars:

'B.J. Freeman' has silvery-gray leaves with occasional scattered small dark specks. The foliage stands quite upright. This larger plant is available in 10 to 14-inch diameter containers and grows to forty inches tall and one foot wide. 'Gabrielle' is an improved cultivar.

'Emerald Beauty' also known as 'Maria' is widely used. It was originally collected in the wild in the Philippines. It grows more compactly and upright than 'Silver Queen' with narrower and thicker foliage. It has better cold tolerance than 'Silver Queen'. Each leaf has angled, light gray-green obvious bands and small flecks on a deep, dark green background. The fleshy leaf petioles are usually covered by the foliage. 'Emerald Beauty' develops insignificant pale green spathes or inflorescence that require removal. (See foot note #1, p. 25.) Because 'Emerald Beauty' is a smaller plant, it usually is sold in containers with a diameter of up to 10 inches.

'Silver Queen' is the most widely used aglao worldwide and is believed to be a cross between A. curtisii and A. treubii. It has the most arching and wide, horizontal appearance of any other aglaonema, especially when placed in low light. The short leaf petioles are hidden by the many lance shaped leaves. Each leaf has dark green irregularly splotched bands which run on an angle to the equally dark midrib. The background is a silvery-gray-green. This old standby happens to be the least cold tolerant of all. Chilling injury is characterized by leaf spots, either yellow or gray, that turn into holes on older leaves. A physiological problem that rarely occurs but is worth mentioning is "bent tip" characterized by leaf tips that droop downward especially during the summer months. The cause is thought to be excessive watering or light.

Other cultivars include:

'Manila Pride' has predominantly dark green foliage with light green markings and pink leaf petioles. It is a large, upright plant.

'Maria Christina' combines the coloration of 'Silver Queen' and the compactness of 'Emerald Beauty'. It is tolerant of cool temperatures.

'Moe Moe' which is patterned with yellow speckles.

'Peacock' is colorful with dark green spots upon a silvery-green leaf. The leaves have a yellow-green midrib and very light green leaf petioles with some green spots and streaks.

'Rachel' has green speckled leaves; similar in shape and pattern to 'Emerald Beauty' but more upright to thirty-four inches. It is cold tolerant to 40° F., resistant to mealybugs and stem rot.

'Romano' and 'Royal Ripple' have wavy margins.

'San Remo' is a very dark green plant with silvery-white markings.

'Stripes' has lush, very dark green foliage highlighted by angled narrow silver stripes. (See color plate 1.) It is a large size yet compact plant that is cold tolerant to 45° F. 'Margarita' is similar with light pink leaf petioles.

Bay Series: These compact plants will tolerate a little more light than most and are cold tolerant to 45° F.

'Diamond Bay' has a sparkling white center and irregular bright green margin.

'Emerald Bay' is an improved 'Silver Bay' with more prominent green coloration.

'Golden Bay' has a golden midrib, a larger silvery-pewter center than 'Silver Bay' and with white leaf petioles.

'Silver Bay' has a silvery-pewter center covering much of the leaf and an irregularly spattered very dark green margin. The leaves are wider than most aglaos.

Elite Series: Plants are well noted for their increased tolerance to cooler temperatures, as low as 45° F. Some are upright growers, have wavy leaf margins and/or showy white or light green leaf petioles.

'Amelia' is a short compact cultivar with an extremely dense growth habit. Tri-colored foliage are variously marked with silver-gray on a darker green background.

'Black Lance' has dark green leaf margins with the center portion of the leaf in two shades of silver green. 'White Lance' has silver-green leaves with few green spots and margins. Both are tall and upright plants with very long and narrow stiff foliage and pale green leaf petioles. 'Brilliant' is an upright grower with very broad leaves boldly variegated with silver-green, yellow-green, light green and dark green streaks and spots.

'Deborah' is very showy with abundant silvery-white and yellow-green markings on the midrib and central leaf bordered in dark green. The highly visible thick white leaf petioles are a good identifying feature. 'Queen of Siam' is a very large sport (a naturally occurring mutation) available in larger size containers. 'White Rain' is the smaller version.

'Green Lady' has tri-colored foliage with areas of silver in the center accented by two shades of green at the leaf margin. This cultivar has a dense growth habit.

'Illumination' has white leaf petioles, glossy silver-green upper leaf surfaces with dark green, yellowish-green and white spots and streaks.

'Jubilee' and 'Jubilee Petite' are short, compact but very full plants named for the boldly striped leaf coloration. 'Abidjan' is very similar.

'Mary Ann' looks similar to 'Emerald Beauty' but has a compact growth habit.

'Painted Princess' has sharply tapered foliage uniquely marked with two shades of silver-green on a dark green background. It really stands out in a low light area with its paint spattered coloration. It has a compact and dense growth habit.

'Patricia' is a compact grower with narrow, sharply tapered foliage. This foliage is almost solid silver except for a green midrib and small spots of green near the margins.

'Rhapsody in Green' has similar coloration as 'Black Lance' with wider foliage and lower growth.

'Royal Ripple' has attractive rippled, wavy leaf margins. The foliage is prominently marked with two shades of silver-green on a dark green background. This cultivar has a low growth habit, perfect for a tall ground cover. 'Romano' is very similar.

'Silver Frost' has a dark green irregular pattern along the midrib while the majority of the leaf is silvery-gray. It is a larger size cultivar with a striking presentation.

'Stars' differs from the others with having white to yellow-green speckles over much of the dark green foliage. Dark silver-green blotches are also visible. The growth is upright.

Stars of India Series: These are cold tolerant to 40° F. and have excellent pest and disease resistance.

'Emerald Star' has dark forest green, thick leaves with irregular, cream to yellow "stars". Upon closer inspection, the dark green appears irregularly along the margin and blends in with a lighter dark gray-green background. The foliage is somewhat wider than many aglaos and also has a wavy margin. The dense, upright growth provides a sense of formality and elegance.

'Jewel of India' has thick leaves predominantly light gray-green, slightly outlined and splotched with dark green accents. (See color plate 1.) The leaves are long and narrow with ever so slightly wavy margins. It is a full yet compact plant with a more horizontal appearance.

'Silver Ribbons' has a silvery center with dark green margins on narrow leaves. The margins are curled so that it resembles a ribbon. The plant is upright growing.

'Silverado' has wider and pointy leaves that are silver-pewter with a thin green margin.

Related species:

A. pseudobracteatum, golden aglaonema, is attractively blotched with yellow, cream, white, pale and dark green. The leaf petioles are white. Many cultivars are very light and bright with splashy colors, great for lightening up a dark area. Most are susceptible to chilling injury.

Alocasia x *amazonica*
Alocasia
Araceae or Arum Family
Hybrid of *A. lowii* and *A. sanderana*, both native plants of southeast Asia
Light: From medium to high
Soil: Moderately moist

If you are looking for plant with tremendous visual impact, choose an alocasia. These are striking plants with large, colorful foliage than lend that sought after tropical look. (See color plate 1.) The arrowhead shaped dark green foliage has a raised, contrasting thick white midrib and prominent narrower white veins and wavy white leaf margins. The undersides are purple. Each huge leaf that grows to two feet long slightly overlaps the next one producing stepped layers. If you peer beyond the leaves, you'll see that each leaf is attached to a thick and strong fleshy light green leaf petiole emerging directly from the soil. Actually, it's attached to an underground rhizome (thickened storage stem.)

Temperature: Warm, above 65° F. is preferred.

Humidity: High, over 50%, if possible.

Overall shape: Upright and erect but wide with its huge leaves.

Texture: Bold.

Availability: The large ones are best suited for large size containers, up to 14-inches in diameter, but newer cultivars are available in table top sizes and are two feet tall.

Placement: At an entryway to a gala ball or similar event; or as a specimen plant in an sunny atrium—maybe next to a waterfall or a pool; it provides a splashy appearance. As specimen plants in the smaller sizes.

Be aware that: Mealybug is an occasional problem. *Alocasia* and the related plants contain a sap that may cause a burning sensation upon contact with skin. If ingested, a swelling of the throat and airway is possible.

Helpful hints: Phototropism is quite strong in this plant and a ¼ turn rotation every week may be necessary.

Cultivars: These are more tolerant of interior conditions.

'Argentea' with very prominent silvery contrasting veins. (See color plate 1.)

'Wentii' is table top size.

Related species:

A. x 'Black Velvet' or *A. micholitziana* has the name of black velvet that perfectly describes the foliage. The veins are silvery-white. The leaves are oval shaped—up to one foot long and six inches wide—with leaf petioles from twelve to eighteen inches long making this suitable for a table top garden or specimen planting.

A. cuprea is table top size with oval-shaped foliage. It has metallic coppery tones on the rippled dark green leaves. The veins are sunken, forming an attractive leaf pattern.

Related plants:

Colocasia esculenta 'Yellow Splash' is just one of the many different elephant ear plants. They are larger than alocasia, but are similarly tropical looking.

Xanthosoma lindenii has foot-long arrow-shaped foliage prominently marked with white veins. The long leaf petioles have dark green stripes contrasting with the light green color. They are smaller than alocasia, but are similarly tropical looking, and are more versatile.

***Alpinia zerumbet* 'Variegata'**
Variegated Shell Ginger
Zingiberaceae or Ginger Family
A cultivated variety from native
**   plants of the Pacific Islands**
Light: High
Soil: Moist

Certainly, the ginger plants are very lush and tropical looking. This one has foliage with irregular, diagonal, bright yellow and bright green stripes on either side of the light midrib. This showy foliage is narrowly elliptical and eighteen inches long. The foliage is densely packed along short, bamboolike stems that emerge from underground rhizomes—similar looking to the ginger used in cooking. New plants emerge from the base of the plant after flowering. (See color plates 1 and 2.)

The pendant sprays of white flowers resemble small orchids. When in bud, they are ivory and waxy and open one at a time from the base to reveal yellow and red throats.

Length of bloom time: The flowers last for many months usually blooming in spring. But use this plant for its foliage alone.

Temperature: Warm, from 70 to 95° F.

Humidity: Moderate.

Overall shape: Upright with horizontal focus on the foliage.

Texture: Bold.

Availability: In 8 to14-inch diameter containers usually two to five feet tall.

Placement: As specimen plants. As a tall groundcover in a sunny atrium.

Be aware that: Phototropism is quite strong in this plant and free standing containers should be turned one-quarter of a turn every week.

Helpful hints: This plant may need to be cut back after blooming. *Heliconia* is very similar looking.

Other ginger plants:

A. aureocarpa, red-backed bamboo ginger, has fine foliage resembling bamboo. The gray-green leaves are dark red on the underside. It is two to three feet.

A. purpurata, ornamental red ginger, is known for its showy red inflorescence and is a popular cut flower. The glossy, narrow lance-shaped foliage are arranged in pairs.

Burbidgea scheizocheila, golden brush orchid ginger from Malaysia, is a clumping ginger that has bright orange-gold, spicy scented inflorescence (Similar to that of bromeliads, see footnote #2, p. 25) that resemble upside down brushes atop orange flowerstalks that arise to three feet. Cut inflorescence back when finished flowering. The glossy green foliage makes a neat and attractive tall groundcover or background planting.

Ginger-like plants:

Billbergia pyramidalis 'Striata' is a bromeliad that has a similar looking inflorescence composed of erect club-shaped spikes surrounded by showy colorful bracts. The stiff and leathery foliage is irregularly striped bright green and bright yellow. The plant is eighteen inches tall.

Calathea burle-marxii 'Blue Ice' is not a ginger, but has similar looking foliage. The cultivars are known for their beehive shaped inflorescence similar to bromeliads. This cultivar has iridescent light blue bracts. 'White Ice' and 'Green Ice' have those colors. The actual small, yellow flowers are embedded in the center. The plant is four to six feet tall.

Anthurium x *cultorum*
Anthurium, Flamingo Flower
Araceae or Arum Family
Hybridized from native plants of tropical America and Hawaii
Light: On the brighter side of medium
Soil: Moderately moist

If you are so lucky to have an atrium or well lighted area, then use anthuriums known for their inflorescence. (See footnote #1, p. 25) The usual color of the spathe is red or white, with a naturally waxy sheen; however, anthuriums include all shades of pink, orange, red, purple, green, and even brown. Combinations with the top half pink or red and the bottom half green are available. The upright spadix inside varies in color from white, yellow and orange through red and green. Some spadices have bands of three colors. It's easy to see why these were initially very popular as cut flowers.

The leathery foliage has an exaggerated arrowhead shape. Sometimes the foliage is elliptical. Tall anthuriums have few and large inflorescence; others have a more compact growth habit with small but many blooms.

Anthuriums are epiphytic—they have aerial roots absorbing nutrients from water, air and dust particles—and are often planted in a fir bark medium. High humidity and high light are necessary for further flowering.

Length of bloom time: Long-lasting, up to a month or so.

Temperature: Intermediate to warm, from 65 to 85° F. (See "Lady Series" below.)

Humidity: High humidity allows for a longer bloom time.

Overall shape: Upright and erect with full foliage.

Texture: Medium.

Availability: In the 6-inch diameter container the plant is two feet tall. The miniatures with many small blooms are half that size and are often sold in 4-inch diameter containers.

Placement: Used especially in contemporary and art deco design. Also used as an accent plant where color is desired. Use the minis on a table or counter in a simple and elegant decorative container. Anthuriums are as dramatic as orchids so place them where they can be viewed up close.

Be aware that: If soil is too wet, *Pythium* and *Rhizoctonia* fungal diseases may develop.

Helpful hint: Remove spathes as soon as they are past their prime.

Cultivars include:

'Amigo' is tri-colored—red, white and green.

'Anaconda' is salmon and green.

'Athens' is a blush pink.

'Bestino' has large white spathes edged in green that turn to pink and then again to green. The leaves are small.

'Excellent' has a green and white spathe and a golden yellow spadix.

'Fruffles' has wavy leaf margins.

'Kingston' has very large (six inches long and four inches wide) wine-red spathes with bold, dark green foliage.

'Mary Jean' has a white spathe with a pink spadix tipped in green.

'Mazie' has a small dark red spathe with a white spadix.

'Nicolien' is different with nearly black-green foliage and bright pink spathes.

'Nicoya' is round-shaped with a crimson spathe and a pink spadix tipped in white.

'Pacora' has a red spathe and a white spadix.

'Patino' is orange.

'Paula' has a large red spathe with a pale yellow spadix. (See color plate 1.)

'Pink Frost' and 'White Frost' have very large spathes upon substantial plants.

'Pure Vida Red' is dark red with long and narrow dark green foliage.

'Purple Plum' has numerous purple spathes held above the glossy, dark green foliage.

'Ramona' has dark red spathes and dark green foliage.

'Rubino' grows compactly with ruby-red spathes that darken with age.

'Showbiz' has a dark red spathe and a purple spadix. The flowerstalk is red-purple.

'Sonette' has a white spathe and a light pink spadix.

'Sophia' is red with a green edge.

'Southern Blush' is peach.

Hot Series:

'Orange Hot' and 'Red Hot' with intense orange and red tulip-shaped spathes held well above the compact, glossy green foliage. Available in 8-inch and larger diameter containers.

Lady Series:

'Lady Anne' is white, ' Lady Beth' is pastel pink with a tulip shape, 'Lady Carmen' is red-pink, 'Lady Jane' is dark pink and 'Lady Ruth' is raspberry. These are compact plants with small but abundant flowers and dark green foliage. They exhibit a tolerance of cool temperatures between 50-60° F. and excellent disease resistance.

Smalltalk Series:

'Smalltalk Lavender,' 'Smalltalk Pink,' 'Smalltalk Red' and 'Smalltalk Salmon' grow about ten to fourteen inches tall and are available in 3 to 8-inch diameter containers. The heart-shaped spathes are three to four inches long. They exhibit good disease resistance.

Aphelandra squarrosa
Zebra Plant, Saffron Spikes
Acanthaceae or Acanthus family
A native of tropical America, especially Brazil
Light: From medium to low
Soil: Moderately moist

This is a plant where you get double for your money. It has extremely showy foliage: lance shaped dark green leaves with white midrib and veins forming zebra stripes. And an equally showy yellow inflorescence which consists of a dense cluster of colorful bracts, thus its other common name, saffron spikes. The true tubular flowers appearing among the bracts are yellow, orange or red.

Length of bloom time: Long-lasting, six weeks or so.

Temperature: Intermediate to warm, from 65 to 90° F. Keep out of drafts.

Humidity: Moderate.

Overall shape: Wide and horizontal, with a vertical inflorescence.

Texture: Medium.

Availability: In the fall, one plant per 4 to 6-inch diameter container where it is from eight inches to one foot tall.

Placement: On a table or desk, as a substitute for bromeliads. Where bold color is desired.

Be aware that: Although pests are infrequent, mealybugs may occur.

Helpful hint: After the inflorescence declines, either remove it or replace the plant.

Cultivars include:

'Apollo' and 'Red Apollo' both have more white to cream variegation. 'Red Apollo' has red undersides on the leaves and red leaf petioles.

'Dania' has dark green foliage with prominent midrib and veins. (See color plate 1.)

'Louisae' has yellow bracts tipped in red with dark green foliage with prominent midrib and veins.

'Silver Cloud' has much white variegation.

Araucaria heterophylla
Norfolk Island Pine
Araucariaceae or Araucaria Family
**A native of that island in the South
  Pacific**
Light: From medium to low
Soil: Moderately moist

The Norfolk Island pine, not a true pine, has traditionally been used around the winter holidays. But, it is increasingly seen in the interiorscape throughout the year. When multiple plants per pot are used, then the effect is more generic.

The drooping, horizontal branches appear in whorls, then layers along the sparsely needled trunk. And those needles are so soft. The older this tree becomes, the quicker it grows, often producing an entire tier of branches each season. This brightly colored green new growth contrasts well with the rest of the dark green foliage. Truly, an easy maintenance plant with many tolerances. (See color plate 1.)

Temperature: Warm, from 75 to 95° F., but will tolerate low temperatures to 45°F.

Humidity: Will tolerate low humidity.

Overall shape: Pyramidal.

Texture: Finely textured needles upon a medium textured tree.

Availability: In 8 to 17-inch diameter containers. Approximately four to five feet tall in a 14-inch container.

Placement: Well suited for high traffic areas. As a massed background plant or as a specimen tree.

Be aware that: Although rarely troubled by pests, spider mites may develop in warm, dry locations.

Helpful hints: The root mass is small compared to the top growth; therefore, staking may become necessary. The lower the light, the more the branches droop. Not necessarily a bad.

Related species:

A. bidwilii, bunya-bunya pine or monkey puzzle tree, has a name that refers to the sharp edges of the flat, glossy foliage as it spirals around the stems. It's a puzzle even for a climbing monkey. I have seen specimens fifteen feet tall. Place in a "Look, but do not touch area."

Asparagus densiflorus 'Sprengeri'
Sprenger or Plume Asparagus, Asparagus Fern
Liliaceae or Lily Family
A cultivated variety from native plants of South Africa
Light: Medium
Soil: Moderately dry

These plants are not true ferns but are related to the edible asparagus. The needle shaped foliage does resemble that of the asparagus plant. The light green foliage actually consists of cladophylls (flattened stems that look like and photosynthesize as leaves.) The true leaves are located at the base of the cladophylls and are small spines. The upright and wide spreading branches arch gracefully and take up much space as they mature.

Temperature: Intermediate, from 60 to 70° F., but tolerates as low as 50° F.

Humidity: Moderate.

Overall shape: Low and draping when young. Taller as the plant matures.

Texture: Delicate.

Availability: In 6 to10-inch diameter containers and hanging basket sizes. Table top size is another choice.

Placement: As a specimen plant or as a substitute for ferns. As a finely textured fill-in contrasting with flowering plants.

Be aware that: Leaf yellowing occurs under low humidity. Spider mites are the most common pest.

Helpful hint: As the plants mature, spines appear. Since water is stored in the large white underground tubers, these plants can go without watering for quite a while.

Another cultivar:

'Myersii,' Myers or foxtail fern is stiff and angled upward resembling a foxtail. (See color plate 1.)

Aspidistra elatior
Cast-Iron Plant
Liliaceae or Lily Family
A native of China and Japan
Light: From medium to very low. Tolerates as low as 20 foot-candles. Nearly in the dark!
Soil: Moderately dry to dry

This Victorian parlor plant that can withstand abuse and neglect—and extremely low light. After I had been working in the industry for about nine months, I was called to the housekeeping department. The director was concerned about a plant in the men's executive rest room. I told her that I knew nothing about a plant being there and thought this an unusual request of a female. I asked a male housekeeper to move the plant into a nearby hallway and sure enough, it was a cast-iron plant. I cleaned it, watered it and trimmed a few dried leaf tips and then had him put it back. From then on, I followed this maintenance pattern once every six months. Can anything be easier than that?

So much for how much care this plant requires. If aspidistra is placed in a medium light level then water it more often and it'll grow—not necessarily a desired characteristic. Although aspidistra has elegant, leathery, glossy dark green elliptical foliage, the two variegated cultivars are so much more interesting. The thick and strong leaf petioles may be long, short or nearly nonexistant but they are attached directly to thick rhizomes (thickened storage stems) which are sometimes visible at the soil surface.

Temperature: A wide range, from 50 to 90° F.

Humidity: Moderate, but will tolerate low humidity.

Overall shape: Upright with slightly arching foliage.

Texture: Bold.

Availability: In 8 to 14-inch diameter containers with the larger sizes being from two and one-half to three feet tall and as wide.

Placement: Place in hard to reach locations

away from windows, such as under a stairway. In a heavy trafficked area.

Be aware that: Pests include spider mites. Older plants may develop tipburn, as a result of fluoride buildup.

Helpful hint: Try this easy to maintain plant that has a wide range of tolerances.

Cultivars include:

'Milky Way' has small white dots or "stars" on the foliage. It is subtle, yet an interesting pattern. The foliage is narrower—two to three inches and shorter—eighteen inches long. It is resistant to spider mites.

'Variegata' has one of the most striking and interesting leaves of all plants. The leaves are long, up to two feet, and five inches wide. This provides plenty of room for white variegation that appears lengthwise in various irregular widths and often stops at the midrib. Sometimes, half the leaf is green and the other half is striped. (See color plate 1.) If too many new leaves appear all green, remove a few. Fertilizing this cultivar reduces the amount of variegation.

***Aucuba japonica* 'Variegata'**
Gold Dust Plant, Japanese Laurel
Cornaceae or Dogwood Family
A cultivated variety from native
**   plants of Japan and temperate**
**   Asia**
Light: From medium to high
Soil: Moderately dry

The first time I was introduced to this plant was when a client asked me if I could get a plant for her. She described it as a plant with yellow splotches and it came from Cuba. It's interesting how facts get misinterpreted. The gold dust plant is another aptly named plant. Whether it is "spotted" as a specimen plant or massed in an atrium, the gold dust plant is easily noticed. It has five inch long leathery elliptical foliage with pointy tips. Mature foliage has slightly serrated leaf margins. (See color plate 1.)

If you look at the glass as half-empty, then you might say the splotches look like the plant is diseased. Otherwise, the color pattern of the gold dust plant provides a great contrast when planted among other foliage plants.

Temperatures: Cool to intermediate, from 45 to 75° F.

Humidity: It tolerates low humidity.

Overall shape: Upright with full horizontally held foliage

Texture: Medium.

Availability: In 8 to 14-inch diameter containers where the larger sizes are three feet tall.

Placement: Near a drafty doorway, anywhere a "spot" of color is needed.

Be aware that: It is suseptible to spider mite infestations.

Helpful hint: This plant may require pruning.

Cultivars include:

'Goldiana' has more yellow specks.

Bambusa vulgaris 'Striata'
Feathery Bamboo
Graminaceae or Grass Family
A cultivated variety from native plants of tropical Asia
Light: On the brighter side of medium to high levels
Soil: Moderately moist

Bamboo is a large, ornamental grass with perfectly round culms (canes.) It is those culms that first attract attention. They are bright yellow with vertical dark green stripes every so often. These stripes abruptly stop and start again at the horizontal nodes. This ornamentation leads the eye on a vertical adventure. (See color plate 1.)

Overhead, narrow feathery foliage adds a soft touch to the straight and narrow culm from which it emanates. Bamboo grows to twenty-five feet.

Temperature: Warm, from 70 to 90° F., but tolerates cool temperatures well.

Humidity: Moderate.

Overall shape: Tall and airy.

Texture: Bold culms and delicate foliage.

Placement: Sunny atriums, en masse to enhance the eye-catching culms.

Availability: The 21-inch diameter containers are five to ten feet tall whereas 26-inch diameter containers have plants twelve feet and taller. Six to twelve culms are planted per container.

Be aware that: Yellow foliage is a sign of iron deficiency. Watch out for spider mites, too.

Helpful hint: This plant grows and old culms may need to be removed.

Other bamboo plants:

Phyllostachys nigra, black bamboo, has green culms that turn to a rich black with maturity. The prominent horizontal nodes have a white lower edge.

Beaucarnea recurvata
Ponytail Palm, Elephant Foot Tree
Agavaceae or Agave Family
A native of Mexico and Texas
Light: From high to medium
Soil: Moderately dry to dry

This is a curious plant that really is like no other. And it is not a palm. The thick trunk with a bulbous base is most intriguing. It resembles an elephant's foot, thus its one common name. (See color plate 1.)

The other, ponytail palm, describes the foliage. It arises from a whorl of leaves along the top of the trunk looking like a pony's tail. The long and narrow, leathery yet supple leaves recurve and gracefully "weep" downward way past the plant base and often beyond the base of the decorative container. Place this plant on a stand to raise it off the floor.

Since the base of the trunk stores water, be judicial with the watering to avoid stem rot. Ponytail palm is a very slow growing plant, another reason why it doesn't require much water.

Temperature: Warm, from 75 to 90° F. are preferred, but tolerates as low as 50° F. and as warm as 95° F.

Humidity: Medium but tolerates low.

Overall shape: Upright and arching gracefully.

Other forms: From short, squatty bush size plants to tall tree height. Multiple trunks with those swollen centers fused together are an eye-catching sight.

Texture: A combination of bold trunks and delicate foliage.

Availability: In 6 to 14-inch diameter containers.

Placement: Out of the main stream of traffic, unless they are treelike. They add interest to a larger table top arrangement.

Be aware that: The leaf margins are sharp and pests are uncommon, so a feather duster is appropriate for cleaning this plant.

Helpful hint: This plant has a wide range of tolerances along with easy maintenance.

Begonia x *hiemalis* [1], *B.* x *elatior*
Rieger Begonia, Hiemalis Begonia
Begoniaceae or Begonia Family
Hybridized from *B. socotrana* and
B. tuberhybrida
Light: Medium
Soil: Moist

These hybrid begonias were bred in England in 1883 and were the first flowers developed specifically for the commercial market. England dominated the market until the 1930s during which time they were the most popular houseplant in Western Europe. In 1955, Otto Rieger of Germany released many excellent cultivars and began calling them Rieger begonias. Beginning in 1978, Jim Mikkelson of Ashtabula, Ohio, grew and promoted them for the American market.

The colors range from reds to corals, peaches, oranges, whites and yellows including combinations. The flowers may be single or double, some with fringed margins. Many of the double flowers resemble miniature roses. These plants are not masses of color but rather clusters of beautiful, individual flowers set against a background of large green leaves. (See color plates 1 and 5.)

Improvements include: stronger stems for easier transportability, longer bloom time and increased disease resistance.

Length of bloom time: The long-lasting flowers often bloom for four weeks or more. Remove dried blossoms; this also encourages reblooming.

Temperature: Cool-intermediate, from 50 to 75° F.

Humidity: Moderate.

Overall shape: Rounded.

Texture: Medium in foliage, delicate in flower.

Availability: They are forced into bloom year-round usually available in 6-inch diameter containers. Miniatures are also available.

Placement: Massing these plants provides more color. Individual placement in areas close to the public so they can see the beauty of the flower.

Be aware that: The foliage is succulent and the plant is often staked. Once in place, remove the string and stakes if they are visible. Rieger begonias are susceptible to powdery mildew. Proper air circulation and low humidity will prevent this disease. Keep the foliage dry when watering to prevent bacterial blight, *Xanthomonas begoniae*, small water-soaked spots at the leaf margin and gray mold, *Botrytis*, also appearing on the stems or flowers. Root rot, *Pythium*, may also occur.

Helpful hint: Do not allow this plant to wilt; the buds dry up and fall off.

Cultivars include:

'Baladin' has very dark red double flowers.

'Balamon' has bright orange-red double flowers.

'Berseba' has lilac-pink double flowers.

'Bina' with light pink double flowers.

'Fayal' with pale pink-peach double flowers and very dark green foliage.

Netja Series: All have double flowers.

'Asani' has coral pink flowers with medium green foliage.

'Jutta' has deep yellow flowers with rose margins.

'Kleo' has deep salmon pink flowers.

Spectrum Series: The wide range of sizes and colors is great in these double flowers.

'Barkos' is the number one selling Rieger begonia in Europe, with rich red flowers and dark green foliage.

'Moonbeam' has pale yellow flowers.

'Pink Chablis' with delicately pale yellow flowers with a salmon-orange margin and salmon-orange buds.

Takora Series:

'Takora Orange' has orange double flowers.

'Takora Yellow' with golden yellow double flowers with fringed margins.

---

[1]   These are complex semi-tuberous hybrids combining the large, colorful flowers of *B. tuberhybrida*, composed of several tuberous species from Peru and Bolivia with the short-day characteristics of *B. socotranta*, a fibrous type from Saudi Arabia.

Begonia* x *rex-cultorum
Rex Begonia
Begoniaceae or Begonia Family
Hybridized from native plants of Central and South America and Asia
Light: Medium
Soil: Moderately moist

These begonias are known for their colorful foliage and varied leaf texture and shape. During the winter, they may bloom with clusters of delicate pale pink or white flowers. They are the result of a cross between *B. rex* and various rhizomatous begonias.

Temperature: Cool-intermediate, from 60 to 75° F.

Humidity: Moderate.

Overall shape: Rounded.

Texture: Bold.

Availability: Usually in the 4 to 6-inch diameter containers where they are one foot tall.

Placement: As a specimen plant where all may admire. As a substitute for flowering plants.

Be aware that: Crown and root rot may occur, so water properly. Keep the leaves dry to prevent leaf spot disease. Insects are usually not a problem.

Helpful hint: The larger leaf begonias tend to flop.

Cultivars include:

Decorative, ruffled foliage:

'Kismet' has silvery-pewter foliage with radiating dark green midribs and veins.

'Uncle Remus' has a crimson to rose center that fades to a silvery-green with dark green midribs, veins and leaf margins. This is a miniature form that is six to ten inches tall.

Spiral leaf foliage:

'Escargot' with a wide band of pewter coiled at the leaf base then swirled around the massively large, dark green foliage. It really does look like a colorful coiled snail. (See color plate 1.) This is one of the first releases by Gen Plant breeder Dick Alderen. He takes rare species, propagates them and returns a portion to the wild or back to the botanic garden from which they originated. This cultivar is resistant to disease, tolerates neglect and is very easy to maintain.

'Fortune Cookie' has a metallic silvery-bluish center that is pink along the leaf margins.

'Mexicross' has a very dark leaf splashed with lime green splotches and blooms with clusters of pure white flowers. It is a hybrid between *B.* x *rex-cultorum* 'Cleopatra' and *B. boweri*. 'Tiger' is a very similar cultivar.

'Persian Swirl' has many shades of green, gray and silver.

'Raspberry Swirl' has a red center on a dark green leaf.

Other related begonias:

B. masoniana, iron-cross begonia, has a bumpy surface with a wide dark brown iron crosslike image dominating the leaf. Small reddish flowers are grouped in clusters held above the foliage.

B. semperflorens-cultorum 'Bull's Eye' is a fibrous begonia suited for indoor use. It has a large red central bull's eye upon a large green leaf.

__Bougainvillea__ **spp.[2]**
Bougainvillea, Paper Flower
Nyctaginaceae or Four-o-clock
Family
Hybridized from native plants of
Brazil
Light: On the brighter side of me-
dium
Soil: Moderately dry

The showy colors of pink, red, yellow, orange, peach and violet all with varying shades, scream "tropical" in this vining plant. The one inch diameter inflorescence is composed of three colorful bracts (modified leaves appearing as petals) surrounding tiny white flowers. The petals are papery thin and translucent. Bougainvillea typically blooms in late summer but many cultivars are repeat bloomers.

The foliage is dark green, oval and pointy at the tip and acts as a great backdrop for the many flowers. The stems become woody with spines as they mature.

Length of bloom time: The colorful bracts last several months.

Temperature: Intermediate, from 65 to 75° F. , but tolerates as cool as 45° F. although leaf drop may occur.

Humidity: Moderate to high.

Overall shape: Variable, from vining to shrublike.

Texture: Medium.

Availability: In 10 to14-inch diameter containers.

Placement: Haven't you seen a trellised wall with bougainvillea reaching the ceiling? Or small plants cascading gracefully from large containers?

Be aware that: Scale insects may occur.

Helpful hint: The vining form requires staking and/or pruning and quickly fill a large area. The selection of compact varieties is lower growing.

Cultivars include:

'Harrisii' has a stunning green and white variegated leaf with bright magenta inflorescence. It is a compact grower. (See color plate 1.)

---

[2]   Most hybrids are derived from *B. glabra* and/or *B. spectabilis*. When these two were crossed, *B.* x *spectoglabra* resulted. *B.* x *buttiana* is a cross between *B. glabra* and *B. peruviana*.

Bucida buceras
Black Olive
Combretaceae or Combretum Family
A native of south Florida and the West Indies to Panama
Light: High, but acclimates to medium levels
Soil: Moist

When you got it, flaunt it. Thirty-foot high ceilings in an atrium area merit the expense and use of the black olive tree. These big trees have very dark green, glossy foliage similar to a ficus leaf shape. The branches grow in symmetrical horizontal tiers for a formal and elegant appearance. Often the width is three-quarters the height of the tree, so a great canopy envelops those who walk beneath. (See color plate 1.)

And, like the ficus tree, it is prone to lose its leaves with changes in environmental conditions. This is most obvious within a week after installation. Sometimes, the trees lose all of their leaves. They will quickly refoliate within a couple of weeks, but still this is a fact that everyone involved should be aware of. No wonder that new installations are set in place as soon as the dust settles, before clients move in. There seems to be no easy way to predict which trees will defoliate, but keeping a moist root ball at all times especially prior to installation, may help.

Temperature: Intermediate, from 60 to 70° F.

Humidity: As high as possible, but will adapt to moderate and low levels.

Overall shape: A huge tree.

Texture: Medium.

Availability: The 17-inch diameter container plant is eight to ten feet, the 32-inch is fourteen to eighteen feet and the 48-inch is eighteen to twenty-two feet. Field grown specimens may be taller and are balled and burlapped for delivery.

Placement: These are often planted in a row on either side of a walkway.

Be aware that: Insecticides may turn the foliage yellow. Clean with a soap solution to combat scale, mealybug or spider mites.

Helpful hint: Once the black olive shed its leaves, that will not happen again, unless the tree dies.

Cultivars include:

'Shady Lady'

'Table Top' (which is that size)

Caladium* x *hortulanum
Fancy-Leaf Caladium
Araceae or Arum Family
Hybridized from native plants of
    South America, especially Brazil
Light: Medium
Soil: Moderately moist

This is the same plant, derived from *C. bicolor* and other minor species, that is used outdoors and for the same reasons—colorful foliage. Whether the foliage is predominately pink, red, cream, light or bright green, or a combination, they all are very attractive. The most prominent color follows the midrib and veins creating some intricate patterns. Each leaf is attached to a sturdy but flexible leaf petiole which arises from an underground tuber.

Improvements include: dwarf sizes, new foliage shades and shapes, and tubers more resistant to rot.

Temperature: Warm, from 70 to 90° F. Protect from cold drafts.

Humidity: High to moderate.

Overall shape: Dense and upright.

Texture: Bold.

Availability: In late spring and seasonally throughout the year typically in 6-inch diameter containers.

Placement: Add for an unexpected touch of color or as a substitute for flowering plants. Use as a large scale groundcover planting.

Be aware that: When watering, avoid using cold water. Used for the short term, pests should not be a problem.

Helpful hints: With these bright color combinations, use caladium as an economical choice as a substitute for flowering plants. I always receive compliments when I plant them as a summer groundcover surrounding large kentia palms. This unexpected touch of tropical heart-shaped foliage surprises and pleases people. They'll last for a month or so. Then, go back to using flowers.

Cultivars include:

'Candidum' is an older cultivar that is predominantly white with dark green veins. Available as eighteen-inch tall plants.

'Carolyn Whorton' or 'Carolyn Wharton' is similar to 'Fanny Munson' but has more splotches of dark green along with a dark green leaf margin. Available as sixteen-inch tall plants. (See color plate 1.)

'Fanny Munson' nearly the entire heart-shaped leaf is hot pink with red veins. Great for Valentine's Day. Available as sixteen-inch tall plants.

'Frieda Hemple' has a large bright red heart shape inside each light green leaf. Great for Valentine's Day. Available as fourteen-inch tall plants.

'Mrs. Arno Nehrling' has a red midrib and veins that predominate the creamy green leaf edged in solid green. Available as sixteen-inch tall plants. Another great color combination to brighten up an interior plantscape.

Miniatures:

'Miss Muffett' grows six to eight inches and has ruffled foliage. Green is the predominant color of the foliage with cream veins surrounded by shades of hot pink. Burgundy splotches appear in the green area.

Calathea spp.
Calathea
Marantaceae or Arrowroot Family
Bred from native plants of Central and South America
Light: Low but acclimates to a medium level
Soil: Moist

What colorfully patterned foliage the *Calatheas* have. The large foliage—up to one foot long—decorates an entire area and can be used in place of blooming plants or as floor plants. The extremely showy foliage has many shades of green, pink and purple often with undersides of red-purple. These have traditionally hard to maintain but many improved cultivars are more durable and pest resistant.

Temperature: Intermediate to warm, from 65 to 90° F. are preferred.

Humidity: From high to moderate.

Overall shape: Upright and wide.

Texture: Bold.

Availability: In 6 to 14-inch diameter containers. The plants vary in height from one to three feet.

Placement: In a bed surrounded by other plants where it can be looked upon from above. As a substitute for flowering plants.

Be aware that: Spider mites are the main pest.

Helpful hints: This plant is often short-lived; leaf damage is due to low humidity. It is also sensitive to soluble salt build up and fluoride tipburn on older leaves.

Cultivars include:

'Corona' has round foliage that is light green with a wide, dark green margin. It has a quiet look, rather than heavily patterned. It is available in the 4 to 6 inch-diameter containers for table top gardens as well as 8 to 10-inch diameter containers as floor plants. A 6-inch plant is fifteen inches tall and as wide, a 10-inch plant is twice the size.

'Medallion' is a very decorative plant with busy-looking patterns. The one-foot long foliage has light green angled blotches along the midrib, then scalloped dark green, followed by a narrow area of white and light green along the widemargins. The undersides of the leaves are red-purple. The plant grows upright to three feet. (See color plate 1.)

'Picta Royale' has similar but less distinctive patterning than 'Medallion'. It has a low and spreading habit.

Related species:

C. equadoriana 'Velvet Touch' with velvety dark green foliage and a light green midrib and veins.

C. kennedyeae 'Helen' has foliage that looks similar to *Maranta leuconeura* var. *kerchoviana*, rabbit's tracks, but with larger dark green "tracks" on either side of the leaf and a wide, dark green leaf margin upon a silver-gray green background. The undersides are purple. A 6-inch diameter growing container is one foot tall.

C. lancifolia, the rattlesnake plant, looks rather different beginning with the long and narrow foliage with subtle light and dark green markings, wavy margins, and dark red-purple on the undersides. The leaves are very thin and pliable and have soft hairs mostly obvious when touched. The dark red leaf petioles have soft red hairs which more prominent. This species is two feet tall.

C. makoyana, the peacock plant, has prominent dark green markings and thin dark green lines along both sides of the midrib all upon a light green background. It is easy to maintain, and is eighteen inches tall.

C. ornata 'Rosea-linneata' is most striking with sets of two or three white to light pink pinstripes separated by a dark green background with the underside being red-purple. This pattern is repeated throughout the leaf. It definitely brightens up a dark area. It is often grown in the smaller sizes where a 6-inch plant is fifteen inches tall.

C. rufibarba, fuzzy feather, has a different presentation with velvety, solid green foliage and a ruffled margin. The undersides are red-purple. It has a more upright habit, twenty inches tall in the 6-inch diameter container. It is more durable than other *Calatheas*.

C. vitatta, scribe leaf, has small elongated oval leaves with green veins upon a silvery background. This plant is one foot tall.

C. zebrina, the zebra plant, has velvety foliage with lime green stripes upon a dark green background. It is three feet tall.

Related plants:

Stromanthe amabilis is a similar looking plant but on a smaller scale. The oval, pointy leaves are six to nine inches long and two inches wide. They are banded with dark green on a light green background. The foliage is more compact and dense. It is a tougher plant that acclimates to low light levels and requires less watering than *Calathea*. This durable plant tolerates high levels of soluble salts and fluoride without showing leaf damage and is resistant to spider mites. The cultivars are available in 4 to 6-inch diameter containers and hanging basket sizes.

'Triostar' has irregular, distinctive streams of dark green splash on the cream colored foliage. The elongated foliage is oval and glossy with dark red undersides. The new foliage is tightly curled and dark red. Very eye catching.

'Burle Marx' has dark green diagonal stripes on both sides of the midrib upon a bright yellow-green background. The undersides are purple. These low-growing plants are one and one-half to two feet tall.

Caryota mitis
Fishtail Palm
Arecaceae or Palm Family
A native of southeast Asian rain forests and India
Light: From medium to high
Soil: Moderately moist

The fishtail palm is a favorite with its unusual foliage shape. The leaflets have ragged edges resembling a goldfish tail. The dichotomous (fanned) veining adds to the effect. Each frond is bipinnately compound typical only of this genus of palms. (See color plate 2.)

Usually the fishtail palm is grown with many green stems that are hidden by an abundance of foliage. This palm also is available as a tall tree. In this case, the foliage is perched atop a thick tan trunk which contrast nicely. This plant readily suckers from the base.

Temperature: Warm, from 70 to 95° F.

Humidity: As high as possible, but will adapt to moderate and low levels.

Overall shape: Shrubby or treelike with foliage resembling a deciduous tree more than a palm.

Texture: Bold.

Availability: Multistemmed, in 10 to 17-inch diameter containers. The 14-inch is five and six feet tall. Trees which may grow to twenty feet, are available upon request.

Placement: In an atrium in rows serving along a pathway. Or in a large planter box. As a specimen plant.

Be aware that: The two-spotted spider mite is endemic to this plant and usually requires prophylactic applications of a miticide. *Helminthosporium* fungus, with numerous brown round leaf spots may occur with overwatering. All in all, this is an easy to maintain palm.

Helpful hint: If the foliage turns yellow, add supplemental iron rather than fertilizer. Fertilizer causes rapid growth.

Chamaedorea elegans
Parlor Palm
Arecaceae or Palm Family
A native of Mexico and Guatemala
Light: Medium but acclimates to
    low
Soil: Moderately moist

Remember what those Victorian parlors looked like? Think of the conditions—cool with low light and that's where this palm is most useful.

This is a compact and delicate pinnately compound palm with rich, dark green foliage. These suckering palms have many plants per container to create a full look. (See color plate 2.)

Temperature: Warm, from 75 to 95° F. but will tolerate temperatures as low as 50° F.

Humidity: Moderate to low.

Overall shape: Upright and full with outwardly arching foliage.

Texture: Delicate.

Availability: In 10 to 14-inch diameter container from three to occasionally five feet tall. Table top size is another choice.

 Placement: In many classic interiors for formal balance. A pair of parlor palms would be nice along an entryway. As smaller specimen floor plants.

Be aware that: Spider mites and mealybugs seem to be endemic without the use of systemics. These palms are sensitive to soluble salt buildup so fertilize less often than other palms.

Helpful hints: When looking for a tropical look in a small area, try these durable palms. This palm is often incorrectly labeled as *Neanthe bella*.

Chamaedorea seifrizii
Reed Palm
Arecaceae or Palm Family
A native of Belize, Guatemala and
    the Yucatan peninsula
Light: Medium, but acclimates to
    slightly lower levels
Soil: Moderately moist

The reed palm, similar to the parlor palm, also creates a neat and formal appearance but on a larger scale. The entire plant is narrow with leaves extending from the base to the top. The uniformly-sized leaflets along the leaves resemble bamboo foliage. These leaves are tough and strong, making this plant a good choice for highly trafficked areas. When purchasing, look for the containers that have the most individual plants. These suckering palms grow well when crowded. (See color plate 2.)

Temperature: Warm, from 75 to 95° F. are preferred, although it does well in cooler temperatures.

Humidity: Moderate.

Overall shape: Upright and full with slightly arching foliage.

Texture: Medium.

Availability: From the 10-inch diameter container which is three feet tall to the 21-inch diameter container which is eight feet tall. Twelve-foot tall plants are available upon special request.

Placement: This is an elegant and neatly appearing palm that is often preferred where verticality is desired.

Be aware that: With the tougher foliage, spider mites and mealybugs rarely occur.

Helpful hint: This is an easy to maintain plant that has a wide range of tolerances.

Related species:

C. cataractarum, cascade palm, resembles the areca palm, *Chrysalidocarpus lutescens*, but has very dark green foliage. The 10-inch diameter containers are three feet tall and the 14-inch sizes are five feet tall.

C. erumpens, bamboo palm, has slightly wider and fewer leaflets per frond than the reed palm. The two terminal leaflets are substantially wider, an easy identification feature. The leaves are slightly pendulous rather than stiff as those of the reed palm. (See color plate 2.) The prominent horizontal node markings on the trunk resemble that of bamboo, a very desireable characteristic. Dried tan leaf sheaths are attached the trunk. This is an area that may harbor pests and disease. These dried sheaths are easily removed by twisting them with your hand until they easily separate. Bamboo palm requires medium light levels. Both this species and *C. seifrizii* have been interbred with results often called "Florida hybrid palms".

C. hooperiana, Maya palm, resembles the kentia palm, *Howea forsteriana*. This species is tolerant of low light levels as well as low humidity, and it is pest-resistant.

Chlorophytum comosum
Spider Plant
Liliaceae or Lily Family
A native of South Africa
Light: From medium to low
Soil: Moderately dry

Who isn't familiar with the spider plant with its graceful, arching look? (See color plate 2.) And with good reason, this is a very easy plant to grow and maintain. Many people don't know that the straight species plant has solid green leaves. It's the cultivars that are striped. All long and narrow leaves arise from a central rosette attached to fleshy underground rhizomes (thickened storage stems.) In the winter when days are short, the spider plant sends forth leafless runners which terminate with small white flowers. Plantlets then develop at these ends. They may be removed or allowed to hang and become a decorative part of the plant.

Temperatures: Intermediate to warm, from 65 to 90° F., but will tolerate temperatures as low as 35° F. for short periods of time.

Humidity: Moderate is best.

Overall shape: Fountainlike, upright and arching.

Texture: Medium.

Availability: In the hanging basket size or smaller growing containers.

Placement: As a hanging basket, or in a shelf planter, as groundcover, or in table top gardens.

Be aware that: On rare occasion, scale insects may infest the plant, most commonly along the runners.

Helpful hints: Tipburn occurs in low light, low humidity, as a buildup of soluble salts or fluoride damage. Usually underwatering is not the problem since this plant stores water in its rhizomes.

Cultivars include:

'Picturatum' has a wide pale yellow stripe or stripes down the center of the leaf and thin green leaf margins.

'Variegatum' has a white stripe down either side of the leaf margin. The central leaf portion is green.

'Vittatum' has a wide white stripe or stripes down the center of the leaf and thin green leaf margins. (See color plate 2.)

Chrysalidocarpus lutescens
Areca Palm
Arecaceae or Palm Family
A native of Madagascar
Light: From medium to high
Soil: Moderately moist

This inexpensive palm is best used as a "throw-away" palm. Within a few months of being on site, the stems turn yellow and the foliage develops a yellowish tinge. It no longer looks like a prime specimen. The pinnately compound leaf is large, long and graceful. (See color plate 2.) The many yellowish thin trunks have black lenticels (prominent pores used for gas exchange) which are sometimes mistaken for insect problems or disease.

Temperature: Adapts to a wide range, but warm, from 70 to 90° F. It tolerates as high as 95° F.

Humidity: Moderate to high.

Overall shape: Visible vertical stem centers with tall and arching leaves.

Texture: Medium.

Availability: The 10-inch diameter containers holds plants three to four feet tall whereas the 14-inch size holds plants six feet tall. Limited availability of the 24-inch diameter containers hold plants twelve to fifteen feet tall.

Placement: Used for any temporary location, such as upon a stage, or for seasonal plantings. This palm also works well where a taller, full palm is desired.

Be aware that: When using areca palm for a short term, pesticides become unnecessary. Otherwise, use a systemic pesticide to prevent spider mites, mealybugs and scale insects. Fertilize to keep this plant looking healthy. For a quick greening up, spray the foliage with a dilution of Super-Thrive[3].

Pink rot, also known as *Gliocladium* blight, affects stressed palms. The first sign of this fungus is a dark brown dead area along the stem close to the soil. At this time, treatment with a fungicide may save the plant. Eventually, all portions of this palm except for its roots become infected. Stem cankers are darkened depressed areas with masses of orange to pink spores. The stem exudes a gummy substance. Avoid open wounds and make sure to disinfect pruning tools when removing dead leaves.

Helpful hint: Try *Chamaedorea cataractarum*, cascade palm instead.

---

[3]   Superthrive is a solution of fifty vitamins-hormones developed by Dr. John A.Thomson's Vitamin Institute, Box 230, North Hollywood, CA, 91603.

Chrysanthemum x *morifolium,*
Dendranthema x *grandiflora*
Chrysanthemums, Mums
Asteraceae or Aster Family
Hybridized from native plants of
   China[4]
Light: Medium to low levels
Soil: Moist

Although mums are the number two flowering plant in yearly sales, they are North America's highest value year-round flowering plant. Alas, mums have been and remain, by all means, a workhorse in the industry. They are long lasting and durable. Availability, low maintenance and low cost adds to their appeal. A wide range of flower colors, shapes and sizes are constantly being developed. Pastel colors such as creams, pinks, apricots, mauves, lavenders and variations thereof predominate during the spring and summer; whereas bold autumnal colors such as corals, salmons, oranges, bronze, dark and cherry reds and purples preside during the fall and winter. Light and bright colors such as the whites and yellows remain popular all year long. Bicolors are increasingly popular.

According to Yoder Brothers, Inc., perennial top-sellers are: 'Pelee' (red-yellow bicolor daisy), 'Miramar' (yellow daisy), and 'Surf' (white decorative) for fall. The bronze and orange daisy and decorative-types continue to make a strong showing (Pelee-type mums); 'Miramar,' 'Shasta' and 'White Blush' (both white daisy-types) and 'Kory' (yellow decorative) for spring. The bicolors in soft shades of pink and lilac are gaining popularity. Summer and winter best sellers are yellow, white and pink/lavender decorative-type mums. Runner ups are coral/salmon daisy-types.

What is normally thought of as the "flower" really is composed of numerous outer ray flowers (petals) and central disk flowers (centers) together forming an inflorescence. Commonly, the term "flowerhead" is used.

There are three types:

Decorative mums consist of hundreds of petals that form a cushion without a distinct center. (See color plate 2.) The button mum is a type of decorative mum with short, stiff petals tightly compacted forming a molded looking flowerhead.

Daisy mums are exactly as they sound; they resemble daisies with one or two rows of open and flat petals and clearly visible centers. (See color plate 2.)

Anemone mums which has a showy pincushionlike center occasionally in a contrasting color.

The distinction between decorative, daisy and anemone mums sometimes becomes blurred. Some cultivars have more rows of petals than a daisy mum but are not as full as decorative mums; others almost look like an anemone mum but are not as distinct.

This is how the industry keeps reinventing mums so that they are interesting, different and ever popular.

Other shapes of the ray flowers:

Quill-shaped—with long, thin tubes. A plant with very narrow quills are called spider mums.

Another modification of the quill-shaped mum is **spoon-tipped**. The quills become showy tips in the shape of a spoon bowl.

Quill, spider and spoon mums usually are daisy-types, but may be decorative-types. (See color plate 2.)

Length of bloom time: The Floral Marketing Association and the Society of American Florists have distinguished five stages of flower development. Purchase mums at Stage 2 (one-quarter to one third of the buds are open) for maximum longevity of three to four weeks. Stage 4 (two-thirds to three-quarters of the buds are open, nearly full bloom) is ideal for instant, short-term color.

Temperature: Avoid extremes. Intermediate, from 65 to 75° F.

Humidity: Moderate.

---

[4]   Mums have been used in the Far East as early as 500 B.C., although numerous countries claim origin.

Overall shape: Mounded. Single stem pot mums are upright.

Texture: Medium.

Availability: The 6 to 8-inch diameter containers are most common. The 10-inch size and miniatures are also available. The 12-inch color bowl is low and wide and filled with color. Mums are naturally a short-day crop but they are forced into bloom year-round.

Placement: Mums can be used in high traffic areas or where instant color, long-lasting flowers and durability are desired.

Be aware that: Wilted mums do not revive with watering. Insects that may arrive with mums are thrips. Insist on clean replacements.

Helpful hints: Some improved qualities of mums are: a full canopy of color, larger flowerheads, a wider range of color, more diversity in flower forms and increased longevity.

Miniatures:

Fleurettes: These very long-lasting daisy mums are the result of breeding a wild Asiatic species with pot mums. The flowerhead is one and one-half inches or smaller and are sold in 2½ to 3½-inch containers and 4 to 6-inch containers that may be grouped in 6 to 8-inch hanging baskets or 5 to 12-inch shallow containers.

Cultivars include:

'Finesse' is a bicolor with the red-bronze ray flowers and yellow towards the base. The center is light green.

'Giselle' is red with yellow centers.

'Papillon' is dark lavender with yellow centers. 'Cherry Papillon' is that color.

'Rochelle' and 'White Rochelle' have spoon-tipped ray flowers with green centers. 'Rochelle' is lavender with white spoons.

Cherie Series:

'Apricot Cherie' is one of many colors, all with green centers. Others are: 'Bronze Cherie,' 'Dark Cherie' with dark pink, slightly serrated ray flowers, 'Soft Cherie' is light pink, 'Yellow Cherie' and 'White Cherie'.

Elmira Series:

'Elmira' is bicolored—the light pink ray flowers have dark pink towards the base.

'Frosted Elmira' is pink.

'Yellow Elmira' is pale yellow.

Standard size:

The following are sold in 4 to 8-inch diameter containers.

Cultivars include:

'Ayers' is bright salmon-orange with a green-yellow center.

'Bruce' is a red daisy mum with a yellow center.

'Cachi' is a yellow anemone mum with a red pincushion center.

'Chesapeake' is an improved yellow daisy mum with a green center. The foliage is very dark green.

'Cook' is a red daisy mum with a green-yellow center.

'Copper Piano' is a bicolor decorative-type with orange-bronze at the tips and golden bronze at the base of the ray flowers. The flowerhead is four to five inches wide.

'Coral Nashville' is a daisy mum in coral with a green center. The flowerheads are three inches wide.

'Dark Pink Blush' has dark pink ray flowers with a light green center. The flowerheads are five inches wide.

'Duluth' has dark red-purple ray flowers with silvery-pink centers and a light green center. The flowerheads are nearly three inches wide.

'Elliot' is a velvety red daisy mum with a green center.

'Etna' is a pink and white bicolor daisy mum with a pink center.

'Festive New Orleans' is a multicolored daisy mum, three inches wide. The rose-pink ray flowers have creamy yellow to ivory towards the bases. The center is bright yellow.

'Fito' is an orange daisy mum with a green center.

'Honey Gilroy' has bright yellow flowerheads five inches wide.

'Ivory Eugene' is a daisy mum with ivory-white flowerheads four inches wide and a green center.

'Jose's Sunset Lady' is a decorative mum with pink, then red towards the center.

'Kodiak' has ivory-tinged white flowerheads five inches wide.

'Lewis' is a purple daisy mum with green-yellow center.

'Pink Graceland' is a daisy mum pink mum with an ivory-chartreuse center. The flowerheads may be six inches wide.

'Regal Nashville' is a bicolored daisy mum with deep rose-purple ray flowers with yellow towards the base and a green center.

'Reno' is a vibrant orange daisy mum with a lime green center. The two and one-half inch wide flowerheads fill a fifteen by fifteen-inch plant.

'Rose Delano' has some bicolored ray flowers, rose-lavender and creamy-yellow towards the base. Others are rose-lavender. The flowerheads are over five inches wide.

'Royal New Orleans' is a bicolor daisy mum with purple ray flowers with white towards the base. The center is light green.

'Salmon Springfield' is that color with five-inch wide flowerheads.

'Scott' is a daisy mum spoon-tipped purple mum with a green center.

'Tasman' is a white daisy mum with a green-yellow center. What this mum lacks in flowerhead size—two inches wide— it makes up for in sheer number of blooms.

'Trenton' is a white decorative mum with a trace of ivory towards the base. The four and one-half inch wide flowerheads fill a fifteen by fifteen-inch plant.

'Trumbel' is a red decorative mum.

'Valentin' is a light pink daisy mum with a green-yellow center.

'Ventoux' is a white anemone mum with a brown center.

'White Billings' and 'Yellow Billings,' a bicolor with dark and bright yellow ray flowers, are both daisy-types with a green center. The flowerheads are five inches wide.

'Yellow Kodiak' has decorative quill-shaped ray flowers of brilliant yellow with five-inch wide flowerheads.

'Yellow Piano' is a decorative-type with bright yellow ray flowers. The flowerhead is five inches wide.

Danville Series:

'Danville' is a bright rose-pink anemone mum.

'Orange Danville' and 'Yellow Danville' are others.

Davis Series:

'White Davis' is a white daisy mum that is yellow towards the base of the ray flowers. The center is light green. Others include: 'Bronze Davis,' 'Coral Davis,' 'Pink Davis,' 'Purple Davis,' 'Red Davis' and 'Yellow Davis.'

Time Series: Some of the many cultivars are:

'About Time Purple' is a dark purple decorative mum.

'Astro Time' is a light green spider mum.

'Chisel Time' is a spoon-tipped daisy mum with rust ray flowers and white towards the base.

'Compare Time' is a burgundy daisy mum with a yellow-green center.

'Doing Time' is a double daisy mum with bright yellow ray flowers with orange towards the base.

'Energy Time' is a spoon-shaped daisy mum with brick red ray flowers with orange to dark yellow towards the base.

'Grace Time' is a purple quill-shaped mum.

'Lunar Time' is a daisy mum with cream ray flowers and red-purple towards the base. The center is yellow-green.

'Machismo Time' is a double daisy mum with red ray flowers tipped in yellow. The center is green.

'Mogul Time' is a spoon-tipped daisy mum with white quills and red-purple spoons. The center is yellow.

'Mosaic Time' is a spoon-tipped daisy mum with dark pink quills and lavender-frosted spoons. The center is yellow-green.

'Pixie Time' is a small, anemone mum with a dark pink pincushion center surrounded by light pink.

Cissus rhombifolia
Grape Ivy
Vitaceae or Grape Family
A native of the West Indies and
northern South America
Light: Medium but acclimates to
low levels
Soil: Moist

Grape ivy is a good alternative to using English ivy; it is rugged with easy-care. The leaves are grouped in threes, with the center one the largest—total width is four inches. The thin, glossy, deep green leaves look almost metallic with brown veins. The margins are slightly lobed with pointed tips. The new growth is tinged bronze. Along the vine, are coiled tendrils, like a grape vine. The leaf petioles and vines are red.

Temperature: Intermediate to slightly warm, from 65 to 80° F. Temperatures over 82° F. cause the plant to decline.

Humidity: Moderate to high.

Overall shape: Mounding, vining and trailing.

Texture: Medium.

Availability: In 6 to10-inch diameter containers and hanging basket sizes. Table top size is another choice.

Placement: Massed in shelf containers, hanging baskets, lovely growing on a totem, or as underplantings of large specimen trees.

Be aware that: Mealybugs and spider mites may occur as may powdery mildew.

Helpful hint: Grape ivy is a fast grower and may require pruning. Overwatering or cold drafts may cause leaf drop.

Cultivar:

'Ellen Danica,' oak-leaf ivy, is a sport (a naturally occuring mutation) of grape ivy. The larger trifoliate leaf with many lobes resembles an oak leaf. This is a very attractive cultivar. (See color plate 2.)

Related species:

C. antarctica, kangaroo vine, has heart-shaped bright shiny green leaves have widely serrated margins. It makes great underplantings.

A similar plant:

Tetrastigma voinierianum, chestnut vine, is a native of the jungles of Vietnam. If you are looking for a fast growing, vining plant, this is it. The woody stem climbs about five feet a year and quickly fills a trellised wall, or acts as a screening material to quickly hide mechanical structures. It can also withstand severe pruning. With its three to five leaflet, attractively resembling the shape and texture of the chestnut tree leaf, it also resembles the kangaroo vine, *C. antarctica* but with a coarser texture. It prefers medium light but acclimates to low levels. A warm temperature, from 70 to 90° F., allows it to thrive in high, dry areas.

x *Citrofortunella mitis, Citrus mitis*
Calamondin Orange
Rutaceae or Citrus Family
**Intergeneric hybrid of *Citrus
    reticulata*, a mandarin and
    Fortunella spp., a kumquat**
Light: High
Soil: Moderately moist

The calomondin orange is the citrus plant most conducive to indoor culture. What a conversation piece when someone walks into a lobby and sees miniature oranges. This upright tree has glossy, leathery, oval green leaves two to four inches long. The leaf petioles are winged and attached to woody stems.

Fertilize the calamondin orange when growth begins in spring to insure fragrant white flowers. Then, green fruit about two inches in diameter slowly turn bright orange by the fall. Sometimes, fruits and flowers appear on the same plant. The tree remains a focal point throughout the season.

Temperatures: Warm, from 70 to 90° F. for the growing season; intermediate, from 65 to75° F. if undergoing winter dormancy.

Humidity: Moderate.

Overall shape: Treelike or shrublike.

Texture: Medium.

Availability: In 10 to 21-inch diameter containers where the plants are three to twelve feet tall.

Placement: A tropical setting, in an atrium along a path where people walk.

Be aware that: Mealybug and spider mites may become pests.

Helpful hints: Prune to keep within bounds. Avoid temperature extremes to avoid leaf drop.

Cultivars include:

'Variegata' with white margined foliage is a much more attractive plant. (See color plate 2.)

Codiaeum variegatum var. *pictum*
Croton
Euphorbiaceae or Spurge Family
A native of the Moluccan Islands
      between New Guinea and the
      Philippines
Light: On the brighter side of me-
      dium but acclimates to lower
      light levels (with loss of bright
      colors)
Soil: Moderately moist

The crotons have large, leathery leaves that offer spectacular color. Magenta and orange mixed with contrasting lighter colored, usually yellow or pink, midribs and veins offer great contrast. Throw in some shades of pink, burgundy and cream for added color. Sometimes the leaf margins are irregular or wavy, adding extra interest.

The leaves have very short leaf petioles and are whorled along the green stem, suggesting a dense and heavy feeling to the plant.

Temperature: Intermediate to warm, from 65 to 90° F., leaf drop may occur if exposed to cold drafts.

Humidity: Average to high humidity.

Overall shape: Stiff and upright with nearly horizontal foliage.

Texture: Bold.

Availability: In 8 to 14 inch diameter containers which are from two to four feet tall. Three or four plants per large container are required for a full look. Table top size is another choice.

Placement: In a sunny atrium, ideally alongside a water feature. As a substitute for flowering plants. Also, to brighten up a poorly lit area.

Be aware that: Spider mites are the worst pest; mealybug or scale insects may also appear. Many improved cultivars are insect-resistant.

Helpful hint: Under inadequate light, the foliage loses its bright coloration to dark green but keeps the light colored midribs and veins, not necessarily all bad.

Cultivars include:

'Banana' is predominantly yellow with a wavy margin.

'Curly Boy' has a wavy margin.

'Glauca' has slender, olive-green foliage with a hint of lavender in the new foliage. It has a very upright habit.

'Gold Dust,' the gold dust croton, has much smaller foliage, elliptical in shape, with gold flecks.

'Mammy' with brightly colored red and green foliage with yellow midribs and veins. The narrower and more upright foliage has an attractive wavy margin. (See color plate 2.)

'Norma' with red, orange and yellow variegations on the more rounded, green foliage. It also is a more compact plant, fifteen inches tall.

'Oak Leaf' has a lobed leaf margin in fall colors.

'Petra' has yellow, orange and red clearly defined veins and margins upon a green background. It also is a more compact plant, fifteen inches tall.

'Stoplight' has very narrow leaves that emerge yellow and lime green, then turn bright red eventually maturing to red-black with narrow red margins.

Cordyline terminalis
Hawaiian Ti Plant
Agavaceae or Agave Family
**A native of India, east Asia, Malay-
sia and Polynesia**
**Light: On the brighter side of me-
dium but acclimates to lower
levels (with loss of bright colors)**
Soil: Moderately moist

This plant is prized for its spectacularly colored foliage—some of the brightest in the industry. The multicolored, elliptical leaf is dominated
by reds, red-purples, purples and shades thereof
with only a trace of green. The foliage grows
upright before slightly arching and is attached to
fleshy leaf petioles that wrap around the cane.
These flexible gray canes are marked with horizontal bands indicating leaf scars.

Temperature: A wide range from 45 to 95° F.

Humidity: Moderate to high.

Overall shape: V-shape.

Texture: Bold.

Availability: In 8 to 14-inch diameter containers. The 10-inch container has a plant thirty
inches tall. Table top size is another choice.

Placement: Often used in a well lit area as a
replacement for flowering plants. As a mid-height
border plant. As individual specimen plant where
all may appreciate the brightly colored foliage.

Be aware that: Some cultivars become riddled
with spider mites. *Erwinia* bacterial soft rot occurs with overwatering.

Helpful hints: This plant is closely related to
the *Dracaena plants* but is less durable. Under
low light, the foliage loses its bright coloration.
Many improved cultivars are insect-resistant.

Cultivars include:

'Baby Doll' has green foliage with a narrow red
margin.

'Glauca' contains predominantly white foliage.

'Kiwi' has red and green striped foliage.

'Purple Prince' and 'Red Prince' are two of the
most insect-resistant and stable ti plants.

'Red Madam' has a dark red-black leaf bright-
ened by pink and/or red splashed tops and margins.

'Red Sister' has irregular vertical bands of red,
red-violet and pink. It is susceptible to spider mite
infestation.

'Sherbert' is a stable red, pink and green variegation.

'Tricolor' has green and cream striping over most
of the leaf with pink margins.

'Xerox' has dark purple foliage with wide sections
of magenta on the new foliage that become narrower with maturity. (See color plate 2.)

Crassula ovata, C. argentea
Jade Plant
Crassulaceae or Stonecrop Family
A native of South Africa
Light: From high to medium
Soil: Moderately dry

The jade plant is a succulent with thick, glossy bright green oval to round leaves. When the jade plant is used in brighter light a red leaf margin develops. The foliage is directly attached to green, succulent branches growing in many directions which are then attached to thick tan stems. The eye-catching contrast makes an strong architectural statement. (See color plate 2.)

After a cool winter dormancy, delicate small white starlike flowers may develop. This is a durable plant with many tolerances and easy maintenance.

Temperature: Cool to intermediate, from 55 to 75° F. are preferred; but will tolerate as low as 40° F. and as high as 100° F.

Humidity: Tolerates low levels.

Overall shape: Shrublike.

Texture: Bold.

Availability: In 8 to 14-inch diameter containers. The typical height as a floor plant is three feet tall. Also in the table top size. Bonsai plantings are another choice.

Placement: As a specimen plant especially in Asian-themed rooms. The leaves are easily broken off when bumped, so place the jade plant in a low traffic area.

Be aware that: Mealybugs may develop at the leaf axils (the junction between the leaf petiole and stem.) Avoid leaf shine; it damages the foliage.

Helpful hints: The jade plant grows best in a soil mixture containing sand. It is often planted in a small shallow clay container where it drains well and is allowed to become root bound.

Cultivars include:

'Tricolor' has foliage that is dark green, light green and cream.

'Variegata' has foliage with cream and green coloration blending together.

Cryptanthus bivittatus
Earth-Star Plant
Bromeliaceae or Pineapple Family
A native of Brazil
**Light: From high to the brighter
   side of medium**
Soil: Moderately dry

The earth-star plant looks like a starfish. The narrow and serrated foliage radiates from a central rosette. This foliage nearly always has prominent dark green stripes running down the center and leaf margins, contrasting nicely with lovely pastels filling in.

The many cultivars are striking, with bronze-pink, pink, ivory and coppery-green coloration. Some are dwarf, just a few inches across, and others are giant, up to sixteen inches wide. The plant remains attractive for up to six months.

Temperature: A wide range from 55 to 85° F., and can tolerate short periods of cooler and warmer temperatures.

Humidity: Adapts to low humidity although moderate is preferred.

Overall shape: Low and wide.

Texture: Medium.

Availability: In small growing containers or as part of a table top bromeliad garden.

Placement: This unusual presentation makes it suitable for placement on desks, tables, even in the middle of a pond on a protruding rock.

Be aware that: *Cryptanthus* needs very little soil since it is an epiphyte—growing in tree crevices with aerial roots absorbing nutrients from water, air and dust particles. The roots cling to whatever material it touches. Sometimes the plants are mounted on a dab of sphagnum moss glued to driftwood, rock or other decorative items.

Helpful hint: It is okay to splash some water of the foliage when watering.

Cultivars include:

'Elaine' has very dark green foliage striped horizontally with white. The wide margins are deep magenta. This is a larger size plant, six to ten inches tall and one foot to sixteen inches wide.

'Pink Starlight' and 'Starlight' have brilliant striping along with wavy leaf margins. (See color plate 2.)

Cycas revoluta
Sago Palm
Cycadaceae or Cycad Family
A native of southern Japan
Light: Medium, but acclimates to low levels
Soil: Moderately dry

The sago palm is among the most primitive of all living seed plants and the oldest—200 million years. Members of this family are gymnosperms but unrelated to any other group of living plants. They are formal, neat-looking plants that resemble palms or ferns but are distinctly different.

The leaflets look like plastic. They are stiff with sharp tips. The margins are strongly revolute (rolled backwards.) The pinnately compound leaflet arrangement does resemble a palm frond. The leaves arise from the center—a short and squat trunk that is reduced to a large brown terminal bud covered with thick and loose, dark brown fibrous hairs. The combination of bright green smooth leaves and a rich brown shaggy trunk is a striking contrast of texture and color.

(See color plate 2.) These are slow growers; one tier of leaves grows every year or two. Being very easy to maintain with a wide range of tolerances, they are well-suited for indoor use.

Temperature: Tolerates a wide range, from 55 to 95° F., and will withstand temperatures below freezing for brief periods.

Humidity: Moderate to low.

Overall shape: Low with a widely spreading crown; occasionally palmlike with a trunk and terminal leaves as large specimen plants.

Texture: Bold trunk, medium foliage.

Availability: The 10-inch diameter container is two to three feet tall; up to 21-inch diameter containers with 10 feet tall plants.

Placement: Away from traffic; however, the tall tree forms are fine with the foliage high above overhead.

Be aware that: Scale insects or mealybug may become a problem. Avoid getting the terminal bud wet when watering.

Helpful hint: These are tough plants. Try them.

Interesting fact: The tall, treelike *Cycas* are sometimes imitations composed of fabricated material.

Cyclamen persicum
Cyclamen
Primulaceae or Primrose Family
A native of the Mediterranean region
Light: Medium
Soil: Moist

The cyclamen has been a collector's item in Western Europe since the seventeenth century. Improved breeding methods in the mid-1800s allowed it to become the leading containerized flowering plant in Europe. The United States quickly joined rank. Breeding is continually going on in Europe and Japan.

The fragrant blossoms rise well above the foliage upon long and thin green stalks and look as if they were blowing in the wind. They appear in various shades of pink, purple, red, salmon and magenta. They may also be white or bicolored with darker eyes or flamed with a very narrow white picotee (margin.) The petal edges may be fringed. Some flowers are double.

At the base, a thick mound of large heart-shaped leaves with silver tracery and burgundy on the underside cover the soil. This foliage is nearly as attractive as the blossoms and will last for months. Improvements include unusual bicolored flowers with smaller, more silvery foliage.

Length of bloom time: Depending upon the temperature, cyclamen stays in bloom from three weeks to two months. Purchase in the mature bud stage.

Temperature: Cool, from 55 to 60° F. Avoid drafts and sudden temperature changes.

Humidity: Moderate to high.

Overall shape: Round base, tall flowerscapes.

Texture: Bold in foliage and delicate in flower.

Availability: This is a naturally winter blooming plant and is available from September through May available in many sizes. Miniatures are also available.

Placement: Cool, bright locations; as a seasonal bloomer welcoming spring. In classic decors.

Be aware that: Keep the crown dry when watering. If the temperature is too warm or the light is not bright enough, cyclamen foliage quickly yellows. Cyclamen mites causing flower disfigurement are the only pest, but growers address this problem.

Helpful hint: Try the many cultivars that are heat tolerant.

Miniature size: (Available in 3 to 4 ½-inch containers. The micro-mini—2 ½-inch is another choice.)

Compact Mini Series. 'Compact Spotted' which is white with a medium to dark, large purple eye. Each plant produces up to one hundred flowers. Other colors are available.

Dixie Series. Available in seven colors and a mix, all with foliage strongly marked with silver. Colors include: 'Dark Red,' 'Light Lilac' and 'Salmon with Eye'.

Inferno Series. Available in fourteen colors, such as 'Laura' which is cherry red and 'Violetta' which is purple.

Metis Series. 'Scarlet Red' and 'Pure White' are two popular colors. A total of eleven colors including pink, salmon and lavender are featured, some of which are scented and are covered with long lasting flowers that have good tolerance to higher temperatures. Available from September through March.

Miracle Series. This includes eight solid colors, one having a red eye; a separate flamed with a very narrow white picotee (margin) mix is available.

Marvel Series. Several colors are scented.

Musical Series. Available in nine colors.

Intermediate size: (Available in 4 to 5-inch containers.)

Compact Series. 'Spotted' which is white with a from medium to dark, large purple eye.

'Spotted Purple' in purple with an even darker purple eye. Each plant produces up to one hundred-forty flowers. Other colors are available.

Laser Series. 'Laser Fuchsia' has petals with deep burgundy centers surrounded by fuchsia. Other colors are available with some that are scented. These are compact plants with intermediate-sized flowers.

Latinia Series. 'Bright Rose,' 'Deep Salmon,' 'Purple,' 'Scarlet Red,' 'Wine Red' and 'Pure White Compact' have long lasting flowers held far above the foliage.

'Rose with Eye Improved' and 'White with Eye' both have magenta eyes.

'Rose Flame' and 'Salmon Flame' are those colors, respectively, with a very narrow white picotee (margin.) These fragrant flowers have a good tolerance to higher temperatures. Available from September through February.

Libretto Series. All the standard colors, some with dark eyes, are available. The abundant flowers have shorter stalks than most and foliage is small. The entire plant forms a rounded shape.

Standard size: (Available in 4½ to 7-inch containers.)

Concerto Series. All of the following are compact growers with flowers centrally held.

Available in fifteen colors such as 'Apollo' which is solid white, 'Magenta Catya' which is fuschia-magenta with a dark eye, 'Salmon Lucia' which is a solid, deep salmon with a dark eye.

Halios Series. 'Deep Rose Improved' has fluorescent rose-colored petals. (See color plate 2.)

'Pure White,' 'Pure White Improved,' 'Rose,' 'Salmon Rose,' 'Bright Salmon,' 'Scarlet Salmon,' 'Bright Scarlet,' 'Scarlet Red,' 'Magenta,' and 'Purple'.

'Rose with Eye' and 'White with Eye Improved' have magenta eyes.

'Deep Red Flame,' 'Rose Flame,' 'Magenta Flame,' 'Purple Flame' and 'Salmon Flame' are those colors, respectively, with a barely visible white picotee (margin.)

Maxora Series. Similar to the Sierra Series with ten colors available.

Sierra Series. 'Sierra Deep Red,' 'Sierra Deep Rose,' 'Sierra Deep Salmon' and 'Sierra Light Purple' which have such colors.

'Sierra Pink' has pale pink blossoms with a mottled mauve eye.

Extra large size: (Available in 6-inch or larger containers.)

Pannevis Series. Available in eight colors such as 'Boheme' with wine red flowers, 'Bolero' with mid-lilac flowers and 'Romeo' with scarlet red flowers.

Super Series. Available in all four sizes. Colors include: 'Light with Eye,' 'Neon Pink,' 'White' and 'Wine Red'.

Dianthus **spp.**
Carnations
Caryophyllaceae or Pink Family
**Bred from native plants of Europe
     and Asia**
Light: Medium
Soil: Moderately moist

In the spring, carnations are sold for outdoor use. However, they are occasionally used indoors to add temporary yet abundant color. The typical carnation flower is single or double, in many colors such as white, yellow, pink, peach, lavender, purple, red and maroon. Many are flecked or laced with another color or have a contrasting picotee (margin.) Some have a spicy scent. The foliage is narrow and not very prominent.

Length of bloom time: Usually about one week or two.

Temperature: Intermediate, from 65 to 75° F., but will tolerate cooler temperatures.

Humidity: Moderate.

Overall shape: Low and dense.

Texture: Delicate in foliage, medium in flower.

Availability: In spring, and seasonally at other times of the year, in 4 to 6-inch diameter containers. Miniatures are also available.

Placement: Any cool area where a splash of color is desired.

Be aware that: These are short-lived but easy maintenance flowering plants.

Helpful hint: These are not traditionally thought of as an indoor plant, so surprise your client.

Cultivars include:

'Diorama' has pink with a rose center and semi-double flowers.

'Discovery' has red double flowers.

'Dimple' has purple semi-double flowers.

'Igloo' has pure white flowers.

Adorable Series: These are shorter plants with double flowers.

'Essence' has creamy yellow flowers with a pink picotee (margin.)

'Lacy' has yellow flowers with a maroon picotee (margin.)

'Mango' has orange flowers.

'Morango' has melon-colored flowers.

'Yellow Lacy' has yellow flowers.

Romance Series: These are taller with slightly more open, full flowers.

'Playtime' has flowers with numerous red-purple thin stripes heavily concentrated toward the outer edges and forming a red-purple picotee (margin.) The inside of the petals is a contrasting light yellow.

'White Passion' has large white flowers.

'Whisper' has numerous red-purple thin stripes heavily concentrated toward the outer edges and forming a red-purple picotee (margin.) The inside of the petals is a complimentary light pink. (See color plate 3.)

***Dieffenbachia* spp.**
Dieffenbachia, Dieffs, Dumbcane
Araceae or Arum Familly
Bred from native plants of tropical
   America
Light: Medium
Soil: Moderately dry

Dieffenbachias are known for their splashy, dashy foliage. The huge and stiff, elliptical leaves are broad and flat, perfect to see the variations of spotted and colorfully patterned foliage. All shades of green including lime green, all shades of yellow from bright to pale, and cream through white may be present. The green leaf petioles are attached to the flexible cane, usually covered by the foliage. Improvements include: new colors and patterns with compact growth.

Temperature: Intermediate to warm, from 65 to 85° F. Chilling injury occurs when lower than 50° F. and heat injury occurs in those over 90° F.

Humidity: Moderate, but tolerates low.

Overall shape: Upright and then angled outward.

Texture: Bold.

Availability: In 6 to10-inch diameter containers. The 10-inch size often has 3 ppp. (three plants per pot) where they are two and one-half to three feet tall. Table top size is also available.

Placement: As an unusually patterned plant among plain green ones. As an individual specimen floor plant. In an atrium where people can look down upon this accent of color. As a substitute for flowering plants.

Be aware that: Spider mites are the most common pest. Be most careful not to overwater because *Erwinia*, a bacterial blight, and *Fusarium*, a fungus, occur. *Erwinia* leaf spot looks water soaked and proceeds to stem rot while *Fusarium* causes a leaf spot that is round and papery looking. Purple stem spots with red margins develop as the disease progresses.

Dieffenbachia contains a sap that may cause a burning sensation upon contact with skin. If ingested, a swelling of the throat and airway is possible. Hence, the common name of "dumb cane".

Helpful hint: The foliage is brittle, so be careful when moving or grooming.

Cultivars include: The majority of cultivars are derived from *D. amoena* and the smaller *D. maculata.*

'Bali Hai' is speckled white on a dark green background.

'Camille' has predominantly creamy white leaves with cream midribs and thin green leaf margins. The entire plant is compact and is eighteen inches tall. (See color plate 7.)

'Camouflage' has huge green leaves with various sizes of dark green, gray-green and light green splotches. Each leaf also has a cream colored midrib and central area which also has splotches. It truly resembles a camouflage attractively presented without any brown color. The plant is four feet tall. (See color plate 3.)

'Excellent' is pale, lime green with a prominent white midrib and a subtle green leaf margin.

'Exotica' is a classic dark green leaf with a splotchy white center.

'Exotica Compacta' is two feet tall.

'Green Magic' has solid green leaves each with a thick, white midrib. It is a compact plant that is fifteen inches tall.

'Hi Color' has lime green foliage with a cream colored midrib and an irregular dark green margin.

'Mars' has yellow speckles on lime and dark green foliage.

'Octopus' has green foliage with white spots.

'Panther' has green foliage with lime green spots.

'Picta' has a snowy white interior with bright green margins.

'Rudolph Roers' has a yellow leaf with a green midrib and margins.

'Sparkles' has leaf variegation somewhere between 'Camouflage' and 'Starbright' with irregular splashes and spots of dark green, lime green and pewter with a prominent white midrib. It has compact growth upon two to three feet tall plants.

(See color plate 3.)

'Starbright' has mostly cream colored leaf with delicate dark green splashes and narrow, dark green leaf margins. The entire leaf is narrower than others.

'Sterling' has dark green foliage with a very prominent white midrib and subtle white along the midrib and veins.

The Tropic Series: All are known for the large, lightly colored central area.

'Tropic Dawn'

'Tropic Marianne' has bright yellow leaves with dark green margins.

'Tropic Snow' has a large central striped area of cream and lime green then edged with dark green splotches and leaf margins. The midrib is green.

'Tropic Snow Compacta' is a smaller version of 'Tropic Snow'.

'Tropic Sun' has yellow variegation and is similar to 'Tropic Snow'.

Dizygotheca elegantissima
False Aralia, Spider Aralia
Araliaceae or Aralia Family
A native of the New Hebrides Islands, north of New Zealand
Light: Medium
Soil: Moderately moist

Don't you just love pronouncing this scientific name? It's even more fun than rolling *Gleditsia triacanthos*, the honey locust tree, off your tongue. The most distinguishing feature about false aralia is its foliage. It looks like as if it isn't even real. The palmately compound leaves are coppery purple-brown with a greenish cast, a rather unusual color on an unusual plant. The leaflets are very narrow—only one quarter inch—and long with serrated margins. The spidery looking foliage on the false aralia gives this treelike plant a see-through quality. (See color plate 3.)

If you are lucky enough to inherit an older tree, then you'll see some mature foliage. Although it resembles the younger foliage, it is generally longer, wider, thicker and lobed. Look at those mature trees a little closer and you may be surprised with the two types of foliage. The mottled, cream colored stems offer great interest and contrast. Many plants per container are used to give a full look, since this plant rarely branches.

Temperature: Moderately warm, from 70 to 80° F.

Humidity: Moderate.

Overall shape: Upright and vertical.

Texture: Delicate.

Availability: As a shrub, usually in the 6 to 10-inch diameter containers. The 14 to 26-inch container sizes are twelve feet tall and three feet wide. Tree forms as well as table top sizes are also available.

Placement: As a specimen planting where an exotic look or strong architectural definition is desired. As an interesting snip added to a table top garden.

Be aware that: This plant is susceptible to spider mites and soft scale insects.

Helpful hint: Once you have success with this plant, leave it in place. Moving it may cause lower leaf drop.

***Dracaena deremensis* 'Janet Craig'**
Janet Craig Dracaena, J.C.
Agavaceae or Agave Family
An all green sport (a naturally
   occurring mutation) of
   'Warneckii' dracaena
Light: Medium, but acclimates well
   to low levels
Soil: Moderately dry

Here is an excellent example of a *Dracaena* used for low light areas. Janet Craig has whorls of glossy, dark green strappy foliage that arch and then gently fall downward creating a formal elegance. The parallel veins are slightly depressed causing a subtle pattern. The leaf bases overlap as they directly wrap around the sturdy but flexible canes. If lower leaves are removed, then the tan canes with horizontal nodes becomes visible.

Janet Craig may remind one of an imitation plant—it is a very slow-grower so it doesn't require much pruning— but it also is known for its easy maintenance.

Temperature: Intermediate to warm, from 65 to 90° F. Occasional brief, exposure to temperatures of 50 to 60° F. is tolerated.

Humidity: Tolerates low humidity, moderate is preferred.

Overall shape: Treelike, tall and somewhat narrow.

Various forms:

Staggered cane—The typical staggered canes have multiple plants per pot at various heights, such as 4-3-2 (feet) in a 10-inch container, offering a full and consistent composition from top to bottom. This is the most commonly available form.

Bouquet Narrow leaves are staggered along the cane. The 3-4 ppp grow five to six feet tall in a 10-inch diameter container.

Bush—All of the 3 ppp. (plants per pot) are three to four feet tall and nearly as wide in a 10-inch diameter container.

Cutback—Multibranched on each cane, 3-4 ppp. are five to six feet tall in a 10-inch diameter container.

Tip cuttings—Many short tips are used for shelf planters or table top gardens.

Texture: Medium-bold.

Availability: In 6 to 17-inch diameter containers. Larger sizes upon special request.

Placement: Janet Craig is a great specimen plant against a light backdrop. The solid, dark green foliage is very restful to the eye. The tall and narrow forms and cultivars are great for small offices, tight spaces, corners, restaurants and bars.

Be aware that: Control the watering to control most problems. It's that easy. If overwatered, then brown leaf spots surrounded by a bright yellow ring may appear on the new foliage. This is a highly visible fungal disease, *Fusarium moniliforne*, that should be promptly treated with a fungicide. Rarely are insects ever a problem.

Helpful hints: The durable leaves are easy to clean. If you need to remove a leaf, hold it near the tip and tear in half lengthwise along the midrib. Pull the two sections in opposite directions and back around the cane until they detach.

Other cultivars include:

'Compacta' has foliage that is shorter and closer together forming a bird's nest-like look. The entire plant is shorter, narrower and very versatile for tight, low-light areas. Available as staggered canes and tips. The 10-inch diameter container cane plant has 3 ppp. with the tallest cane at thirty inches tall. The tips, grown in a 10-inch diameter container also has 3 ppp. with an overall height of about twenty-four inches.

'Costarricana' has wide, medium green, corrugated foliage with dark green canes. Good cold tolerance is exhibited.

'Lisa' has leaves that are slightly narrower and much shorter, but still maintain the elegant look. It is disease resistant. This is another plant perfect for tight spots. (See color plate 3.)

'Machiko' has light green foliage with deeply depressed parallel venation creating a corrugated look. It is also available as a cutback which creates a narrow plant. The 10-inch diameter container has 3-4 ppp. available from five to six feet tall.

Dracaena deremensis 'Warneckii'
Warneckii Dracaena
Agavaceae or Agave Family
A native of tropical Africa
Light: Medium, but acclimates well
**   to low levels**
Soil: Moderately dry

Warneckii dracaena is another easy-care plant with whorls of strappy, green leaves with two prominent white stripes along the margins. The rest of the leaf has various shades of gray-green along with white, depending upon light conditions. The foliage is somewhat narrower but stiffer than the Janet Craig but is visually softened by the striping. (See color plate 3.) If lower leaves are removed, then the tan canes with horizontal nodes becomes visible.

Temperature: Intermediate to warm, from 65 to 90° F. Occasional brief exposure to temperatures of 45° F. is tolerated.

Humidity: Tolerates low humidity, moderate is preferred.

Overall shape: Tall with long and arching foliage.

Various forms:

Staggered cane—The typical staggered canes have multiple plants per pot at various heights, such as 4-3-2 (feet) in a 10-inch container, offering a full and consistent composition from top to bottom. This is the most commonly available form.

Bouquet—Narrow leaves are staggered along the cane. The 3-4 ppp. grow five to six feet tall in a 10-inch diameter container.

Bush—All of the 3 ppp. (plants per pot) are three to four feet tall and nearly as wide in a 10-inch diameter container.

Cutback—Multibranched on each cane, 3-4 ppp. are five to six feet tall in a 10-inch diameter container.

Tip cuttings—Many short tips are used for shelf planters or table top gardens.

Texture: Medium.

Availability: In 6 to 17-inch diameter containers. Table top sizes are also available.

Placement: The many forms and cultivars provide different options. Tips are used as a mid-height groundcover. Use where some contrast is desired.

Be aware that: Under low light, the coloration diminishes. Rarely are insects or disease ever a problem.

Helpful hints: This is a very versatile plant because of its wide range of light level tolerances.

The durable leaves are easy to wash periodically to remove dust. If you need to remove a leaf, hold it near the tip and tear in half lengthwise along the midrib. When you get close to the cane, pull the two parts in opposite directions and back around the cane until both parts detach.

Other cultivars include:

'Gold Star' is striking with wide yellow margins.

'Lemon Lime' is also very striking with wide and bright lime green stripes. The 10-inch diameter container holds 3 ppp. and grows to about twenty-eight inches tall. (See color plate 3.)

'Lindenii' is similar to 'Gold Star' with more distinct yellow margins.

'Rikki' was discovered as a sport (a naturally occurring mutation) in a propagation field in Costa Rica. The bright yellow color that runs in bands along the midrib of the deep, rich green leaf is repeated again and again. Each container is filled with many of these colorful plant tips. The color remains bright in low light placement, a real advantage. (See color plate 3.)

***Dracaena fragrans* 'Massangeana'**
Corn Plant
Agavaceae or Agave Family
A native of northern Guinea in
**   western Africa**
Light: Medium, but acclimates to
**   low levels**
Soil: Moderately dry

The corn plant is invaluable as one of the work horses of the industry. It is the most durable of the genus. It's easy to see why this is called the corn plant, with wide yellow and narrow green stripes in the center of the leaf and wide margins of bright green upon the strappy leaves.

The foliage grows in arching whorls at the terminal ends of the thick, strong canes. These tan to gray canes are horizontally patterned and offer interesting contrast. (See color plate 3.)

Temperature: Intermediate to warm, from 65 to 95° F. are preferred but tolerates as low as 55°F.

Humidity: Tolerates low humidity, moderate is preferred.

Overall shape: Tall and slender with immature leaves; once they reach full size, they are long and arching.

Various forms:

Staggered cane—The typical staggered canes have multiple plants per pot at various heights, such as 4-3-2-2 (feet) in the 14-inch diameter container, offering a full and consistent composition from top to bottom. This is the most commonly available form.

Branched standard—This type has a thick cane that was cut off within one foot of the base and then multiple canes, usualy four, emerged slightly below that spot and grew upward and outward symmetrically. This form has a very formal and elegant look.

Stumps—These are so very different looking. One is used to looking up high for corn plant foliage but, here, it is close to the ground. The

single cane was cut off about a foot from the base at a mature age—those stumps are sometimes near a foot in diameter. Then the typical whorls of leaves grew. This is a very heavy-looking plant and truly makes an architectural statement.

Trees or standard—All the foliage is at one height upon a bare, single stem.

Texture: Thick trunks exploding with terminal whorls of bold greenery.

Availability: In 10 to 17-inch diameter containers with plants from four to eight feet tall. Larger sizes to twenty feet may be special ordered.

Placement: The branched standard makes a great focal point in a grouping. With all the various forms and cultivars available, the corn plant is adaptable to most interiorscapes.

Be aware that: The corn plant is often put in a dark area where it slowly loses its variegation. These easy-care plants suffer most commonly from brown leaf tips which is an indication of fluoride tipburn, prolonged low humidity, or lack of water. Rarely are insects ever a problem.

Helpful hints: The canes often have small root systems making then unstable. In order to stabilize new arrivals, corn plants arrive with styrofoam inserted in the center secured with clear tape around the outside. Do not remove this packing material until the corn plant is in its final location. If the canes begin to lean later on, insert short bamboo stakes for support behind the cane well into the soil.

The durable leaves are easy to wash periodically to remove dust. If you need to remove a leaf, hold it near the tip and tear in half lengthwise along the midrib. When you get close to the cane, pull the two parts in opposite directions and back around the cane until both parts detach.

Other cultivars include:

'Santa Rosa' has reversed coloration. Now, the wide light cream margins appear on either leaf margin as well as spattered through the center. (See color plate 3.) This cultivar retains variegation under low light, although it changes to lime green. Not your plain old corn plant. Give it a try.

Dracaena marginata
Marginata, Marge, Red-edged Dracaena, Madagascar Dragon Tree
Agavaceae or Agave Family
A native of Madagascar
Light: Medium, but acclimates well to low levels
Soil: Moderately dry

This *Dracaena* has a different appearance than others because of its delicate foliage and canes. The foliage is very narrow and long with thin red margins. Each leaf is directly attached to the canes and appears in densely whorled rosettes at the terminal ends. As the plants mature the lower leaves "weep" and arch ward creating a soft effect. In higher light, foliage remains upright and horizontal. The canes are slender and flexible with crescent-shaped leaf scars which add an interesting texture. (See color plate 3.)

The marginata is another work horse of the industry. Because of its durability and easy-care, it is constantly being reinvented to create excitement.

Temperature: Intermediate to warm, from 65 to 90° F.

Humidity: Moderate.

Overall shape: Tall with cascading rosettes.

Various shapes and forms:

Staggered cane—The typical staggered canes have multiple plants per pot at various heights, such as 4-3-2-2 (feet) in the 14-inch diameter container, offering a full and consistent composition from top to bottom. This is the most commonly available form. A more elegant form is one "with character" in which case many of the canes are trained to grow horizontally before going upward. (Weights are added to the young canes causing this effect.) The architectural interest is stunning.

Candelabra—Four plants are grown closely to the center of the container and extend horizontally in four different directions before again growing upward, like a candelabra. It is most often seen growing about two feet tall in a 6-inch diameter container.

Heavy trunk—This form is similar to the tree form but has many very thick trunks closely spaced that branch with many whorls of foliage. These are also available "with character". The heavy trunk form consists of older, larger plants in 17-inch diameter containers which is seven and one-half to nine feet tall and four to five feet wide at the crown.

Multicane cutback—Sometimes, this is called the exotic-shaped form. This has the general appearance of the staggered form but is narrower, but features natural curves and bends in the canes. The multicane cutback in a 14-inch diameter container has 7-10 ppp. from five and one-half to six feet tall.

Tip cuttings—Many short tips are used for shelf planters or table top gardens.

Tree or standard form—These have a single cane trunk two to three feet high then branches of multiple heads. The tree form's total height in a 14-inch diameter container is from five and one-half to six feet.

Texture: From medium to delicate.

Availability: All forms are available in 10 to17-inch diameter containers. Table top sizes are also available.

Placement: Anywhere that elegance and softness is desired. In those hard to fill poorly lit areas, such as conference centers or meeting rooms.. A nice compliment to red foliage or flowers. Those "with character" are especially beautiful along a simple, light colored backdrop. The cutbacks are great along narrow hallways or in dark corners.

Be aware that: The marginatas are very susceptible to spider mite infestations. Often a systemic insecticide is used prophylactically. Don't use a feather duster. That's a perfect way to spread mites. *Fusarium moniliforme* leaf spot may also occur. The leaf spots may be tan to red-brown surrounded by a yellow or orange halo. Spray with a fungicide.

Helpful hint: Be careful when transporting, especially marges "with character" to avoid breaking off the foliage rosettes.

Cultivars include: All of these cultivars require medium light to maintain variegation.

'Colorama' has wide leaf margins of magenta with some stripes of cream upon a dark green background.

'Magenta' has that color on both top and undersides of foliage that is harsh and is more difficult to incorporate in the interior plantscape.

'Tricolor,' the rainbow tree, with foliage that has colorful stripes of green, cream with a rose pink margin. It is less susceptible to *Fusarium* leaf spot.

Dracaena reflexa
Reflexa, Pleomele, Malaysian Dracaena
Agavaceae or Agave Family
A native of Malaysia
Light: Medium, but acclimates well to low levels
Soil: Moderately dry

The short, stiff foliage appearing upon usually shrubby plants gives another look to the *Dracaena* genus. The dark green leathery foliage grow from five to seven inches long and one inch wide. Each leaf is tapered to a pointed tip and is directly attached to and loosely whorled along the entire green cane. The canes become gray with age yet remains flexible and supple.

Temperature: Cool-intermediate to warm, from 55 to 90° F.

Humidity: Moderate to low.

Overall shape: Many canes planted in a pot achieve a medium sized shrub or tree form.

Texture: Medium, instead of foliage being long and narrow, it is short and stubby.

Availability: Generally sold in larger diameter containers from 10 to 14-inches, but also available in 6-inch diameter containers. Larger containers to 36-inches as nine to twelve foot tall trees are elegant.

Placement: To add structure or height to an area. In a background planting. Along a wall. Suitable for use in a highly trafficked area.

Be aware that: Rarely are insects ever a problem although scale and spider mites may occur. Reflexa is very sensitive to overwatering.

Helpful hint: This is a tough and durable plant with low maintenance requirements. A wide range of temperature and humidity tolerances make this a very versatile plant.

Cultivars include:

'Song of India' has green foliage with wide creamy to bright yellow margins. The midrib as well as thin parallel veins are also banded yellow. (See color plate 3.) Available in diameters from 6 to 14-inches.

'Song of Jamaica' has yellow to light green bands lengthwise down the center of the leaf which are lost if placed in the low light interior plantscape. Available in diameters from 6 to 21-inches.

Related species:

D. draco, dragon tree dracaena, has long, stiff gray-green leaves growing in rosettes upon thick green stems. It is native to the Canary Islands.

D. sanderiana, ribbon plant, lucky bamboo or Chinese forcing plant, is a native of Cameroon in western Africa. This is a more delicate *Dracaena*. It has strappy leaves that are edged in white but have a twist to it; the canes gracefully bend at right angles and curl in various directions. This is a small architecturally interesting plant for a table top gardem.

D. surculosa, gold dust dracaena, is unlike other *Dracaenas*. Not only is the foliage spattered yellow to cream, it also is elliptical in shape and appears individually upon long wiry leaf petioles. This is a table top size plant adding color to mixed plantings. It is somewhat short-lived compared to other *Dracaena* plants. 'Florida Beauty' has foliage with more cream spatters than green background.

Epipremnum aureum
Golden Pothos, Pothos
Araceae or Arum Family
**A native of the Solomon Islands, in
   the west Pacific east of New
   Guinea**
**Light: Medium, but acclimates to
   low levels**
Soil: Moderately dry

We've all seen the basket of golden pothos hanging in that dark corner, Anyplace, U.S.A. But thankfully, there are several colorful cultivars on the scene. It can be unquestionably said that this is the perfect plant for harsh locations—low light, low humidity— with low maintenance requirements.

The foliage is heart-shaped and thick with irregular golden coloration. Sometimes half of a leaf is golden while the other half has only a few markings. The glossiness is due to a thick cuticle, ideally suited to retain as much water as possible within the leaf, especially under low humidity. The mature leaves, which are seldom seen indoors, are deeply lobed.

The leaf petioles are long, thick and flexible. A long groove extends along the top all the way to the green stem. Thick white aerial roots form at the leaf nodes along the stem.

Temperature: Warm, from 65 to 90° F., but tolerates to 95° F.

Humidity: Low.

Overall shape: Full and trailing or climbing.

Texture: Medium.

Availability: In 6 to 14-inch diameter containers, also in hanging basket sizes and assorted sizes including height as totems. As a pyramidal form trained on a bamboo teepee. Table top garden sizes, too.

Placement: Most often massed as general groundcover or underplantings of containerized trees. Great for locations under stairways, hanging baskets, shelf planters, or narrow areas as pyramidal forms or growing as totems.

Be aware that: Mealybugs are an occasional problem.

Helpful hints: In very low light areas, golden pothos will lose its variegation. Prune pothos to maintain a full plant. The older foliage turns bright yellow with even a suggestion of overwatering.

Cultivars include:

'Hawaiian' is a larger plant with foliage up to four times the size of golden pothos. This cultivar is truly stunning especially on a totem.

'Jade' is solid green and a nice alternative when used as a groundcover to tie together variegated plants.

'Marble Queen' has many ivory to white irregular markings on the foliage which not only brightens an area but has a fresh, clean look. (See color plate 3.)

'Neon' has solid lime green foliage which adds a futuristic or art deco look and is best highlighted in a black container. Keep in low light to prevent burning of the foliage. (See color plate 3.)

Related species:

E. pictus 'Argyraeus,' satin pothos, has satiny blue-green foliage with silver spots and margins.

Erica gracilis
Heather
Ericaceae or Heath Family
**A native of the south peninsula of
     South Africa, in the rocky hills**
Light: From medium to high
Soil: Moist

The many species of heather are all lovely. They have abundant sprays of small flowers which cover the plant. The flowers may be white or shades of pink through lavender. The foliage is needle-like upon shrubby plants.

Length of bloom time: A number of weeks. (See Helpful Hint: below.)

Temperature: Cool, from just above freezing to 75° F.

Humidity: Low.

Overall shape: Upright and vertical.

Texture: Delicate.

Availability: Usually in the fall, sometimes in the spring, in 6-inch diameter containers where the plant is eighteen inches tall.

Placement: As an interesting and unusual blooming plant. In hard to reach locations.

Be aware that: Grab this plant when you see it; it's readily purchased.

Helpful hint: Although heather prefers moist soil, if it dries out, the flowers retain their intense color—and no one really knows that this is now a beautiful dried flowering plant.

Related species:

E. persoluta 'Sachi,' Sachi heather, has deep pink flowers. (See color plate 3.)

Eucharis x *grandiflora*
Amazon Lily
Liliaceae or Lily Family
**A native of Colombia in the Ama-
     zon River basin; a naturally
     occurring hybrid**
Light: From medium to low
Soil: Moist

The Amazon lily is a prime example of a cut flower now being grown as a potted plant. The flower blooms sporadically, usually in late winter and then again in summer. But sometimes it blooms in other seasons. The sweet fragrance of the white daffodil-like flower permeates an entire area. These flowers droop in graceful clusters of four, although occasionally in clusters of three, five or six. (See color plate 3.)

The foliage is equally as spectacular and it remains that way for all to enjoy year-round.

The many straplike and arching leaves spill over from the base. They are naturally so glossy that it looks like leaf shine has been applied. The parallel veins are obvious and reinforce the soft shape of the leaves.

Length of bloom time: From two to three weeks.

Temperature: Warm, from 70 to 90° F. Chilling injury occurs below 60° F.

Humidity: Moderate.

Overall shape: Low V-shape.

Texture: Bold.

Availability: Usually planted with six bulbs to a container in the 14-inch diameter container where the plants are two feet high and up to four feet wide. The 10 and 12-inch diameter sizes are availble, too.

Placement: En masse in a tall, raised bed area where all may inhale this floral aroma as they walk by.

Be aware that: Mealybugs congregate along the midrib on the underside of the foliage, so clean that area regularly to prevent problems.

Helpful hint: The foliage alone is a reason to use the Amazon lily; the flowers are an added bonus.

Eugenia myrtifolia
Eugenia
Myrtaceae or Myrtle Family
A native of the American tropics
Light: Medium
Soil: Moderately moist

This tree fills a real slot in the interiorscape as a substitute for a sculptured ficus tree. The foliage is smaller than that of a ficus tree but resembles it in shape—elliptic, glossy, dark green and leathery. It is compactly arranged, almost forming rosettes, along the stem. (See color plate 3.)

This is a many branching tree creating a very full and lush look. It takes well to being sheared. It also resembles a myrtle plant to which it is closely related.

Temperature: Intermediate to warm, from 65 to 90° F. Chilling injury occurs below 65° F.

Humidity: Moderate.

Overall shape: Formally shaped trees.

Texture: Delicate.

Availability: The standard size is the 14-inch diameter container with a four ball topiary form is seven feet tall and two and one-half feet wide. Smaller sizes as three or two ball topiaries and as standards are available.

Placement: In formal locations such as in front of pillars, columns and/or white backgrounds.

Be aware that: Pests are usually not a problem. Pruning may be required.

Helpful hint: Few plants have such a formal look. Take advantage of it.

Euphorbia milii
Crown of Thorns
Euphorbiaceae or Spurge Family
A native of Madagascar
Light: Medium
Soil: Dry

This plant has seen recent improvements such as large flowers in many colors allowing the crown of thorns to reclaim its popularity. The inflorescence consist of a pair of colorful bracts (actually modified leaves resembling petals) and a yellow button center (these are the true flowers.) The bright green oval foliage adds a good background and hides the spiny stem.

Length of bloom time: The colorful bracts last many months.

Temperature: Tolerates a wide range, from 40 to 95° F.

Humidity: Tolerant of low humidity.

Overall shape: Upright and full.

Texture: Medium.

Availability: Year-round in 4 to 8-inch diameter containers.

Placement: In a dry location where other flowering plants do not survive.

Helpful hint: These easy-care succulents with wide tolerances act as both flowering and foliage plants.

Cultivars include:

'Minerva' with very large, red inflorescence.

Supergrandiflorum Series: All inflorescence have enormous blooms, three inches in diameter, and are clustered everywhere as full bouquets. The large dark green foliage hides the small spines on the stem. The plants are compact and grow to less than a foot.

'Apple Blossom' has a white base with irregular splotches of bright pink to pale pink from halfway up to the bract tips.

'Coral' is a solid deep red with slightly magenta overtones.

'Raspberry Peach' has a yellow-peach base with irregular raspberry pink markings from halfway up to the bract tips.

'Salmon' has a light cream base with splatters of bright pink from halfway up to the bract tips. (See color plate 3.)

'Yellow' is a soft, pale yellow color.

Short and Sweet Series: These are constantly flowering. The softly thorned stem is an improvement as is the compact size.

'Rosalie' has dark red-orange inflorescence.

'Saturnus' is peach.

'Venidas' is yellow.

'Vulcanus' is red-orange.

Related species: The following are known for their foliage.

E. lactea, the candelabra plant, a native of the East Indies, is stiff and upright, resembling a candelabra. It grows to fifteen feet tall. The stems and branches are actually cladophylls (flattened branches that look like and photosynthesize as leaves) that have a light green stripe down the center. Small cladophylls keep on branching off the tips as new growth occurs. The entire plant is equipped with sharp spines. An easy plant to maintain.

E. ingens resembles the saguaro or southwest cactus. It is tall and narrow with just enough branching to make it interesting. Small spines run vertically along the edges.

E. tirucalli is known as the pencil tree and has branches pencil-thin cladophylls.

E. trigona, the African milk tree, is similar to the candelabra plant but with a concentration of cladophylls near the terminal ends.

Euphorbia pulcherrima
Poinsettia
Euphorbiaceae or Spurge Family
A native of Mexico
Light: Medium
Soil: Moderately moist

Pulcherrima means "the most beautiful" and it's easy to see why. This flower was cultivated by the Aztecs over 2,000 years ago. In 1825, Joel Poinsett, the first U. S. ambassador to Mexico, saw them growing as shrubby perennials in the countryside. He brought them back to California and by the late 1800s they were sold commercially for the Christmas season.

The 1960s saw many genetic improvements such as new and long-lasting colors, sizes and forms. Some early cultivars were: 'Annette Hegg' with red bracts from Norway, introduced in 1964; 'Guthier V-10 Amy' white, pink and marbled sports, 1976; 'Eckespoint Lilo' with bright red bracts, dark green foliage with excellent retention, 1988. The yellows, whites, salmon, orange, and purples followed. Variegated foliage; oak leaf-shaped foliage and bracts; bicolors; crinkled foliage and bracts; miniature and roselike forms are other developments.

Points, as they are called in the industry, are the best seller of all blooming plants. Red is still the color of choice with nearly 80% of the market[5] captured. Pink, white, peach/salmon/apricot, yellow, mixed and bicolors are far in the backstretch. Colors such as orange and plum have advantages, too— they both open the season in the fall and are less linked with religious holidays. Many improved cultivars are introduced each season.

Length of bloom time: Bright light and cool temperatures, as well as breeding, extend the bloom time to four weeks or longer. Dark green foliage is an indication of long-lasting color.

Temperature: Avoid extremes. Intermediate, from 65 to 75° F. are preferred. Temperatures above 75° F. are just as damaging as are low ones. Drafty locations quickly cause chilling injury.

Humidity: Moderate; dry air promotes leaf drop.

Overall shape: From low and rounded to the standard tree size that grows for many a year. Traditionally, 6-inch points are placed on a wooden form in the shape of a Christmas tree that may reach thirty feet.

Texture: Bold.

Availability: From the micro minibloom in a one-inch diameter container, upward through the 6 to 8-inch diameter growing container, to the 10-inch hanging baskets. Larger containers with up to nine multibranched plants create a five foot diameter circle of color and may be used for hanging baskets or container plantings. Watering one container saves time. A tower of points, the same as towers of annuals for the outdoors, is also available, as are standards.

Be aware that: Poinsettias should be sleeved and boxed when delivered to prevent chilling injury. Make sure to remove sleeves immediately to prevent leaf drop due to a concentration of ethylene gases. Plants placed in low light also may experience leaf drop. The sweet potato whitefly has been a problem in poinsettia production.

Helpful hints: The colorful bracts which are thought of as flowers are actually modified leaves. Cyathia[6] are small yellow or red 'buds' located in the center of the plant. They should be tightly closed. Open or missing cyathia indicate a plant that is past its prime.

Look for foliage all the way down to the soil surface. Make sure the plant is full with good branching and stiff stems. A general rule of thumb is that the plant should be 2 ½ times taller than the container's diameter

Interesting fact: These plants are photoperiodic and must have no light from sundown to sunup—approximately for fourteen hours each

---

[5]   "Why We Buy: Poinsettias"; Martinez, Steve F. and Rappaport, Barrie; *GrowerTalks*; July, 2001.

[6]   Single female flower without petals and sepals surrounded by individual male flowers all enclosed in a cup-like structure called a cyathium (singular; cyathia, plural).

night—during bract initiation for eight to ten weeks sometimes less, in September or October.

For easier organization, color categories are designated.

Red cultivars include:

'Bonita' with coppery red bracts.

'Carousel' with curled and ruffled outer bracts while the inner bracts are smoother and held close to the center. This distinctive combination gives the appearance of motion—like a carousel. (See color plate 3.)

'Celebrate II' has dark red bracts and dark green leaves.

'Christmas Bells' with intense red bracts and prominent cyathia.

'Christmas Day' is similar to 'Spotlight'.

'Christmas Dream' is similar to 'Cortez Red'.

'Christmas Eve' with large, dark red textured bracts and dark green foliage.

'Christmas Season'

'Christmas Time' is similar to 'Freedom Red'. All of the Christmas cultivars are in the First Class Series.

'Cortez Fire' has some orange undertones and is in the Cortez Series.

'Cranberry Punch' and 'Redberry Punch' have small, pointed, bracts with slightly ruffled edges and oak leaf-shaped bracts and are in the Punch Series.

'Deluxe Red' is well suited for 4-inch containers.

'Festival Red' with intense red bracts and deep green foliage.

'Freedom Fireworks' has long, narrow pointed bracts.

'Freedom Bright Red' is an improved cultivar in the Freedom Series.

'Freedom Red' is the number one selling cultivar with 59% of the market in 2000[7].

'Galaxy Red' has smooth bracts with an upright growth habit.

'Holly Point' with dark red colored bracts and large foliage that resembles a variegated holly leaf with dark golden yellow margins.

'Jester' has upright bracts. It is well suited for 4 to 6-inch containers.

'Jolly Red' with very large bracts.

'Lilo Red' is part of the Lilo Series.

'Malibu Red' has dark red bracts with a sheen. The top bracts have a slight upward tilt. It is well suited for the 4 to 6-inch containers.

'Orion Red' has large, dark red bracts with dark green leaves on an upright plant.

'Peace'

'Pepride' with oak leaf-shaped bracts and foliage.

'Peterstar Red' with oak leaf-shaped bracts and foliage.

'Petoy Red' with very large bracts and is part of the Petoy Series.

'Pizarro' has deep notches on the oak leaf-shaped bracts and leaves.

'Prestige Red' is filled with large bracts.

'Red Angel' has dark green foliage upon upright plants.

'Red Baron' has burgundy red bracts with a waxy sheen.

'Red Elf' has dark red bracts with compact growth.

'Red Sails' with very large red bracts.

'Red Splendor' with very dark red bracts and very dark green foliage.

'Red Velvet' with velvet-like large bracts.

'Santa Claus Red' with medium red bracts held horizontally. The Santa Claus Series includes four other colors.

'Silverstar Red' has silver-green and white variegated leaves upon compact plants and is part of the Silverstar Series.

'Sonora Red' and 'Sonora Dark Red' have dark green, oak-leaf shaped foliage and is one in the Sonora Series.

---

[7]   "The Good, the Bad, and the Ugly", Feb. 2001, p.94, *Greenhouse Grower Magazine.*

'Splendor Red' has dark green foliage and is in the Splendor Series.

'Spotlight Dark Red' with dark pink-red rippled bracts.

'Victory Red' has bright red bracts with dark green leaves.

'Winter Rose Crimson,' 'Winter Rose Dark Red' and 'Winter Rose Red' really do resemble a rose. The foliage and bracts are reduced and compressed to form a roselike cluster creating a series of differently shaped points. Extending poinsettia sales through Valentine's Day and beyond is the idea behind the marketing plan. 'Winter Rose Curly Red' has curled foliage and bracts which form a rose-like sphere. One in the Winter Rose Series.

'Xenia Red' with red oak leaf-shaped bracts and foliage.

Pink cultivars include:

'Champagne Punch' is light pink with oak leaf-shaped foliage. See 'Cranberry Punch'.

'Coco Hot Pink' has rose-pink bracts with dark green foliage.

'Cortez Hot Pink' has rose-pink bracts with some white mixed in.

'Cortez Purple Rose,' 'Festival Rose,' 'Freedom Rose' and 'Sonora Hot Pink' are deep rose-pink.

'Liberty Bright Pink' has soft pink bracts with bright red veins.

'Nutcracker Pink' and 'Nutcracker Salmonstar' are part of the Nutcracker Series.

'Pepride Pink' with oak leaf-shaped bracts and foliage.

'Peterstar Pink' with oak leaf-shaped bracts and foliage and is in the Peterstar Series.

'Santa Claus Pink' with medium pink bracts held horizontally.

'Silverstar Pink' has pastel pink bracts with silver-green and white variegated leaves upon compact plants.

'Winter Rose Pink' with tightly compressed rose-like colorful bracts.

White cultivars include:

'Angelika White' has true white bracts.

'Cortez White' has white bracts with yellow undertones.

'Freedom White' is more of a cream color than true white.

'Lilo White' has dark green foliage.

'Malibu White' has yellowish white bracts and is well suited for the 4 to 6-inch containers.

'Nutcracker White' and 'White Christmas' have white bracts with medium green foliage.

'Pearl' with very large bracts.

'Peterstar White' with oak leaf-shaped bracts and foliage.

'Santa Claus White' with a pure white color.

'Silverstar White' has pure white bracts and some cream-colored ones with silver-green and white variegated leaves upon compact plants.

Snowcap' is a creamy white color.

'Sonora White' has dark green, oak leaf-shaped foliage.

'Spotlight White' is a creamy white color.

'Whitestar' has large bracts and an upright growth habit.

'Winter Rose White' with tightly compressed rose-like colorful bracts.

Peach/Salmon/Apricot cultivars include:

'Champagne' and 'Spotlight Apricot' are similarly apricot-pink colored.

'Freedom Salmon' has salmon-pink bracts with occasional cream.

'Heirloom Peach' is salmon-pink. The silvery gray-green foliage has a white margin. It is in the Heirloom Series.

'Maren' is a rich, salmon-pink with light green foliage.

'Noblestar' has a light pink-salmon color.

'Nutcracker Salmonstar' has large, rose-salmon colored bracts and is in the Nutcracker Series.

'Sonora Salmon Pink' is reddish pink with dark green, oak leaf-shaped foliage. It is in the Sonora Series.

'Success Coral' is more of a deep pink with coral undertones and is in the Success Series.

'Winter Rose Peach' with tightly compressed rose-like colorful bracts.

Yellow cultivars include:

'Goldfinger' is golden yellow.

'Lemon Drop' a pale creamy yellow.

'Lemon Snow' has light yellow bracts and dark green leaves.

Marble:

'Cortez Marble' with is pale pink and creamy white bracts.

'Marblestar' with less cream along the margins.

'Pepride Marble' has lavender and cream bracts with oak leaf-shaped foliage.

'Peterstar Silverbells' and 'Silverstar Marble' are soft pink with white margins and green foliage with silvery-white margins.

'Sonora Marble' has cream-colored bracts with irregular pale pink markings along the midrib and has dark green, oak leaf-shaped foliage.

'Spotlight Marble' has large, muted rose-pink centers that cover at least half of the bract with yellow to white cream margins. The foliage is dark green. It is in the Spotlight Series.

'Winter Rose Marble' with tightly compressed rose-like bracts.

Other bicolored and multicolored cultivars include:

'Goldstar Pink' has medium pink bracts with a yellow band down the center. The leaves are dark green.

'Monet,' 'Monet Twilight,' and 'Santa Claus Candy' have soft shades of pink, rose and cream intermingled.

'Monterrey Pink' has bracts that transition from rose-pink to from medium to light pink, some with light green veins and dark midrib. It has dark green leaves and an upright growth habit.

'Peterstar Silverbells' with bracts that are predominantly apricot pink with irregular creamy margins.

'Pink Ribbon' is a cross between 'Monet' and the Winter Rose poinsettia with larger, looser flowerheads.

'Puebla' has dark pink covering most of the bract surrounded by irregular creamy margins.

'Strawberries and Cream' has dark pink and cream variegated bracts.

Speckled cultivars include:

'Amazone Peppermint' has pink bracts with small red flecks and medium green foliage.

'Jester' is similar to 'Jingle Bells 3' but has wavy leaf margins.

'Jingle Bells 3' has red bracts with pale pink and white speckles. (See color plate 3.) 'Jingle Bells 4.0' is well suited for 4 to 6-inch containers. 'Cortez Jingle' is similar.

Orange cultivars include:

'Christmas Cookie' has bright orange bracts. Best for 4 ½ to 6-inch diameter containers.

'Peterstar Orange' which comes in a deep orange-red color with medium green foliage, perfect for fall.

'Sonora Fire' is orange-red with dark green leaves.

Purple cultivars include:

'Cortez Burgundy' has bracts that color.

'Plum Pudding' has light purple plum-colored bracts.

'Purple Reign' has lavender bracts.

Exacum affine
Persian Violet, German Violet
Gentianaceae or Gentian Family
A native of the island of Socotra,
    south of Yemen in the Arabian
    Sea
Light: Medium
Soil: Moist

This cheery and neat looking flowering plant is covered with small lavender, blue or white five petaled flat flowers with contrasting bright yellow anthers that form an eye. Sometimes, double blooms are available. The flowers make up for size by sheer number. (See color plate 4.) They are also sweet smelling—similar to a weak lily of the valley scent. And, by the way, this is not a true violet.

The oval, glossy green foliage has prominent veins and is pointed at the tip. The leaves are abundant on this full and compact plant.

Length of bloom time: Up to three months if purchased in the mature bud stage with some flowers open.

Temperature: Intermediate, from 65 to 75° F.

Humidity: Moderate.

Overall shape: Low mounded.

Texture: Delicate.

Availability: They are available year-round in 6 to 10-inch diameter container size where they are one foot tall and at least as wide. Table top and miniature sizes are also available.

Placement: Single specimens or massed for a large area of color. As a quiet color, complimenting any yellow flowers.

Be aware that: This is a problem free plant. Discard this flowering plant after blooming.

Helpful hint: Persian violet is a relatively inexpensive plant.

Another related plant:

Eustoma grandiflorum, lisianthus or prairie gentian, is a native of North America. The plants are filled with deep blue-lavender colored rose-like flowers. Two improved cultivars bred in Illinois are:'Forever Blue' which has single flowers splayed open revealing prominent yellow centers. It is 10 inches tall in the 6-inch diameter container. 'Sapphire Blue' has miniature double flowers held more tightly with petals that recurve (curve backwards.) It is 6 inches tall in the 4-inch diameter container. The foliage of both cultivars is a complimentary and restful gray-green color with simple and opposite leaves. Other cultivars are available with pink or white flowers.

x *Fatshedera lizei*
Aralia Ivy, Fatshedera
Araliaceae or Aralia Family
Intergeneric hybrid of *Fatsia* and
Hedera genera
Light: Medium
Soil: Moist

In this case, *Fatsia japonica*, Japanese fatsia, and *Hedera helix*, English ivy, were accidentally, but successfully, crossed and bred in France in 1940.

Aralia ivy features the best characteristics of both parents. The foliage resembles that of English ivy—dark green, shiny, leathery, five lobed leaves–but it is large like the Japanese fatsia. It is an elegant and formal vining plant. (See color plate 4.)

Temperature: Cool, from 60 to 70° F., but tolerates as low as 45° F.

Humidity: Moderate.

Overall shape: Usually grown on a totem so it is upright and vining.

Texture: Medium-bold.

Availability: Aralia ivy will grow to about six feet in the 14-inch diameter container.

Placement: It is great for planters on either sides of a stairway or an entryway.

Be aware that: Cool temperatures tend to discourage spider mites. Keep and eye out for signs of overwatering—leaf spots and root rots.

Helpful hint: It does well using a subirrigation system.

Fatsia japonica
Japanese Fatsia
Araliaceae or Aralia Family
A native of Japan
Light: Medium
Soil: Moist

Japanese fatsia is a large, upright and wide-spreading shrublike plant that forms horizontal layers of foliage. The dark green, often tinged with burgundy, leathery leaves which grow to fifteen inches in diameter consist of seven to eleven serrated lobes. Each lobe gracefully narrows where it joins the central base then widens as it fans out, becoming narrow and pointed towards the tip. The midribs and veins are very prominent and add to the ornamental value. (See color plate 4.)

The leaves have very long, dark green leaf petioles and each plant is single stemmed so many plants are planted together. The Japanese fatsia has some of the most attractive foliage of any plant. Lower leaves will drop if not watered enough, but root and stem rots occur with overwatering.

Temperature: Cool, from 60 to 70° F., but tolerates as low as 45° F.

Humidity: Moderate.

Overall shape: A wide and sprawling shrub.

Texture: Bold.

Availability: In 10 to 14-inch diameter containers

Placement: Near a water feature. Or an area where a large, tropical look is desired.

Be aware that: Mealybugs and scale insects may be occasional problems.

Helpful hint: Give this plant plenty of room. It also does well using a subirrigation system.

Ficus benjamina
Weeping Fig
Moraceae or Mulberry Family
A native of India, southeastern Asia, and northern Australia
Light: Medium, but some cultivars acclimate to low levels
Soil: Moderately moist

The weeping fig was introduced to the interiorscape in the late 1950s. Since then, it has appeared in nearly every office building and indoor shopping mall. It's easily recognizable with its recessed midrib which causes both halves of the oval leaves to be angled upward in comparison. The extended leaf tips droop gracefully as do the tips of the branches, thus its common name. The branches are many creating a nice, full appearance. The smooth trunk is beige-gray.

The old weeping figs were notorious for losing most of their leaves if the plant was moved. Not a pretty picture. They may also lose leaves when the soil is allowed to dry out. This happens because natively, they grow where there is a wet and dry season. As the dry season becomes evident, they shed their foliage. So, when watering is lessened, similar to the dry season approaching, the weeping fig drops its leaves.

Fortunately, the weeping fig has come a long way in the last number of years. Cultivars with welcomed improvements have taken over the market.

Temperature: Intermediate to warm, from 65 to 95° F.; although it will tolerate brief exposures to 55° F.

Humidity: Moderate.

Overall shape: Like a tree or shrub

Various forms.

Trees and standards—The trunk may be straight or shaped into:

Corkscrews including single, double and triple—two or three plants growing separately but in spiral synchrony in the same container. (Anytime the spiral or cylindrical shape occurs, young plants were trained to grow along different size diameters of PVC pipe.)

Double helix—two single corkscrew trunks intertwined like DNA.

Closed or open braids—three plants tightly woven or loosely woven together.

Open weave— numerous plants loosely woven but in an evenly spaced cylindrical form.

Multitrunk—many trunks on a treelike plant.

Shrubs—many, thin trunks with foliage to the base.

Pyramids—trained on a pyramidal bamboo teepee and used as trees especially for the holiday season.

Lollipops—two dimensional circle, like an old-fashioned flat lollipop.

Other shapes such as arches or trellises.

Texture: Medium.

Availability: All sizes from very small for table top gardens through thirty-foot tall specimens which are available at specialty nurseries.

Be aware that: Scale and mealybug are the most common pests. Twig dieback and stem cracks are caused by a fungus, *Phomopsis*.

Helpful hints: Care must be taken when pruning because the stems contain a milky sap which drips from the cut surface. Use a lighted match to seal the wound. The sap may irritate skin or stain carpeting.

Cultivars include:

'Dwarf Nikita' has variegated foliage with an upright habit.

'Golden King' has gray leaves with a green center and an irregular golden yellow leaf margin.

'Jacqueline' has gray leaves with a green center and an irregular cream leaf margin. (See color plate 4.)

'Mini-Frances' is a compact bonsai ficus. The small leaves are a combination of light green and yellow and white with dark green and gray surroundings.

'Spearmint' has narrower, light green foliage edged with cream or light yellow. It has a wide and spreading shape.

'Spire' has typical ficus shaped leaves but they are large, light medium green with a slightly wavy margin. They lack a natural glossy appearance; if this is important, use a little leaf shine. The plant is narrow and upright with mature branches only fourteen inches long. (See color plate 4.) Pruning is unnecessary. It acclimates to low light levels with less leaf drop and requires less watering than other *Ficus* plants. It is cold tolerant to 32° F. A great alternative to the corn plant.

'Starlight' has variegated foliage with a spreading habit.

'Wintergreen' has larger, solid dark green foliage. This cultivar has a spreading habit.

Ficus of the Future Series:

This is an exclusive variety developed in Holland in the late 1980s and since then propagated worldwide. They are long lasting with superior durability and performance and unusual colors and forms. The most significant improvement is the resistance to leaf drop. This is because they are light acclimated by growers under heavy 72% and 83% shade cloth. Many interior plantscapers have gone exclusively to using these improved cultivars.

Standard sizes:

'Indigo' has very lustrous, dark indigo-colored foliage with the new growth emerging dark green. Upon close inspection, the mature leaves have an irregular area along the midrib that is a shade lighter than the margins. The irregularly long internodal spaces between the foliage create an open feel; the branches droop creating the weeping effect. (See color plate 4.) This was the first cultivar of the purple leaf types. 'Indigo' performs extremely well in very low light interiorscapes.

'Midnight' is a sport (a naturally occurring mutation) of 'Indigo' and has lustrous, dark blue to black foliage without variegation. The difference is that the plant has short internodal spaces between the foliage and the branches are upright with a strong apical dominance. It has a very dense appearance and is often seen in a shrub form. (See color plate 4.) Initial leaf drop of inner leaves may occur when placed in very low light.

'Midnight Princess' is an improvement of 'Midnight'. The same blue-black foliage has wavy margins. It has slightly elongated internodal spaces between the foliage with more of a cascading effect. It is a superior plant with good tolerance of low light levels. Consider it for limited floor spaces, in front of pillars, columns and against light backgrounds.

'Monique' has lustrous, bright green leaves with noticeable wavy margins that become accentuated under lower light. A very nice decorative feature. The entire plant is upright and full. It acclimates well to a wide range of light levels. This was the first cultivar in the series.

Miniature sizes:

'Mini-Midnight' is similar to 'Midnight' but with smaller foliage upon a compact plant.

'Rianne' is a bonsai with horizontal branches and twisted internodes looking like an actual bonsai.

'Wiandi' is related to 'Rianne' with smaller foliage and less horizontality. The twisted stems bend at a 90° angle. 'Wiandi' is tolerant of low light.

Other species:

F. maclellandii 'Alii,' commonly called Alii, is one of the slower growing ficus with long and narrow leaves that gracefully droop downward. (See color plate 4.) This species was planted near the entrance of Disney World in Florida growing in allees (long, formal rows.) It adjusts very well to low light and temperature change, but do not allow the soil to dry out to prevent leaf drop.

F. binnendijkii 'Amstel King' or 'Amstel' is another Ficus of the Future cultivar with all those attributes. (See above.) The leaves are similar in shape to 'Alii'; however, twice as wide providing an attractively full look. The new red-green foliage contrasts well with the dark green foliage. (See color plate 4.) It is more durable and less prone to leaf drop than 'Alii'. Some interior plantscapers use 'Amstel King' exclusively.

F. pumila, creeping fig, is a native of China, Japan and Vietnam. This is a tiny *Ficus*. The oval leaves are only one-half inch long. (See color plate 4.) As its name suggests, this fig is great for a groundcover or topiary. The tendrils grasp onto any solid surface and climb. Do not allow creeping fig to dry out; it becomes crispy in a few days. It also requires from high to medium light levels. It is most susceptible to mealybugs. 'Minima' has smaller foliage with a slow growth rate, 'Quercifolia' has lobed foliage, 'Snowflake' has smaller foliage with much white coloration, and 'Variegata' has white variegation.

F. retusa 'Nitida,' Indian laurel, is a native of the Malay Peninsula and Borneo. It has somewhat wider and thicker leaf than the weeping fig. The branches are upright and spreading. It acclimates to low light levels. 'Hawaii' has variegated foliage.

F. stricta 'Nuda' is similar to the weeping fig. The foliage is slightly larger and the trunk is lighter in color and somewhat smoother. This species has an accentuated weeping habit. It acclimates to low light levels.

A similar plant:

Trichilia emetica, Natal mahogany, has a compound leaf arrangement. Each leaflet is larger but similar to the leaf of the weeping fig. It combines the shape of *F. benjamina* 'Monique' with the dard black-green color of 'Midnight.' The overall plant shape is upright and columnar, similar to that of 'Midnight Princess."

Ficus elastica
Rubber Tree
Moraceae or Mulberry Family
A native of Nepal through eastern India, and Burma
Light: From medium to high, but some cultivars acclimate to low levels
Soil: Moderately moist

The rubber tree plant goes in and out of style, and has been doing so since Victorian days. Many colorful cultivars update its look to fit in any major interior plantscape. The thick and leathery, glossy dark green foliage has a recessed light colored midrib causing the leaf halves to be angled upward. The large oval leaves are very neat and tidy looking. The tightly curled red new leaves are held upright offering their own colorful appeal. (See color plate 4.)

Temperature: Warm, from 70 to 90° F., but tolerates temperatures close to freezing and as high as 95° F.

Humidity: Moderate but adapts to low levels.

Overall shape: It most often grows as a low growing and wide specimen with many plants per pot. Rubber trees are very attractive growing as single, upright standard tree or similarly with multistems.

Texture: Bold.

Availability: Most commonly in 10 to 14-inch diameter container but available in the 6 to 8-inch containers.

Placement: A rubber tree is great for sunny lobbies as well as poorly lit areas. It can stand on its own as an individual specimen plant.

Be aware that: Rarely are insects or disease a problem.

When cleaning the foliage, be careful. The leaves tend to break off under pressure. When pruning, a milky sap may irritate skin or stain carpeting. Use a lighted match to seal the wound.

Helpful hints: This is a tough and durable plant and easy to maintain with a wide ranges of tolerances.

Cultivars include:

'Altissima' has irregular, yellow-green leaf margins. (See color plate 4.)

'Burgundy' is an easy to find foliage plant tinged red-purple.

'Cabernet' has burgundy colored foliage. From medium to high light levels are necessary to retain coloration.

'Doescheri' is a muted variegation with patches of pewter, olive green edged in cream. The tightly curled new foliage is red as are the midrib and leaf petioles.

'Green Gem' has irregular, lime green leaf margins. (See color plate 4.)

'Mahogany' has dark mahogany foliage.

'Robusta' has smaller green foliage.

'Sylvie' has wide, irregular cream leaf margins and a pink midrib.

'Tricolor' has irregular markings of green and gray edged in cream. This cultivar is very similar to 'Doescheri' with a cream colored midrib. (See color plate 4.)

Decora Series: All are known for their ability to tolerate low light levels without lower leaf drop. The sheath from which the leaf emerges as well as the leaf petiole is red.

'Decora' has wider and glossier foliage with the undersides tinged red.

'Decora Burgundy' has burgundy-dark green foliage. (See color plate 4.)

'Decora Variegata' has some slight white variegation.

Ficus of the Future Series: (See description under *Ficus benjamina*.)

'Melany' with small foliage that is dark green and glossy. Furthermore, the leaves have shallow ridges which give a faceted texture. Burgundy veins give the entire plant a burgundy undertone. Medium light levels are necessary to retain coloration. Often the trunks are braided for added interest. This cultivar is available in 6 to 8-inch diameter containers and is perfect for a table top planting or as a small indoor shrub.

Ficus lyrata
Fiddle-Leaf Fig
Moraceae or Mulberry Family
A native of tropical Africa
Light: Medium
Soil: Moderately dry

This is a different looking ficus with enormous fiddle-shaped, or more exactly, violin-shaped leaves. Each leaf usually grows to fifteen inches long and half as wide. The thick leaves have a recessed light colored midrib causing the leaf halves to be slightly angled upward. The stiff foliage has a wide, wavy margin that adds depth and dimensionality. Sometimes the new leaves have red flecking. (See color plate 4.)

Each leaf has a short, thick petiole where it attaches to a branch or the stem. The trunk is strongly textured, dark brown and relatively slender.

Temperature: Warm, from 70 to 90° F.

Humidity: Moderate.

Overall shape: Upright and branching, as a multitrunk shrub or single stem tree or standard.

Texture: Bold.

Availability: The 14 to17-inch diameter containers are most common. Smaller sizes are available.

Placement: As a specimen plant; near a large and impressive entryway; a large area that requires such a desired texture.

Be aware that: It is rarely a host to pest and disease problems. The new growth may be removed to maintain desired shape.

Helpful hint: This is a tough and durable plant, with low maintenance requirements.

Cultivars include:

'Compacta' and 'Suncoast Compacta' have shorter internodes so that the foliage is closer together yet the same large leaf size. (See color plate 4.) If you look at the trunk, it is thick and strong. When utilized as a multitrunk shrub, five plants are placed in the growing container to ensure a dense and full appearance. When used as a tree or standard, the ficus has been pruned to ensure the same dense appearance. The foliage is very dark green without any red flecking. This cultivar requires moderately moist soil because of the increased amount of foliage. It acclimates to the medium side of low light levels.

Fittonia verschaffeltii var. *argyroneura*
Fittonia, Silver-Veined Nerve Plant
Acanthaceae or Acanthus Family
A native of Colombia through Peru
Light: Medium
Soil: Moderately moist

This is a small plant with a lot of punch—it has filigree-patterned foliage. The papery, oval, dark green foliage is most attractive with numerous and prominent ever branching white veins. The leaves appear in pairs opposite each other with the larger ones at the base of the plant followed by smaller and smaller ones. The foliage is so very abundant that the thin stems are hardly noticeable. (See color plate 4.)

Temperature: Prefers warmer temperatures of 80 to 90° F.

Humidity: As high as possible to prevent browning of leaf margins.

Overall shape: Low mounding to evenly flat.

Texture: Delicate.

Availability: Table top sizes to hanging basket sizes.

Placement: These are great groundcover plants. Table top gardens, too. Hanging baskets are best located near a water feature.

Be aware that: Mealybug is the only pest that may occur.

Helpful hints: If this plant wilts, it responds well when watered. Flower stalks should be removed as they appear. Cut back any tall shoots.

Cultivars include:

'Nana' has smaller foliage.

Related species:

F. verschaffeltii, red-nerve plant, has dark red veins instead of white. 'Pearcei' is the pink-nerve plant.

Closely related plants:

Hypoestes phyllostachya, polka dot plant, is a native of South Africa, Madagascar, and southeast Asia. This small plant has either pink or white spots on the leaves. The spots are small as if the plant was a cookie decorated with sprinkles, perfect for a splash of color. Or in combination with similarly colored flowers.

Pseuderanthemum atropurpureum is the polka dot plant with red spots.

***Guzmania* spp.**
Guzmania
Bromeliaceae or Pineapple Family
**Bred from native plants of Colom-
    bia and Equador, especially the
    Andean rain forests**
**Light: From medium to slighly
    lower levels**
Soil: Moderately dry

Guzmanias are some of the largest decorative and showy bromeliads with a wide range of inflorescence (See footnote #2, p 25.) A very thick, colorful stalk arises from the center continuing with strappy, colorful bracts in red, orange, yellow or purple or combinations.

The surrounding glossy, straplike foliage is sometimes horizontally banded and colorful on its own. What brilliantly colored, long lasting, easy maintenance plants these are.

Length of bloom time: Purchase plants before the true flowers open so that the color will last from three to six months.

Temperature: A wide range from 55 to 85° F. and can tolerate short periods of cooler and warmer temperatures.

Humidity: Adapts to low humidity although moderate is preferred.

Overall shape: V-shape.

Availability: The 6-inch diameter container holds an eighteen inch to two foot tall plant. Larger sizes are available.

Placement: En masse, anywhere color is desired. As a substitute for flowering plants. Although these plants may be more expensive initially, in the long run they are economical because of the long lasting color, durability and minimal upkeep.

Be aware that: These epiphytic plants—they have aerial roots absorbing nutrients from water, air and dust particles—may become top heavy and need to be weighted down to avoid toppling over.

Helpful hint: The *Guzmanias* as well as the *Vriesias* retain their color better when placed in lower light.

Cultivars include:

'Amaranth' is a dark purple color.

'Attila' is a different looking cultivar with a feeling of lightness. The narrow foliage encircles a delicate flower stalk with red inflorescence emerging in various directions.

'Bolero' has a white inflorescence with some white with green tipped bracts continuing below. Then, the rest of the foliage is bright green. This one has a bright, crisp look with unusual color.

'Cherry' has bright red inflorescence on a smaller plant. (See color plate 4.)

'Christine' is bright red-orange.

'Claret' is red-purple with a compact inflorescence. It grows to twenty-two inches tall.

'Clementina' has a yellow-gold inflorescence.

'Copito' is a low rising cultivar with a pale yellow to cream color.

'Decora' is an old standby, with a rather short red inflorescence.

'Eloy' is low rising with red inflorescence.

'Empire' has low rising red inflorescence.

'Estrella' is one of the lower rising cultivars that resembles a *Neoregelia*. It has a bright red inflorescence.

'Graaf Van Horne' has branching yellow inflorescence upon a red stalk.

'Gwendolyn' is deep magenta with a compact inflorescence.

'Hilda' is yellow.

'Huron' has a orange-red stem and inflorescence upon a compact plant also with short leaves for vertical impact. The 4 ½-inch diameter container is twenty to twenty four inches tall.

'Intro' is another low rising cultivar in a magenta color.

'Irene' has pink-red color.

'Jive' is a lively, hot orange color.

'Kapoho Fire' has red and yellow inflorescence.

'Lemonade' has bright yellow inflorescence.

'Loja' is different looking. The tall inflorescence has short, stiff red bracts and numerous yellow flowers.

'Luna' is one of the darkest colors; a wine-red, close to purple. It has an art deco look both in color and shape. It is very tall, growing to twenty-eight inches, is narrow and sleek looking.

'Mandarine' has low rising orange and yellow inflorescence.

'Marjan' has yellow-gold color. It lasts for fourteen weeks.

'Mikaso' is twenty-six inch tall with long lasting, bright red and yellow inflorescence; long straplike, glossy, dark green foliage with burgundy undersides. The plant is three feet wide. It is a great centerpiece plant.

'Morado' with a dark red flower stalk and loosely clustered red and white inflorescence.

'Neon' is a fluorescent magenta color with a compact inflorescence.

'Ostara' is red with yellow tips.

'Pax' is a peacefully clear yellow color.

'Puna Gold' has golden-yellow inflorescence. (See color plate 4.)

'Rana' has a long red-orange inflorescence. It grows to two feet with upright foliage and lasts fourteen weeks. (See color plate 4.)

'Ruby' has a deep ruby red inflorescence.

'Salsa' one of the broader shaped cultivars with a tomato-red inflorescence tipped in white. Some of the lower red bracts are tipped in green.

'Samba' is rather unusual because the inflorescence is clear yellow that turns orange and then red towards the base.

'Soledo' is yellow combined with a muted, dark pink base.

'Symphony Encore' is full of color. The inflorescence have a central area of tightly concentrated yellow bracts markedly different in shape, too, to the surrounding long and loosely clustered red bracts. The foliage is striped with cream and pink with a dark green margin. (See color plate 4.)

'Tutti Frutti' is tall with a flat red-orange inflorescence.

'Torch' is a very showy cultivar with its prominent bright red inflorescence touched with yellow tips. The yellow knoblike, central protrusions are actually the flowers. The counterbalance of the long, wide, upright, dark green leaves is excellent. Always a show stopper. Grows to twenty-two inches tall.

'Ultra' resembles a *Neoregelia* with a deep magenta starlike center and is great used for groundcover.

Related species:

G. conifera has a cone-shaped cluster of overlapping, spiny red bracts prominently edged in bright yellow.

G. dissitiflora 'Major' is extremely interesting with a pencil-thin bright red flower stalk with the same color continuing as the colorful bracts break off the main stem. Each red bract is prominently tipped with a bright yellow. The bright green, delicate foliage grows close to the base allowing the bright red stem to stand separate. (See color plate 4.)

G. wittmackii has cherry red bracts neatly arranged singly along the colorful flower stalk giving the plant a certain formality. One of these plants on a granite or lacquered wood table makes an elegant statement.

Hedera helix
English Ivy
Araliaceae or Aralia Family
A native of southern Europe, western Asia and northern Africa
Light: From medium to high
Soil: Moist

This trailing and vining plant does best in cool, bright conditions. It makes sense since indoor ivy is the same plant that is used outdoors. The familiar three lobed foliage is most common; however, in older plants, the mature foliage has five lobes. Innumerable shape and color variations appear. Most of the cultivars are self-branching; they slowly grow at a uniform rate, consequently, they don't require much pruning.

Temperature: Very cool temperatures, from 45 to 65° F. are preferred. Temperatures of 32° F. are tolerated.

Humidity: Moderate.

Overall shape: Low and trailing.

Texture: From medium to delicate, depending upon the cultivars.

Availability: In 6 to10-inch diameter containers and hanging basket sizes; sometimes larger if shaped into topiaries or grown on trellises. Table top sizes, too.

Placement: As a groundcover especially near a drafty entryway, or planted in containers surrounding tall plants or with flowering plants.

Be aware that: Spider mites develop in hot, dry locations, so try to avoid using ivy in hanging baskets or as shelf planters. Otherwise, plan on replacing about every three months or at the first sign of decline. Prophylactic miticide applications may also be used.

The variegated plants tend to be unstable and branches may revert back to solid green. Remove them when necessary. Soluble salt damage occurs most frequently on the variegated plants.

Helpful hint: Place English ivy in cool, moist areas and it will grow successfully.

Cultivars include:

Solid green foliage:

'Brigitte'

'Curlilocks' has curled foliage.

'Green Ripple' has curled foliage.

'Midget' is a miniature ivy with narrow, sharply pointed foliage.

'Needlepoint' is a favorite with its narrow, needle-like lobes.

'Pittsburgh'

'Pixie' is a miniature with light green and rounded leaf points.

'Shamrock' looks like its name.

'Telecurl' has curled foliage.

White margined foliage:

'Ann Ganie' with an central area of gray green and minimal white leaf margins. (See color plate 5.)

'Eva'

'Glacier' has widely lobed leaves with a prominent white margin.

'Kokibri'

'Lady Frances' is a miniature with small, star shaped foliage. The interior of the leaf is streaked with pewter sections as well as green. The white leaf margins vary in width. The plant is strongly self-branching. The runners turn upward as the vine grows.

'Mona Lisa'

'Tonny'

'White Wonder'

Golden margined foliage:

'Gold Child' has wide golden margins.

'Goldheart' has a golden center.

'Golden Kolibri'

'Yellow Ripple' has rippled leaf margins.

Related species:

H. canariensis, Algerian Ivy, is a native of Algeria and the Canary Islands. It has much larger and very dark green foliage with red leaf petioles and stems. Its boldness combines well when underplanted with large trees and palms. (See color plates 1 and 5.) It also is great for groundcover in large atriums. 'Variegata' has equally large leaves with a gray green center and an irregular cream colored margin.

Heliconia spp.
**Lobser Claw, False Bird-of-Paradise
Heliconiaceae or Heliconia Family
Bred from native plants of tropical
    America, southeast Asia and
    various Pacific Islands
Light: High
Soil: Moist**

With tropicals always the rage, this plant with showy flowers and some species with showy foliage is a hit. The inflorescence is similar to that of bromeliads and looks like two rows of lobster claws alternating along a flower stalk. The bracts (modified leaves) are red, pink, yellow, orange, or multiple colors including some that are tipped in black. Small white true flowers emerge from among these showy bracts.

The foliage is narrowly elliptical—eighteen inches long and six inches wide—with a light midrib and attached to a central thick petiole. New plants are constantly being created from fleshy, underground rhizomes (thickened storage stems.) When four to seven leaves are present, the plant is ready to send up its lobster claws.

Length of bloom time: The inflorescence last for three to four months usually blooming in summer. But grow this plant for its foliage, too.

Temperature: Intermediate to warm, from 65 to 90° F. Below 60° F. encourages dormancy.

Humidity: Moderate.

Overall shape: Upright with arching foliage.

Texture: Bold.

Availability: In 8 to 14-inch diameter containers where it is five feet tall.

Placement: As specimen plants. As a background plant in a sunny atrium.

Be aware that: Phototropism is quite strong in this plant and free standing containers should be turned one-quarter of a turn every week. This plant is a heavy feeder and requires regular fertilization.

Helpful hints: Purchase this plant with spikes of colorful bracts already visible. This plant may need to be cut back after blooming.

Colorful species:

H. illustris 'Golden Torch' or *H. illustris* var. *aureostriata* is mostly grown for its striking variegated foliage—green, lime green and golden stripes that subtly blend into each other, creating a tropical look. The large leaves resemble that of the ginger plant and grows to eighteen inches long and eight inches wide. This plant is six feet tall. (See color plate 5.)

H. psittacorum 'Andromeda,' parrot's beak, is known for its inflorescence that is composed of red-orange basal bracts surrounding the many red-orange sepals that are banded with green-black tips. The solid green, elliptical foliage has a white midrib. This is not only a smaller plant that grows from three to five feet, it also is less affected by cool temperatures and more infrequent watering. (See color plate 5.)

Hemigraphis alternata 'Exotica'
Waffle Plant
Acanthaceae or Acanthus Family
A native of tropical Asia
Light: From low to medium
Soil: Moist

The foliage of this small plant is very unusual. Rather than looking like a waffle, the glossy oval foliage is puckered. Each leaf is metallic dark green touched with a red midrib and veins. Light is reflected causing the texture to be emphasized. The underside of the foliage is red-purple. The stems are hidden by the masses of foliage. (See color plate 5.)

Temperature: Warm, from 70 to 90° F.

Humidity: High.

Overall shape: Mounding, spreading habit about one foot tall and at least as wide.

Texture: Medium.

Availability: Hanging basket as well as smaller sizes.

Placement: These are small, short plants perfect for a table top garden or a hanging basket. Locate it near a waterfall or water feature. As a temporary, eye-catching, fun plant.

Be aware that: This plant is pest and disease-free.

Helpful hint: The humidity demand makes this a hard-to-place plant.

Hibiscus rosa-sinensis
Hibiscus
Malvaceae or Mallow Family
**A native of tropical countries along
    the Indian Ocean**
**Light: From the brighter side of
    from medium to medium**
Soil: Moist

Hibiscus has been used as flowering shrubs both indoors and out for many hundreds of years in China and Europe. Over the last hundred years, they have become very popular in the United States as well as worldwide.

Whether the brilliant flowers are five inches across or a foot wide, it's easy to see why the hibiscus is so well liked. The flowers look like they are made from crepe paper and may be single, semi-double or double, with or without frilly margins. White and shades of pink through red are the standard colors. The Hawaiian hybrids have the largest flowers in shades of yellow, coral or orange. Nearly all the different flowers have a contrasting darker colored throat although sometimes they are lighter or occasionally one solid color. A very prominent central tube carries numerous stalked stamens and a feathery branched stigma.

The large, glossy, dark green leaves with serrated margins compose most of the shrub that has fragile, woody stems.

Length of bloom time: Each flower lasts a day or two; new buds keep opening during summer. Place in proper light, water well, and avoid temperature extremes to promote blooming.

Temperature: Warm, from 75 to 90° F. Do not expose to sudden drafts or high heat.

Humidity: From high to medium.

Overall shape: Upright and shrublike.

Availability: Common in the 10-inch diameter container, whether as a short or tall shrub or a standard sometimes with a corkscrew or braided trunk. In the latter, they are four to five feet tall. The short shrubs may be only eighteen inches high. Hibiscus is available from early spring through fall and occasionally in the winter.

Placement: Anywhere a tropical floral look is desired. Seasonal interest in an atrium or well lighted doorway entrance.

Be aware that: The sweet potato whitefly is endemic. Spider mites may also occur.

Helpful hint: Provide regular additions of fertilizer.

Cultivars include:

'Jim Hendry' has pale yellow petals with a burgundy center. (See color plate 5.)

'Red Hot' has small—two to three inch wide—bright red blossoms. But it is known for its colorful foliage that ranges from burgundy to green to white when young and matures to many shades of red and bright pink. This is a compact grower that requires half the amount of water that other hibiscus demand and tolerates a wider temperature range from 45 to 85° F. Occasional lower temperatures to 33° F. and high temperatures of 98° F. are tolerated.

Tradewinds Series: If used as a seasonal flowering plant, these are compact growers. If kept longer, then pruning is required.

'Carolina Breeze' has iridescent orange flowers that shimmer in the light; the foliage is medium green.

'Largo Breeze' has orange-bronze flowers.

'Mango Breeze,' 'Paradise Breeze,' 'Raspberry Breeze' and 'Tropical Breeze' are others.

'Candy Wind' has light pink ruffled petals with deep pink throats and stamens. The foliage is medium green.

'Coconut Wind' has coconut white flowers with dark pink throats and medium green foliage.

'Flaming Wind' has soft red flowers with dark red throats and dark green foliage.

'Golden Wind' has vivid yellow flowers with contrasting light orange throats. The stems and leaf petioles have a reddish tint. The dark green foliage has ruffled margins.

'Whirl Wind' has a very large central dark pink throat with a light pink margin. The shiny bright green foliage is very attractive. 'Desert Wind,' 'Sahara Wind' and 'Velvet Wind' are others.

Another related plant:

Abutilon x *hybridum*, flowering maple, has foliage that resembles the maple tree. The flowers resemble large, single hollyhocks and are available in many lovely colors. Flowering occurs in spring and summer, then off and on all year long if given the proper conditions. 'Moonchimes' and 'Kristen's Pink' both have variegated foliage. The foliage is reason enough to utilize these cultivars. The 10 to14-inch diameter container is from three to four feet tall.

Hippeastrum **spp.**
Amaryllis
Amaryllidaceae or Amaryllis Family
Bred from native plants of South America, but most are Dutch hybrids
Light: Medium
Soil: Moderately moist

Amaryllis is used as a short-term flower purchased in bloom and bud. Spectacular, lilylike blooms, each from six to ten inches in diameter, appear in two separate pairs. The first pair opposite each other blooms simultaneously while the other two flowers are in bud. Then, another look is created when the second pair opens allowing for north, south, east and west-facing blooms. The four flowers rise atop a thick, hollow flower stalk that is eighteen inches to two feet tall. Colors range from red, white, pink, salmon, orange, yellow and all colors in between. The white flowers often have muted pink streaks. Some of the flowers are double.

The flowers are most dramatic because they mature before the straplike foliage emerges. Often a second stalk will follow, extending the bloom time.

Length of bloom time: Usually three to four weeks, depending whether a second flower stalk emerges. Cool temperatures and medium light allows amaryllis to bloom longer.

Temperature: Intermediate, from 65 to 75° F.

Humidity: Moderate.

Overall shape: Tall and vertical.

Texture: Bold.

Availability: In 6 inch-diameter containers as a seasonal flower, especially from late fall through early summer.

Placement: Where the lovely blooms can stand above other foliage plants. As a focal point, the flowers are warmly welcomed.

Helpful hint: One-third of the bulb should be visible above the soil surface. It should also be potbound.

Cultivars include:

'Apple Blossom' looks like its name.

'Beautiful Lady' is a deep salmon.

'Christmas Star' is red with a white center.

'Crystal Palace' is a double white.

'Dutch Belle' has muted mauve striations upon a white petal with a white throat ringed with raspberry. The center is green.

'Fanfare' is a double red.

'Orange Sovereign' is a dark red-orange.

'Pico Bello' has peach-pink flowers.

'Red Lion' has very large red flowers.

'Rose Marie' has rich mauve striations with a raspberry throat. (See color plate 5.)

'Salmon Pearl' is a miniature— one foot to eighteen inches tall—with salmon and cream double flowers.

Homalomena 'Emerald Gem'
Homalomena
Araceae or Arum Family
A cultivated variety from native
    plants of India
Light: Medium, but acclimates to
    low levels
Soil: Moderately dry

The heart-shaped foliage has prominent veins forming parallel lines on both side of the midrib. These glossy, leathery, dark green leaves are four inches across. They are supported on strong, narrow, leaf petioles. This creates a formal and elegant presentation along with compact and symmetrical growth. (See color plate 5.)

Temperature: Warm, from 70 to 90° F.

Humidity: Moderate.

Overall shape: V-shape, upright and arching.

Texture: Bold.

Availability: In 6 to 10-inch diameter containers. The 6-inch size is eight inches tall and twice as wide.

Placement: As a neat-looking, strongly textured, tall groundcover. Heavy trafficked areas where people can enjoy its quiet beauty. As an underplanting for tall trees. Or in planters in hard to reach areas.

Be aware that: *Homalomena* is quite insect resistant; however, mealybug may appear on the undersides of the foliage. It is quite disease resistant. Remove any inflorescence that appear.

Helpful hint: This plant is very tough, durable and tolerates many stresses well.

Cultivars include:

'Purple Sword' has has lance-shaped foliage. The dark green leaves have silver markings and purple undersides. (See color plate 5.)

Howea forsteriana
Kentia Palm, Sentry Palm
Arecaceae or Palm Family
A native of Lord Howe Island east
   of Australia
Light: Medium, but acclimates to
   low levels
Soil: Moist

Not only is the kentia palm an elegant palm it also is very durable. These two qualities don't often occur together. This palm has been used indoors since the 1850s. The relatively wide, leathery, deep green leaves magnificently arch. A quick way of identifying this palm is to look for brown hairs on the undersides of the leaves. Some of the leaves are huge; the new ones at the base of the plant are small. Individual plants are quite spindly, therefore three to four plants are grown in a container.

The advantage of being a very slow grower is that the plant does not outgrow its location; the disadvantage is that this is an expensive plant.

Temperature: Intermediate to warm, from 65 to 90° F. but will tolerate cold temperatures to 45° F. and high temperatures to 100° F.

Humidity: Moderate to low.

Overall shape: Tall and arching.

Texture: Bold.

Availability: Most commonly, from 10 to 17-inch diameter containers with 3 ppp. (plants per pot) growing from eight to twelve feet. Taller plants to twenty feet may be special ordered.

Placement: As a showcase plant quite deserving of an executive office or other prominent location. It lends itself to tight spaces. Large plants work well in heavy trafficked area where the leaves reach overhead.

Be aware that: The two-spotted spider mite and Florida red scale are two pests to be on the lookout for. Applying a systemic insecticide/ miti-cide prophylactically may be worthwhile. *Helminthosporium* fungus, with numerous brown round leaf spots surrounded by yellow areas may occur with overwatering. Similar spots on older foliage may be a sign of potassium deficiency. When spots are discovered especially on older leaves, try adding a dose of fertilizer and see if the problem reverses.

Helpful hints: The kentia palm is quite forgiving with occasional overwatering and under-watering. Sometimes, new plants arrive with poorly developed root systems. It's best to go easy on the watering until you evaluate the water uptake. Eventually, the root system develops and is strong.

Cultivars include:

'Keeline,' 'Keeline Wilcox' is a more compact grower make this cultivar great for smaller areas. (See color plate 5.)

Related palms and other plants:

Carludovica 'Jungle Drums' discovered in South America, has palm-like foliage and is a nice alternative to any intermediate size palm. The olive green linear leaflets look corrugated. This plant is at least four feet tall and as wide. Treat it as any palm.

Chamaedorea hooperiana, Maya palm, resembles the kentia palm. This species is tolerant of low light levels as well as low humidity and is pest resistant.

Ravenea rivularis, majesty palm, a native of Madagascar, has similar foliage and grows about the same size as the kentia, but that's where the similarity ends. This palm, along with the areca palm, is treated as a temporary, fill-in plant. The single trunk is short and thick giving rise to individual leaf bases. The lower leaves arise closely from the base. This fast growing palm is ten feet tall and five feet wide in the 17-inch diameter container. Leaf spots, root rots, spider mites and scale insects may be problematic. The majesty palm requires fertilizing to maintain its dark green color. Yellowing of new leaves is typical of an iron deficiency.

Hoya carnosa
Hoya or Wax Plant
Asclepiadaceae or Asclepias Family
A native of southern China through
   Australia
Light: Medium
Soil: Dry

The very thick, waxy and succulent light green leaves appear along a stiff stem. The entire plant trails or climbs in an attractive manner. The rounded clusters of small, waxy, star-like flowers appear each spring sweetly perfuming the air. These flowers are usually very light pink to white but some cultivars are bright pink. This is a very rugged plant related to the milkweed.

Temperatures: Intermediate to warm, from 65 to 90° F., but will tolerate slightly cooler temperatures.

Humidity: All levels, from low to high.

Overall shape: Upright and trailing.

Texture: Medium.

Availability: In 8 to 10-inch hanging basket sizes.

Placement: Hanging baskets or in shelf planters, any very dry and bright area.

Be aware that: Mealybugs rarely occur but if they do, they'll be in the leaf axils (the junction between the leaf petiole and stem.)

Helpful hint: This is a very clean, durable, easy-maintenance plant that does not shed leaves, important for overhead plantings.

Cultivars include:

'Alba' has white flowers.

'Compacta' has foliage that grows very close together creating a dense, full appearance.

'Exotica' has pink and yellow variegated foliage surrounded by wide green margins. The vine is bright magenta. (See color plate 5.)

'Krinkle Kurl' is a good description for the thick, folded leaves that curl backwards.

Hydrangea macrophylla
Big-Leaf Hydrangea
Saxifragaceae or Saxifrage Family
**A native of Honshu, the largest
    Japanese island**
Light: Medium
Soil: Moist

This is the flowering plant that screams "old-fashioned" and has traditionally been available in the spring especially sold for Mother's Day. But it is forced into bloom from Valentine's Day through Memorial Day. Naturally, the hydrangea is a perennial shrub. It has been popular in Europe for centuries. Because of the long cropping time, large area of bench space required and great watering demands, this is an expensive flower. It goes in and out of popularity in the United States often related to economic conditions.

The billowy inflorescence is composed of showy, sterile flowers and resembles a snowball viburnum. The lacecap hydrangea is a variation with a large center area composed of small, fertile flowers surrounded by a single circle of large, showy sterile flowers. (See color plate 5.) The color of the flower is determined by soil pH manipulated by adding aluminum, iron sulfate or limestone during the growing phase. If the pH is greater than 6.0, then the flowers are pink, if it is more acidic and less than 5.0, then the flowers are blue. Levels between those two numbers produce lavender flowers. White flowers are not affected by soil pH; they simply do not contain any color pigment. All flowers have a light scent.

The big leaves are oval, serrated and pointed at the tip. They stand up well as they frame the luxurious blooms.

Length of bloom time: Purchase plants when one or two blooms are open and the rest are in various stages of bud maturity. Optimally, hydrangeas last for six weeks.

Temperature: Intermediate, from 65 to 75° F.

Humidity: Moderate to high.

Overall shape: Tall and shrublike.

Texture: Bold.

Availability: In the spring and early summer in 6 to 8-inch diameter containers where they may be three feet tall. Three or four plants are in each container.

Placement: Anywhere where all may see, certainly a spectacular specimen plant.

Be aware that: Hydrangeas are hard to maintain, but they are worth it. They require copious amounts of water. When I used them, I had a dilemma—I didn't work over the weekend and knew the hydrangeas would wilt (they do not recover.) I always asked someone who worked close to where the hydrangeas were located to add a cup of water to each plant day and night.

Using a subirrigation system is another good idea. DriWater is another option. (See footnote #3, p. 10.) A recent development in subirrigation for blooming plants in 6 to 8 inch diameter containers is a product called Sippers[8]. Four porous spikes are inserted into the bottom of the growing container. The plant is then placed in a decorative container and water is added until it reaches the base of the growing container. Half of the spike is in the soil and half is in the water allowing the water to be drawn upwards.

Helpful hint: Taller hydrangeas may become top heavy and may require extra support.

Cultivars include:

'Hamburg' is a light rose-pink hydrangea with many rounded blooms and strong stems.

'Stockholm' has clear, shining red blooms and strong, dark green foliage.

'Saturn' is a pink and white bicolor variety.

---

[8]   Sippers are offered by Primescape Product Company, P.O. Box 710, Deerfield, IL 60015.

Kalanchoe blossfeldiana
Kalanchoe
Crassulaceae or Stonecrop Family
A native of Madagascar
Light: From high to medium
Soil: Moderately dry

These durable and easy maintenance succulents are filled with a myriad of small but powerfully colorful flowers. They were introduced in Germany in 1932 by Robert Blossfeld and have been bred by the Swiss and the Americans ever since. These compact, neat and attractive plants have been the number one flowering plant in Denmark and rapidly became important to the United States market.

The small four petaled flowers, most often with yellow centers, appear in multiple clusters upon strong flowerstalks. The flower shape varies from flat and open to bell-shaped. The colors extend the full spectrum from white and yellow through orange and reds, from pastels through bright fluorescent pink and orange. The fluorescent colors are so striking that people frequently stop and admire. (See color plate 2.) For fall, the rust and apricot colors blend well. Kalanchoes are also available in bicolors.

The thick, shiny, scalloped, large green leaves offer a rugged contrast to the flowers.

Length of bloom time: Kalanchoes are inexpensive, throw-away plants that last a long time, from six weeks to several months when purchased in mature bud stage. Often, they are replaced every four weeks because of less than optimal light levels.

Temperature: Warm, from 70 to 90° F.

Humidity: From low to moderate.

Overall shape: Full and upright.

Texture: Delicate flowers with bold foliage.

Availability: In 6 to 8-inch diameter containers and table top sizes. Miniatures, too. All are available year-round.

Placement: Massed with a show of color, in among groundcovers, in an area with other succulents or cacti.

Be aware that: Mealybug are the only insect that may become a problem.

Helpful hint: There is no flower drop so upkeep is at a minimum. It's no wonder kalanchoes are appearing everywhere.

Important fact: The preferred pronunciation is kal-an-KOE-ee.

Cultivars include:

'Bingo' with fluorescent pink, long lasting flowers.

'Megan' has soft pink flowers with ivory outer petals and ivory buds.

'Segula' with light pink flowers and red-brown foliage.

'Triade' has soft pink flowers with yellow centers.

Fides Series: (Available in 4 to 6-inch containers.)

Eight colors are available including 'Iztac' which is hot pink, 'Lican' which is rose-purple and 'Mirabella' with bright red bell-shaped flowers.

Forever Midi Series: (Available in small size containers to 4 inches.)

Eight colors are available including 'Midi Hot Pink' with fluorescent pink flowers, 'Midi Frosty Red' with silver-green leaves and a thin white margin, 'Midi Pink Starlet' with dark pink centers and light pink edges giving the appearance of a four-pointed star and 'Midi Sunset Pink' has pale yellow flowers that fade to white, then turn lavender-pink.

Forever Maxi Series: (Available in 6-inch containers.)

Seven colors, all with very large flowers, are available: 'Maxi Antique Pink' which is salmon-pink, 'Maxi Pink,' 'Maxi Orchid' which is dark pink, 'Maxi Red,' 'Maxi Rose,' 'Maxi Salmon' and 'Maxi White'.

Prestige Series: (Available in 4 to 6-inch containers.)

Seven colors including 'Empress' which is cherry red, 'Legacy' which is lavender, 'Majestic' which is rose-red, 'Merit' which is orange and 'Revelry' which is bright yellow.

Revolution Series: All flowers are bicolors on compact plants.

'Revolution Apricot' has light and dark apricot flowers.

'Revolution Rose' has white and rose colored flowers.

Ten Series: The flowers are great for fall coloration.

'Tencotta' is a striking bicolor with soft orange petals and a deep red center. The buds are pink. The colors meld to a terra cotta color.

'Tenflame' has bright, brick red flowers. (See color plate 5.)

'Tenterra' is a very pale peachy-white with dark centers.

Related species: The following are grown for their foliage.

K. tomentosa, panda plant, is grown for its unusual foliage. It has fuzzy, oval, gray-green leaves with brown spots at the margins. It is one and one-half feet tall.

K. beharensis, velvet leaf plant, has velvety, gray-green, foliage with stiff, brown hairs along the leaf margins. The thick, large leaves are shaped like an arrowhead. It's best to keep this one away from where people might be tempted to touch. Although the leaf is velvety smooth, the brown hairs are sharp.

K. pinnata, air plant, is an unusual plant in that new plants form along the scalloped leaf margins. The thick medium green leaves are long and pointy.

Ledebouria socialis
Silver Squill
Liliaceae or Lily Familly
A native of South Africa
Light: Medium
Soil: Moderately dry

What an interesting, easy-care, tough foliage plant guaranteed a "spot" in the interiorscape. Those unusual large green spots upon a silvery background provide great interest. The undersides of the foliage is tinted red. The leaves are fleshy and strappy—less than six inches long and about an inch wide—and are compressed into a central rosette. (See color plate 5.) With many plants in each container, this is a mass of beautiful foliage.

Temperature: Warm, from 70 to 90° F.

Humidity: Moderate.

Overall shape: Low and wide.

Texture: Bold.

Availability: In 10 to 12-inch diameter hanging basket sizes. Table top sizes, too.

Placement: Take advantage of its warm temperature needs and place in hanging baskets or in shelf planters. Massed in containers or used as groundcover.

Be aware that: This is a pest and disease-free plant.

Helpful hints: Take advantage of the easy maintenance requirements of this plant. Usually underwatering is not a problem since the bulbs store water. As an added bonus, sprays of small white flowers may appear.

Cultivars include:

'Silver Leopard' is an especially attractive cultivar with more distinct dark green leopard spots creating stronger contrast.

Leucospermum cordifolium
Pincushion Flower
Proteaceae or Protea Family
A native of South Africa
Light: From from high to the brighter side of medium
Soil: Moderately dry

Originally used as a cut flower from Australia, this potted flower is grown there as well as in Hawaii and California. Just imagine placing these winter brighteners indoors in the northern climes during January, the time of year that everything looks so bare.

The inflorescence take center stage as a four to five inch pincushion of brilliant color: yellow, orange or red. And they are long lasting.

The foliage is three inches long, leathery and pointed. It is directly attached along the strong and stiff stem which angles slightly upward from the soil surface. The terminal ends point upward and surround the inflorescence. (See color plate 5.)

Length of bloom time: Many months.

Temperature: A wide range from cool to warm, 55 to 90° F.

Humidity: Low.

Overall shape: Sparsely shrubby with angled branches.

Texture: Bold.

Availability: In a 6-inch diameter container.

Placement: As a substitute for flowering plants or bromeliads.

Helpful hints: These show stoppers attract attention whenever used. This plant is durable and has easy maintenance requirements.

Cultivars include:

'Flame Spike' with deep orange-red inflorescence.

Plants with similar inflorescence:

Calliandra spp., powderpuff plant, has nearly globe shaped inflorescence of red, pink, or white.

Mimosa pudica, touch-me-not plant, has small, pink, globe shaped inflorescence. The fernlike foliage closes at the midrib when touched.

Lilium longiflorum
Easter Lily
Liliaceae or Lily Family
A native of the Ryukyu islands,
       between Japan and Taiwan
Light: Medium
Soil: Moist

These lilies were discovered in 1777 and became popular plants in Europe where they naturally bloomed in the summer. They were brought to the United States in the mid-ninteenth century and forced into bloom for Easter. Until the 1980s, the Easter lily was the third most popular flowering plant in the United States. It remains a religious symbol for use in churches and homes.

The fragrant, showy, large white trumpet flowers appear in groups of up to eight at the top of the strong flowerscape. The strappy green leaves are eight inches long and one inch wide and appear interspersed along the stem. (See color plate 5.)

Length of bloom time: The flowers last for about one week.

Temperature: Cool, between 50 to 60° F.

Humidity: Moderate.

Overall shape: Upright.

Texture: Medium.

Availability: Usually in 6-inch diameter containers where they are approximately two feet high or taller. They are available in spring.

Be aware that: Tiny thrips that appear deep in the center of the flower are rarely present.

Helpful hint: Removing the yellow anthers from the center of the lily will prevent any yellow staining whether it be on the white petals or anywhere it falls. Remember smelling an Easter lily and ending up with a yellow stain on the tip of your nose?

Cultivars include:

'Ace' was introduced in 1935 and is still being grown. It is from eighteen inches to two feet tall.

'Casa Rosa' is light pink with a dark pink throat. Most of the pink colored cultivars are devoid of scent.

'Croft' is white.

'Howard' is white.

'Nellie White' was introduced in 1955 and is still in production.

'White Elegance' has a large white flower.

'White Heaven' has a large white flower.

Related species:

Many species of lilies, available in a wide range of colors, are lovely accent flowers to use during the spring and summer months.

Liriope muscari
Liriope, Lilyturf
Liliaceae or Lily Family
**A native of Vietnam, China, Taiwan
   and Japan**
Light: Medium
Soil: Moderately moist

This plant looks like an elegant, clumping grass and is used as such. The narrow and glossy dark green leaves—one foot long and three-quarters of an inch wide—arch gracefully. (See color plate 5.)

When conditions are right, usually in late summer, liriope sends up erect spikes extending slightly above the foliage. The spikes are filled with closely packed lavender-blue bell-shaped and fragrant flowers.

Temperature: Intermediate, from 65 to 75° F. but will tolerate as low as 40° F without chilling injury.

Humidity: Moderate.

Overall shape: V-shape clumps.

Texture: Delicate to medium.

Availability: In 6 to 10-inch diameter containers where it is from nine inches to one foot tall.

Placement: As groundcover. As an underplanting of large containerized trees or as a fill in surrounding flowering plants.

Helpful hint: This is an durable, easy to maintain plant.

Cultivars include:

'Variegata' has cream striped foliage.

Livistonia chinensis
Chinese Fan Palm
Arecaceae or Palm Family
A native of China and Japan
**Light: Medium but acclimates to
   low light**
Soil: Moderately moist

This is a very elegant palm with a different look to the foliage. The glossy, fan-shaped, leathery and tough leaves are very broad-spreading, often up to six feet across. Most of the leaflets are fused together and appear pleated for at least half of the leaf. They then split into leaflets that gently droop. Attractive tan fibers hang down from the leaflet tips. These leaves are attached to thorny leaf petioles that emerge from a fibrous trunk. (See color plate 5.)

Temperature: Warm, from 70 to 95° F.

Humidity: Moderate.

Overall shape: As wide or wider than tall with nearly horizontal leaves.

Texture: Bold.

Availability: In 10 to 17-inch diameter containers where the plant is five feet tall.

Placement: In an open area such as a large atrium. As a background planting for a tropical look.

Be aware that: This is an easy-care, durable palm with a good pest resistance.

Helpful hint: Because of the large size of the leaves and small number of them, removing only one frond often changes the look of the plant enough to require replacing.

A similar palm:

Chamaerops humilis, European fan palm, is a native of the countries surrounding the Mediterranean Sea. The soft green leaflets fan out to three feet wide in a stiff manner. They are attached to thorny leaf petioles that emerge from a fibrous, thick trunk. This palm has a variable growth habit and may grow to twelve feet. New growth consists of suckering trunks. This palm is very tolerant of cool temperatures.

Maranta leuconeura var. *kerchoviana*
Rabbit's Tracks, Prayer Plant
Marantaceae or Arrowroot Family
A native of Brazil
Light: From medium to low
Soil: Moderately moist

What colorful foliage all the *Marantas* have. The six-inch long foliage is pale green with pairs of dark green splotches running down either side of the midrib, just like rabbit's tracks. (See color plate 5.) At night, the foliage folds in half along the midrib, resembling a pair of hands praying, thus its other common name.

The large foliage appears on short leaf petioles that are attached to underground rhizomes (thickened storage stems) under the soil surface.

Temperature: Intermediate to warm, from 65 to 85° F. A consistent temperature is most important.

Humidity: From high to moderate.

Overall shape: Low and dense, usually one foot tall and at least as wide.

Texture: Bold.

Availability: Table top size, Also in 6 to 8-inch diameter containers.

Placement: These are small, short plants perfect for groundcover use, low hanging baskets, or table top gardens. One plant is a great decoration for a dining table.

Be aware that: This plant is very sensitive to soluble salt build up and fluoride tipburn on older leaves.

Helpful hint: *Marantas* are not known for their longevity, but rabbit tracks is the easiest to grow. Consistent watering is important.

Related species:

M. leuconeura var. *erythroneura*, red nerve plant, has prominent red parallel veins with light green along the midrib. The rest of the foliage is very dark green. (See color plate 5.)

Monstera deliciosa
Swiss Cheese Plant, Split-Leaf Philodendron
Araceae or Arum Family
A native of Mexico and Central America
Light: Medium
Soil: Moderately moist

This is a large, upright vine—not a true philodendron, but related—that used to be allowed to grow wild in the 1970s. Nothing was given a haircut in those days. Its jungle feeling fell into disfavor, but became popular again. And it should, it's a durable plant with easy maintenance. The large—to one foot wide and long—glossy, leathery green leaves have various shapes. The young leaves are heart shaped, some have a split or two and mature leaves have many "splits" in either side along with Swiss cheese-like holes. (See color plate 6.)

The thick stems become gangly and must be tied together to keep the plant from sprawling. Brown aerial roots emerge from leaf nodes along the stem and reach downward in mature plants.

Temperature: Warm, from 70 to 90° F.

Humidity: It thrives in low humidity.

Overall shape: Either vining and climbing or trimmed back full and wide.

Texture: Bold.

Availability: In 8 to 14-inch diameter containers. Also as four or six-feet tall totems.

Placement: Along a trellis or wall to hide mechanical structures. As a specimen plant in a large area.

Be aware that: Mealybug, scale insects and spider mites occasionally occur.

Helpful hint: This plant grows and requires occasional pruning.

Cultivars include:

'Braziliensis'

'Variegata' has foliage with white and cream markings.

Related species:

M. adansonii is also called the Swiss cheese plant. It is very versatile because of its smaller size— the 10-inch diameter container is two and one-half to three feet tall— and its slower growth rate which lessens maintenance. The smaller foliage is oval to elliptical with many holes on the leaf surface, even on the young foliage. With age, the holes become slits. (See color plate 6.)

Musa acuminata 'Super Dwarf'
Banana Plant
Musaceae or Banana Family
A cultivated variety from native plants of southeast Asia
Light: High but acclimates to medium
Soil: Moist

This small cultivar that grows to three or four feet is very versatile. The leaf petioles and internodes are short, forming a compact plant. But the lance-shaped glossy foliage is very large— growing to three feet long and one foot wide. Before the new foliage opens, it is tightly rolled— an interesting feature. When it fully unfurls, it has red patches that fade with time. The bamboolike, thick trunk is covered with fibrous dried leaf petioles. On occasion, it flowers and bears fruit. If that happens, then the plant develops offshoots while the inital plant dies.

Temperature: Intermediate to warm, from 65 to 90° F.

Humidity: From low to moderate.

Overall shape: Tall and arching.

Texture: Bold.

Availability: Usually in 6 to 10-inch diameter containers where they are three to four feet tall, or in larger containers where the plants are five feet tall.

Placement: In a tropical area where its large leaves can be enjoyed by all. Alongside a pool.

Be aware that: The banana plant is subject to spider mites and mealybugs. Bacterial rots and leaf spots occur occasionally.

Helpful hint: Also try the *Strelitzia reginae*, bird of paradise, for a similar look.

Other banana plants:

M. acuminata has been grown since Victorian days for its enormously large foliage—four feet long and two feet wide. It is available in 10 to 14-inch and larger diameter containers where it is ten feet tall. 'Dwarf Cavendish' is six feet tall with the same size foliage. (See color plate 6.)

Neoregelia carolinae
**Neoregelia, Neos, Striped Blushing
    Bromeliad**
Bromeliaceae or Pineapple Family
**A native of southeast Brazil in the
    Amazon River basin**
**Light: From high to the brighter
    side of medium**
Soil: Moderately dry

This is another colorful plant that is an eye-catcher. A rosette of stiff, strappy, glossy green foliage usually striped with yellow or cream along with serrated margins forms the base of this plant. Shorter, deep red bracts[9] are at the center forming a cup. The actual small white, blue, lavender or purple flowers are located deep inside the cup and usually go unnoticed.

Length of bloom time: Often up to six months. These bromeliads take the prize for longevity.

Temperature: A wide range from 55 to 85° F. and can tolerate short periods of cooler and warmer temperatures.

Humidity: Adapts to low humidity although moderate is preferred.

Overall shape: Low and flat are the keywords for *Neoregelias*. Their shape is so unlike other bromeliads.

Texture: Bold.

Availability: Most cultivars are available in the 4½ and 6½-inch diameter containers where they are less than six inches tall and cover a two foot wide circle.

Placement: As a substitute for flowering plants. Although these plants may be more expensive initially, in the long run they are economical because of the long lasting color, durability and minimal upkeep. En masse in a container or as a groundcover for spectacular color. Great for seasonal and patriotic holidays, Valentine's Day, and any other time in between.

Be aware that: The colors tend to fade unless placed in high light.

Helpful hint: In nature, rainwater collects in the center cup providing a place for frog eggs to hatch and insect larvae to grow. But here, in civilization, water in the cup gives permission for people to throw in things such as gum wrappers. The water also naturally stagnates and must be removed. Therefore, water this epiphyte—growing in tree crevices with aerial roots absorbing nutrients from water, air and dust, particles—at the soil surface.

Cultivars include:

'Deb' has bright red bracts from base to tip surrounded by a few green ones.

'Fireball' is a small, branching plant.

'Flandria' has the dark red center surrounded by most attractive foliage. The foliage is very dark green with a subtle lime green or cream stripe or two. The margin is a wide edge of cream to lime green color. (See color plate 6.)

'Grace' has nearly all red bracts. Only the outer perimeter of foliage is dark green.

'King's Ransom' is a fluorescent dark red color surrounded by dark green foliage.

'Lila' has an almost iridescent lilac color on the short, broad bracts.

'Martin' has red centers with variegated foliage.

'Medium Rare' has red centers with attractive bronze foliage.

'Mocha Mint' has dark reddish-brown bracts with yellow and green spots. It grows more upright than others.

'Perfecta Tricolor' has more coloration than 'Tricolor'.

'Purple Star' develops a solid center of narrow vivid purple bracts surrounded by multicolor leaves of lavender and green.

'Royal Burgundy' has chocolate brown foliage with a few green spots. It is fifteen inches wide.

'Tricolor,' the striped blushing bromeliad, is so named for its central, bright red coloration of the

---

[9]   The center bracts turn red as a sign that flowering is imminent.

strappy leaves, surrounded by green leaves that have a wide ivory stripe down the middle. This light stripe turns pink under high light. (See color plate 2.)

'Ultima' has a dark red center with striking, wide variegated foliage. Most of the foliage is cream to lime green with a few narrow dark green stripes and a wide edge of dark green at the margin. (See color plate 6.)

'Victoria Pink' is deep pink in the center surrounded by dark green foliage.

Nephrolepis exaltata 'Dallasii'
Dallas Fern
Davalliaceae or Davallia Family
A cultivated variety of the Boston Fern which is a native of many tropical regions
Light: From medium to low
Soil: Moderately moist

The biggest challenge in growing ferns is to provide enough light and humidity. The Boston fern (see below) suffers from these problems and is best used as a plant that is frequently replaced in unsuitable conditions.

However, Dallas fern, as well as other cultivars, tolerate interior conditions, especially **low light** and **less humid areas**. Dallas fern has close growing pinnae (leaflets) upon short fronds creating a compact and full plant. (See color plate 6.)

Temperature: Intermediate to warm, from 65 to 95° F.

Humidity: Moderate.

Overall shape: Full and arching.

Texture: Medium.

Availability: Hanging basket sizes.

Placement: Hanging baskets, on a plant stand, or near a water feature. The size makes this fern very practical to use.

Be aware that: Mealybugs are first visible on the undersides of the lower fronds sometimes in the roots. Soft brown scale may become a problem. *Rhizoctonia* fungal root blight espresses itself as brown and black splotches on the fronds and occurs in high soil temperatures above 75° F. *Pythium* fungal root rot expresses itself as yellowing of the fronds, wilting and general stunting. Allow the plant to dry out somewhat and treat with a fungicide approved for ferns.

Helpful hint: If the fronds develop a graying, then the fern has been underwatered.

Other cultivars include:

'Bostoniensis,' Boston fern, with its gracefully arched three foot long fronds with smooth edges, has long been the standard of the industry since its discovery over one hundred years ago as an attractive mutation of the species. It took over the foliage industry in Florida by 1912. As beautiful as it looks, the foliage dries and turns brown unless placed in high humidity.

'Bluebell' is smaller with a golden hue.

'Compacta' is smaller with crinkled pinnae (leaflets.)

'Dallas Jewel' and 'Dallas Ramet' require even less attention to watering and survive in low humidity.

'Fluffy Ruffles' is a medium size fern with fluffy ruffled pinnae (leaflets.) 'Corditas,' 'Florida Ruffles,' 'Frills,' 'Fluffy,' 'Hillii' are similar looking cultivars.

'Marathon' and 'Super' are larger sized plants.

'Rooseveltii' has wavy and bisected pinnae (leaflets.)

'Timmii' has ruffled and twisted fronds that grow upright.

Related species:

N. biserrata 'Furcans,' actually *N. falcata* 'Furcans,' fishtail fern, is stiff and upright and best used for background plantings or in freestanding containers.

'Macho,' actually *N. falcata* 'Macho,' macho fern, needless to say, is very large, but has gracefully arching fronds. Use as a specimen floor plant as well as a very large hanging basket display.

N. cordifolia cultivars are very versatile since they exhibit a tolerance to low light areas as well as a wide range of temperatures and lower humidity requirements.

'Duffii,' lemon button fern, has small, round pinnae (leaflets) that grow along the one foot long fronds. There is a slight lemon fragrance. The overall appearance is upright, stiff and spiky and looks best tucked in with blooming plants. (See color plate 6.)

'Kimberly Queen' has leathery and curly fronds that grow quite large to three feet long. It has a very upright growth habit. It is very tolerant of lower light levels and temperatures to the low 20's.

'Timm's Petticoat' has a dense composition of frilly frond tips. Great for hanging baskets.

'Western Queen,' is an improvement over 'Kimberly Queen' with wavy fronds. It is sometimes sold as *N. obliterata*, Australian sword fern.

Other ferns:

Adiantum raddianum, delta maidenhair fern, doesn't have typical fernlike foliage. The pinnate fronds have small, delicate rhomboid leaflets similar to the shape of the gingko tree leaf. They appear along wiry, thin, black stems that gracefully drape over the edge of the container. Rarely is this plant over one foot tall and wide. (See color plate 6.) Keep moderately moist at all times. High humidity is also required to prevent leaf browning. Limited to locations near waterfalls, fountains, or along the edges of water features. Great used to surround flowering plants. Cultivars include: 'Brilliyttelse,' 'Fragrantissimum,' 'Fritz Luthii,' 'Goldelse' and 'Glorytas'. The last two have yellow variegation.

A. capillus-veneris, southern maidenhair fern, is a more robust and larger version of the above with drooping fronds up to two feet long.

Asplenium nidus, bird's-nest fern, is a striking plant that certainly does not resemble anything typically described as a fern. There's nothing delicate about it. The large (up to four feet long and eight inches wide), shiny, light green single fronds have a rippled effect on either side of the nearly black rachis (midrib.) They arise from a central rhizome (thickened storage stem), partially growing above ground and resembling a fibrous bird's nest.

Sometimes the plant grows hairy aerial roots that protrude over the edges of the container. In the wild, this plant is an epiphyte—it doesn't require soil because aerial roots absorb nutrients from water, air and dust particles. It tolerates low light but thrives in medium levels. Temperatures from 70 to 90° F. are preferred. Keep the soil moderately moist at all times. From medium to high humidity is best. Bird's-nest fern offers a great texture amid other plantings especially near a water feature. Mealybug may appear along the rachis (midrib) on the underside of the frond.

Cultivars Include:

'Antiguum' or 'Antiquorum,' Japanese bird's-nest fern, has slightly narrowed foliage. 'Osaka,' Osaka bird's nest fern, has ruffled margins upon narrow leaves.

Blechnum 'Silver Lady,' silver lady fern, is related to the dwarf tree fern, *B. gibbum* but is only eighteen inches tall. It has an upright and V-shape while the base is nicely filled in with nearly horizontal fronds. The silvery new growth arising in the center of the plant almost gives a feeling of "jewelry" especially when planted en masse. The mature foliage is light green and is palmlike. Each frond has many narrow pinnae (leaflets) along the rachis (midrib.) The fronds are rather wide and the combination is very desirable. Silver lady fern does not shed and keeps its size and shape well. It requires from medium to high light and moist soil. Moderate temperatures are best but this fern is tolerant of temperatures to 20° F. and tolerates lower humidity without browning but, if the soil dries out, the fern turns crispy. The neutral yet elegant color offers a good backdrop to a mid-height planting. It may also be interplanted with seasonal flowers or colorful foliage plants.

Cyrtomium falcatum 'Rockfordianum,' rockford holly fern, has glossy, leathery and dark green foliage resembling a holly leaf. It is mostly upright and slightly arching. Keep soil moderately dry. This fern also tolerates low humidity. With a wide range of tolerances, the holly fern is easily adaptable to the interiorscape. Seek this fern out. Use it in any area where other ferns have a hard time growing.

Davallia trichomanoides or *D. mariesii* var. *stenolepis*, are both called rabbit's foot fern but actually are the squirrel's foot fern. They are closely related ferns known for the rabbit or squirrel "feet" that creep over the edge of the container. These brown and fuzzy protrusions are actually rhizomes (thickened storage stems.) The leathery, very finely divided pinnae (leaflets) grow along a dark brown and wiry rachis (midrib). (See color plate 6.) Keep the soil barely moist. Temperatures below 60° F. cause the plant to lose fronds and become dormant. Great for a 10 inch diameter hanging basket where the "feet" are visible and the fern is two feet tall and wide. This is a long-lasting, easy-care plant that acclimates to low light. 'Mandaianum' has bluish cast fronds with serrated and ruffled margins.

Microsorum diversifolium, kangaroo fern, is similar looking with long creeping rhizomes (thickened storage stems.) The wide and irregularly-shaped leathery, dark green fronds are characteristic of this plant. It features a clustering habit and tolerates a wider range of temperatures.

Pellaea rotundifolia, button fern, is an interesting fern because the pinnae (leaflets) are round. They also are bright glossy green and leathery. They are loosely arranged along a thin, dark brown rachis (midrib.) Button ferns grow from creeping rhizomes (thickened storage stems.) They require from medium to high light levels but tolerate moderate to low humidity and are tough and durable. *P. paradoxa* 'Glowstar' has elongated oval shaped pinnae (leaflets) and resembles a more conventional fern.

Platycerium bifurcatum, staghorn fern, is most unusual with foliage that looks like antlers; thus, its common name. (See color plate 6.) This large, to three feet wide and tall, coarse plant is a very slow grower. At its base, are coverings of concave tan fronds. This epiphyte does not require soil; it gets its nutrition from particles in the air and water. This plant is best grown on a piece of wood attached with sphagnum moss or in wire baskets lined with osmunda. However, it often is planted in soil where it should be kept moderately dry. Place in light that is on the brighter side of medium. High humidity and cool temperatures between 50 and 70° F. are preferable. Fertilize with a foliar spray. Soft brown scale is the main pest. 'Grande' is an even larger version. *P. hillii*, Elk horn fern, is more delicate.

Polypodium 'Green Wave' is very similar to *Blechnum* 'Silver Lady' but is densely packed with curly and dark green fronds.

Pteris cretica, Cretan brake fern is also called ribbon fern. The foliage is wide and ribbonlike. This is another fern that doesn't look typical. It's popularity since Victorian times along with the easy maintenance and many decorative cultivars available make it a good plant to choose for anywhere a small fern is desired. From medium to high light levels are best. Keep the soil moist; if allowed to dry out the fern turns crispy. This low growing fern, six inches to one foot tall and as wide, is especially attractive as a specimen plant. 'Albolineata' has medium green fronds with cream colored centers.

'Childsii' has light green fronds with irregularly fringed margins and crested (forked) tips.

'Cristata' is very striking with dark green, long and slender fronds with cockscomb crested (forked) tips.

'Mayii' has variegated fronds with light centers.

'Parkerii' has larger fronds.

'Rowerii' has small fronds with crested (forked) tips.

'Wilsonii' has bright green fronds with crested (forked) tips.

P. dentata, toothed fern, is a medium-large fern with finely dissected and delicate fronds.

P. ensiformis 'Victoria,' Victoria brake fern, has delicate lacy fronds lobed with dark green pinnae (leaflets) and silvery centers. (See color plate 6.) 'Evergemiensis' has more variegation. The foliage is one foot to eighteen inches long.

Tree ferns include:

Alsophila cooperi, Cyathea australis, C. cooperi or *Sphaeropteris cooperi* (the last one is most widely cultivated in the United States) are all called Australian tree fern. Whatever the name, they have become popular alternatives to tall palm trees. The tree ferns have abundant foliage creating a full look overhead. They often are eight feet tall at a minimum and have finely divided, light green fronds that gracefully weep. The trunk is covered with brown, fibrous hairs. So there is a coarse stem with delicate foliage. A temperature of 65° F is preferred, but it tolerates a wide range. High humidity is best. Place in an atrium with a waterfall nearby. The root systems are very shallow and tall plants may become top heavy. Also, the trunk and fronds are naturally covered with small scales that may irritate the skin or the eyes. Wear eye protection when working with this plant. For this reason, they are often placed on subirrigation systems. 'Brentwood' is an attractive cultivar that is much shorter.

Blechnum brasiliens, Brazilian tree fern, and *B. gibbum*, dwarf tree fern, are respectively, taller and shorter growing tree ferns with large fronds.

Cibotium glaucum or *C. chamissoi*, Hawaiian tree fern, is very graceful with delicate light green fronds and is eight feet tall.

Oxalis rubra
Red-Leaf Oxalis, Shamrock Plant
Oxalidaceae or Oxalis Family
A native of Mexico
Light: Medium
Soil: Moderately moist

This plant has an open habit with attractive foliage and blossoms. The cloverlike foliage consists of three triangular leaflets, each with a distinctive magenta midrib and center pattern, connected at the leaf base where they attach to the long, thin petiole. (See color plate 6.) The three to six delicate white or pink flowers are grouped at the ends of thin, wiry pedicels (flower stems) and keep on blooming for two to three months. These plants grow from corms that store water.

Temperature: Cool, from 55 to 65° F. but tolerates as low as 40° F.

Humidity: Moderate.

Overall shape: Rounded and full.

Texture: Medium in foliage, delicate in flower.

Availability: In 6 to 8-inch diameter containers. In hanging basket and table top sizes.

Placement: As a temporary plant as a substitute for a flowering plant. Where a great contrast in foliage color is desired.

Helpful hint: If the leaves fold up during the day, there is insufficient light or the temperatures are too extreme.

Related species:

O. deppei has solid green foliage with purple splotches at the leaf base. The flowers are red.

O. hirta, small-leaf oxalis, is a quick and very easy grower with numerous, deep pink flowers with yellow centers.

Pandanus utilis
Screw Pine
Pandanaceae or Screwpine Family
A native of Polynesia
Light: From medium to high
Soil: Moderately dry

The screw pine is not a pine, but is thought of as a pine because it forms a large conelike fruit at the terminal end in its native habitat. The glossy, strappy, dark green leaves are spiny-edged and dangerous. The upper leaves are stiff and upright. As the lower leaves mature, their weight causes them to draped downward around the plant as to soften the plant. (See color plate 6.) Where the two types of foliage meet in the middle, the spiral leaf arrangement is visible.

As the lower leaves age, die, and are removed, they leave an attractive spiral leaf base pattern along the thick, tan contrasting trunk. At the base of the trunk, thick aerial roots help to anchor this plant. This slow-growing plant is enjoyable to look at and often invokes the question "What is it?"

Temperature: Tolerates a wide range, from 50 to 90° F.

Humidity: Moderate to low.

Overall shape: X-shaped, not rated!

Texture: Bold.

Availability: In 10 to 17-inch diameter containers; the 17-inch size is five to six feet tall. Specimens up to fifteen feet are available by special order.

Placement: An out-of-the-way but visible area. This has an unusual, architectural shape and is a great specimen plant.

Be aware that: This is a pest and disease-free plant.

Helpful hint: Clean the foliage with a feather duster. This is tough and durable plant with an easy maintenance.

Cultivars include:

'Variegata' with white margins and a white stripe down the middle of each leaf.

Related species:

P. veitchii, variegated screw pine, is a smaller plant.

Pelargonium x *domesticum*[10]
Martha Washington or Regal Geranium
Generiaceae or Geranium Family
A native of South Africa
Light: Medium
Soil: Moderately moist

These compact to medium-size geraniums are especially grown for indoor use. It's interesting that Martha Washington geraniums were developed in Europe.The spectacularly large clusters of blooms sit evenly with the foliage or rise slightly above. The single or double flowers are usually bicolored or splotched. (See color plate 6.) Examples are: white with dark purple or rose center splotches, all the shades of pink with darker centers, purple with contrasting white centers, mauve with dark red markings, salmon with darker markings and white margins. White is the most common solid color available.

The pleated medium to dark green leaves with sharply toothed margins offer a complimentary background. The foliage is soft and flexible making this geranium easy to handle.

Length of bloom time: Purchased in mature bud stage with at least one cluster open, the flowers bloom over the course of several weeks.

Temperature: Warm, from 70 to 90° F.

Humidity: Moderate.

Overall shape: Mounded and full.

Texture: Medium.

Availability: During spring and summer in 5 and 6-inch diameter containers where they usually vary from one to two feet tall.

Placement: Take advantage of this flowering plant when it is available. Sometimes, we get so locked up in ordering a certain thing, we forget to look and see what else is available in season. Everyone wants geraniums outdoors, try using these special ones indoors.

Cultivars include:

'Imperial' is black-purple with a white picotee (margin.)

'Mandarin' has soft red petals with white centers and a white picotee (margin.)

Elegance Series: (All are available in 6-inch containers.)

'Brilliance' has ruffled, large bright white petals with a small red-purple splotch on the upper petals.

'Dapper Burgundy' has red-purple petals with red splotches.

'Debutante' has ruffled, hot pink petals with deep red splotches and white centers.

'Enchantment' has lavender petals with purple splotches.

'Fascination' has three colors combining pink and white petals with carmine red splotches.

'Rapture' has salmon-dark pink petals with dark red splotches. The flowers are so abundant that the foliage is nearly hidden.

'Symphony' has pink petals with burgundy splotches.

'Tiara' has bright white petals with red-purple streaks and splotches.

Maiden Series: (All are available in 5-inch containers.)

Six cultivars are available including:

'Maiden Orange' has soft, chiffon orange flowers highlighted with centers consisting of both dark red and fluorescent pink.

'Maiden Petticoat' has ruffled, white petals with large dark purple centers.

Royal Series: (All are available in 5 to 6-inch containers.)

Six cultivars are available including:

'Excalibur' has cherry-red and light pink flowers.

'Imperial' has dark purple flowers with a narrow white picotee (margin.)

---

[10]   These are derived from *P. cucullatum*, called wildemalva from South Africa; *P. fulgidum* with red flowers, *P. grandiflorum* with white flowers, and *P. angolosum* with purple flowers.

Peperomia caperata
Emerald-Ripple Peperomia
Piperaceae or Pepper Family
A native of Brazil and tropical America
Light: Medium
Soil: Moderately moist

This is a diminutive plant which packs a lot of punch with waxy, green-black, deeply grooved foliage. It has great texture and color. One leaf appears upon each red, hairy petiole. (See color plate 6.) Under proper conditions, peperomia will send up a long, thin flowering stalk. This may be removed to keep the plant looking neat and clean.

Temperature: Intermediate to warm, from 65 to 85° F.

Humidity: Moderate to high.

Overall shape: Low mounding and full.

Texture: Medium.

Availability: In 2½ to 6-inch diameter containers where it is not more than six inches tall with a slightly wider spread.

Placement: These are small, short plants perfect for the table top garden or terrarium.

Be aware that: Mealybugs may congregate in the narrow leaf axils (the junction between the leaf petiole and stem.)

Helpful hint: Even though this is one of the most attractive peperomias, it is one of the most difficult to maintain.

Cultivars include:

'Luna' with red-purple foliage.

Related species:

P. argyreia, watermelon peperomia, is another great foliage plant with the wide, heart-shaped leaves striped like a watermelon.

P. obtusifolia, baby rubber plant or oval-leaf peperomia, is a native of tropical America and south Florida. The baby rubber plant resembles the true rubber plant, *Ficus elastica,* but is not related. It has thick, waxy, dark green leaves with margins that slightly curl upward. They appear on thick, fleshy stems spotted with red. (See color plate 6.) This plant acclimates to low light levels, moderate humidity and moderately dry soil; it's much more durable with easy-care. 'Albomarginata' has a narrow margin of creamy-white upon a gray-green leaf. 'Marble' has creamy-white splotches upon a gray-green leaf. 'Minima' has smaller foliage. 'Variegata' has creamy-white to yellow-green irregular margins with a center of gray and green.

P. scandens, philodendron peperomia, resembles a miniature philodendron plant and trails nicely in a hanging basket.

Phalaenopsis **hybrids**
Moth Orchid
Orchidaceae or Orchid Family
Hybridized from native plants of
    the Himalayas, Southeast Asia
    and North Australia
Light: Medium
Soil: Moderately moist

These very dramatic orchids are simple yet elegant and easy to maintain. The showy inflorescence (See footnote #3, p. 26) is from three and one-half to five inches wide, and lies relatively flat. Many appear along long, arching flowerscapes (a leafless flower stalk rising from the base of the plant) naturally in winter, but are forced year-round. Flowers mature from the terminal end, so there is changing interest from the time the buds form until the last flower blooms. (See color plate 5.)

Colors range from the pure white, *P. amabilis*, discovered by Carolus Linneus in 1753, through the many species and hybrids that are available in various shades of pink and lavender, to colors of green, orange, yellow and bicolors. Colorful patterns of netting or specks add interest to these three to five inch wide blossoms. The most popular color is still the pure white, with lavender close behind.

Length of bloom time: The blossoms last from one to four months. If the scape is cut down halfway after flowering, another one may grow ensuring a second flowering. Some *Phalaenopsis* bloom twice a year.

Temperature: *Phalaenopsis* prefer warm temperatures from 75 to 90° F. during the day with nighttime lows of 65 to70° F.

Humidity: A level above 40% is preferable.

Overall shape: Tall and slender in bloom.

Texture: Delicate in flower with bold foliage.

Availability: Usually 5 to 6-inch diameter containers where the plants are from six to twenty inches tall depending upon the variety.

Placement: Any area which can be viewed up close, in a branch of a tree, or planted singly in a decorative container. Here and there, added to groundcover for interest and surprise.

Helpful hint: Careful watering practices must be addressed. Crown rot, the most common problem, is caused by having the roots remain in standing water. One way of preventing this is to raise the growing pot inside the decorative container and then carefully water. Specially designed orchid containers are made of clay and have several air holes in the sides allowing for excellent air exchange as well as a high evaporation rate.

Cultivars include:

'Angel's Touch' has large, white inflorescence with a yellow center. (See color plate 6.)

'Brother Sophia' has white inflorescence covered with raspberry red spots and margins. The attractive, dark green, shiny foliage has silver markings and burgundy undersides.

'Dorothy Applegate' has a very pale pink inflorescence with numerous pink spots and stripes and colorful margins. The glossy dark green foliage is very attractive.

'Golden Silk' has a pale yellow inflorescence with contrasting pink markings in the center and orange margins. The glossy dark green foliage is very attractive.

'Golden Treasure' features two spikes with bright yellow inflorescence accented by red centers and red flare spots.

'Lio Doro' has scented lilac and yellow-red bicolored inflorescence with glossy dark green foliage.

'Magic Stars' features two branched stalks of long lasting dark red-purple inflorescence.

'The Queen' has white inflorescence with red-purple netting and a red-purple center. (See color plate 6.)

Mystic Series: These have multiple flowerstalks with compact foliage.

'Mystic Golden Leopard Cheetah' has yellow inflorescence with orange centers. Other colors are available.

Other orchids include:

Cattleya hybrids are known for their spectacularly large and fragrant inflorescence. *Cattleya* blooms once a year in winter, but many types are multiple bloomers. They are available in many shades of purple, pink, salmon, red, magenta, white and the many bicolors. Others are green with brown dots, lime green, caramel, mahogany and other novel colors. Some inflorescence may have fringed or frilly petals and sepals. The flowerscapes arise from the plant base. Thick green pseudobulbs are each surrounded by one or two strappy, thick leaves. *Cattleya* is usually from one to four feet tall. They require light levels on the brighter side of medium and prefer intermediate temperatures from 65 to 75° F. The growing medium should be allowed to dry out between waterings.

Cattleya interbreed easily with *Brassavola*, *Diacrium*, *Encyclia*, *Epidendrum* and *Laelia* genera. Try the mini-catts or *Sophrolaeliocattleya*, abbreviated as *Slc.*, which are a more versatile size of one foot. *Slc.* 'Dark Waters' is an intense red. (See color plate 6.)

Cymbidium encompass a wide range of species. The inflorescence, which resembles that of the *Cattleya*, is three inches wide and appears in clusters along the flower stalk. Colors include shades of green, yellow, orange, red, purple and white. *Cymbidium* can grow to four feet tall and become rather ungainly. High light demands and moist conditions are important to maintain. *Cymbidium* are cool-temperature orchids and grow best from 55 to 65° F. The miniatures are very popular with easy maintenance. They are more tolerant of medium light levels and drier soils. 'Pink Diamond' is pale pink with a speckled center. (See color plate 6.)

Dendrobium is another wide and varied genera: some have spindle-shaped pseudobulbs, while others have rounder pseudobulbs. They have many simple blooms of pink, lavender, orange and other various shades clustered along multiple flowerscapes and are capable of repeat flowerings throughout the year. This is an easy to maintain orchid, yet it is four feet tall. High light and moist conditions are best for these. *Dendrobium* prefers intermediate temperatures between 60 and 75° F. Some dendrobiums shed leaves as they go into a cool dormancy period and then refoliate in warmer conditions.

Ludisia discolor or *Haemaria discolor*, jewel orchid, is one orchid known for its spectacular, eye-catching foliage. The velvety dark green leaves have widely spaced but very thin rose colored veins. The underside of the foliage is dark red. The small, white flowers are strung like jewels along a sturdy, upright stalk in winter. (See color plate 7.) Keep the soil moderately moist with from medium to low-medium light levels. This warm-temperature orchid prefers those between 70° and 90° F.

Miltonia, pansy orchid, does resemble a pansy with its broad and flat "face". However, it is larger, and many have a sweet fragrance. Andean miltonias with bright colors such as red, magenta, purple and yellow are widely available. White and pastels are other choices as are the bicolors with colorful center surrounded by white. This is an orchid with attractive long and narrow foliage, an added advantage. They grow best in medium to medium-low light with moderately moist soil. Cool temperatures, from 55 to 65° F. are ideal. 'Red Sky' is brilliant magenta with white margins. (See color plate 7.)

Oncidium altissimum, the butterfly orchid, has so many small—two and one-half inches long, usually bright yellow inflorescence upon long and arching scapes (a leafless flowerstalk rising from the base of the plant.) The clusters of inflorescence is said to resemble swarms of butterflies or dancing ballerinas. (See color plate 7.)

Other *Oncidium* species range in color from shades of pink to lavender and purple and bloom in winter. The long, wide foliage is abundant at the base of the plant. Most *Oncidium* prefer brighter and drier conditions than other orchids but check with suppliers as to specific needs of this diverse group. The humidity should be at least 60% so place this orchid in a grouping, upon a bed of pebbles, or close to a waterfall. Intermediate to warm temperatures from 65 to 90° F. are ideal. Plants in 6-inch diameter containers are twenty inches tall and at least two feet wide.

Cultivars include:

'Gower's Ramsey' has bright yellow inflorescence with contrasting red and yellow striped tips.

'Stefan Isler Lava Flow' which is a mericlone[11] of *Oncidium*-related orchids. It has dark red flowers with contrasting orange tips.

Paphiopedilum, lady's-slipper orchid, has had more hybrids registered than any other orchid. The curiosity in this orchid is the "slipper" surrounded by delicate petals and colorful sepals totaling five inches wide. Only one inflorescence appears atop a thin, delicate stalk. The colors tend to range in the bright yellows, greens, purples and browns and the patterning is magnificent. (See color plate 7.) The petals may be spotted and the sepals may be striped—all on the same plant. They all generally bloom during the spring through fall season and may be repeat bloomers. The foliage is mottled or blotched with other darker or sometimes lighter colors. Few species have solid green foliage. All foliage is shorter and shaped as an elongated oval giving the entire plant grace and beauty even when not in bloom. They are quite easy to grow and are only ten inches tall. The plants with green foliage require cool temperatures from 55 to 65° F. The plants with mottled foliage require intermediate temperatures from 65 to 75° F. 'Green Goddess' has a light green background that fades to white as the petals and sepals extend. The slipper is soft red-purple.

---

[11] Tissue cultured plants originating with meristem tissue. Meristem tissue is undifferentiated, embryonic tissue where rapid cell division occurs.

Philodendron **spp.**
Philodendron
Araceae or Arum Family
Bred from native plants of tropical
   America and the West Indies
Light: Medium, although some
   cultivars acclimate to low levels
Soil: Moderately moist

Philodendron plants have come a long way in recent history with color and habit being most important. Most of the tissue cultured cultivars are self-heading meaning that they are basal branching; they do not climb and do not require pruning. Some are vining types.

The foliage upon individual strong leaf petioles arises from the base of the plant. The crisp, formal, stiff, large elliptical foliage offers a great texture to any interiorscape. The variation of color on one plant is spectacular with many shades of green mixed in with either lime green, orange, red or dark red-black.

Temperature: Intermediate to warm, from 65 to 85° F. Do not expose to temperatures lower than 60° F. or chilling injury occurs.

Humidity: Moderate to low.

Overall shape: Low growing, arching and wide. Occasionally vining.

Texture: Bold.

Availability: The 6 to 14-inch diameter containers are most common. The 6-inch size is one foot and as wide; whereas the 14-inch size is two and one-half feet and as wide.

Placement: Philodendron functions best as a large specimen plant. Place it in an open area where the foliage can be viewed from above. Great for a modern style interiorscape or where a spot of unusual foliage color is desired.

Be aware that: Pests may include mealybugs and spider mites. Overwatering causes leaf spots, rots, and blights.

Helpful hint: Some exciting colors are available, so take advantage of them.

Cultivars include:

'Autumn' with new foliage that is coppery reddish-brown and remains that way under good light. (See color plate 7.) Older leaves eventually change to green. Too much light causes tipburn. Great for autumn displays.

'Black Cardinal' has very dark almost black foliage under medium light turning dark green under lower light. The young foliage is dark red. (See color plate 7.) Older leaves that turn brown indicate *Eucuminia* bacterial disease. It is spread by splashing water so do not use this cultivar en masse. Also, be careful when pruning or removing leaves; the dark sap causes stains.

'Congo' is so formal and elegant looking. The huge glossy dark green foliage has thin white midribs. The thick, tough leaves and fleshy leaf petioles provide great support and prevent any problem with top heaviness. The young foliage varies from purplish red leaves to light lime green. 'Rajo Congo' has a reddish cast to the foliage. Both are very disease resistant.

'Giganta' has medium green large foliage.

'Imperial Green' has rich green foliage that remains so in low light levels. The foliage is more oblong than other cultivars. (See color plate 7.) 'Imperial Red' has foliage with a reddish tinge. It requires a medium light level for color retention.

'Midnight' is a dark colored cultivar.

'Moonlight' has young foliage that is lime green under low light. Too much light causes tipburn. Older leaves eventually change to green. This cultivar is somewhat shorter and wider than others. (See color plate 7.)

'Prince of Orange' is striking with bright orange young foliage under medium light. Older leaves eventually change to green. (See color plate 7.)

'Red Emerald' is one example of the hybrid vining-type climbers. It has large, bright green elongated heart shaped leaves with red leaf petioles, stems and undersides.

Related species:

P. bipennifolium, horsehead philodendron, has foliage that looks like two eyes and a nose of a horse. It is about one foot long and climbs from four to six feet.

Philodendron scandens subsp. *oxycardium*
Heart-Leaf Philodendron
Araceae or Arum Family
A native of eastern Mexico
Light: From low to medium
Soil: Moderately moist

This vining plant is an old standard of the industry. With its ability to tolerate low light and humidity, this plant certainly does well in many harsh environments. The characteristic small heart-shaped leaves that end with a narrow point are glossy green sometimes tinged with dark red. (See color plate 7.)

The leaf resembles that of the pothos plant and it often is hard to tell them apart. The easiest way is to just look at the coloration—pothos most often has variegated foliage. The heartleaf philodendron also is a smaller plant with thinner foliage and thinner and shorter leaf petioles.

Temperature: Intermediate to warm, from 65 to 85° F.

Humidity: Moderate to low.

Overall shape: Mounding and vining.

Texture: Medium.

Availability: In 4 to 10-inch diameter containers. In 10 to 14-inch size pyramidal forms or grown on totems.

Placement: Great for groundcover, as an underplanting for trees growing in a large diameter container, hanging baskets, shelf planters, on totems, or table top gardens.

Be aware that: Mealybugs and scale insects may occur. With proper watering, leaf spot and root rot are avoided.

Helpful hint: This plant may require occasionally pruning.

Philodendron selloum 'Hope'
Dwarf Tree Philodendron
Araceae or Arum Family
A cultivated variety from native plants of southern Brazil
Light: Medium
Soil: Moderately moist

This is a case where the cultivars have such a nice improvement over the straight species, so seek these out. Each leaf has many deep splits and have many shallowly scalloped "fingers" ranked along the midrib. The thick, bright green leaves grow upon fleshy green leaf petioles emerging from the base at an angle. The foliage is large, up to two feet long, but the entire plant is compact and neat growing. (See color plate 7.)

Temperature: Intermediate to warm, from 65 to 85° F., but tolerant of cooler temperatures to 55° F.

Humidity: Medium.

Overall shape: Compact and wide.

Texture: Bold.

Availability: In 10 to14-inch diameter containers. The 14-inch size contains a plant two and one-half feet tall and as wide.

Placement: A room where drama needs to be added. As an accent plant or as screening material.

Be aware that: This cultivar is less sensitive to water stress, pests and diseases.

Helpful hint: Use any of the cultivars. The species plants are sprawling, vining and need to be staked.

Cultivars include:

'Pluto' is a compact cultivar with dark green foliage not as deeply lobed as others. Extremely resistant to pests.

'Xanadu' has glossy, scalloped olive green leaves that are from six to eight inches long and three inches wide. The entire plant grows compactly upon sixteen inch long, fleshy, green leaf petioles. (See color plate 7.)

Straight species:

P. selloum, tree philodendron, has foliage that is among the largest in the industry—up to three feet long and half as wide. (See color plate 7.) People often do a double take when they see the gigantic leaves. These heavy leaves eventually bend over. This fast growing plant becomes vining with age. The 14-inch diameter growing container contains a plant about four feet tall and as wide. Then, it grows. Place it in a large area where the plant will be in scale.

Related species:

P. bipinnatifidum, also called tree philodendron, resembles *P. selloum* but with leaves two-thirds the size.

Phoenix roebelenii
Pygmy Date Palm
Arecaceae or Palm Family
**A native of Laos, northeast India
    and Burma**
Light: From medium to high
Soil: Moist to moderately moist

Because of the very thick, tough foliage, this palm is very durable in the interior plantscape and widely used. It has two attractive forms; one is tall and treelike the other is short and stumpy. The foliage consists of narrow and airy looking pinnately compound leaflets along the large leaves and emerging atop the thick, fibrous trunk. The outer leaves arch downward while the inner leaves remain upright. Thorns grow along the leaf petioles so use the tree form or place the lower growing plants away from trafficked areas. (See color plate 7.)

In older specimens, the trunk has sections that grow thicker farther up the trunk which is very eye catching. The trunk with its many decorative leaf scars may have some mild curves which add an element of flow and eye movement. Curvy double or triple trunks growing very close together are an attractive form.

Temperatures: Warm, from 70 to 90° F., but will tolerate very high, to100° F. and very low temperatures as low as 32° F. for brief periods.

Humidity: Moderate to low.

Overall shape: Full and close to the ground or the more typical tree shape.

Texture: A combination of bold with the trunk and delicate with the foliage.

Availability: In 6 to 17-inch diameter containers; the 14-inch size is usually six feet tall. Larger specimens upon request.

Placement: As a specimen tree, massed as mid-height trees, occasionally as low-growing plants. Also, in a very formal setting.

Be aware that: Pests and disease are usually not a problem. If stressed, then scale, two-spotted spider mites, fungal leaf spot and root rot may occur.

Helpful hint: Fertilize regularly to prevent the following deficiencies: magnesium sulfate (yellow pattern in older foliage, new foliage remains healthy), manganese sulfate (new foliage is yellow green with brown streaks) and potassium (yellowing or spots on older leaves, new foliage dies) and iron (new foliage is bright yellow.)

Pilea cadierei
Aluminum Plant
Urticaceae or Nettle Family
A native of Vietnam
Light: Medium
Soil: Moist

This small plant is another one that packs a lot of punch with its foliage. The oval leaves with prominent silver striping and blotches offer all the color that is needed. Foliage is densely clustered in opposite pairs along a stem usually not visible. (See color plate 7.)

If the aluminum plant is allowed to grow, it gracefully trails. Many interesting species are offered.

Temperature: Intermediate to warm, from 65 to 85° F.

Humidity: High.

Overall shape: Upright and full.

Texture: Medium.

Availability: Table top and hanging basket sizes.

Placement: These plants have traditionally been used in terrariums, but are also used interplanted among flowering plants or in table top gardens.

Be aware that: The limiting factor is low humidity. Mealybug and whitefly may occur.

Helpful hint: Pruning the uneven top growth may be necessary.

Related species:

P. involucrata 'Moon Valley' has deeply puckered leaves brightly colored yellow, green and red-brown. The four inch long leaves grow upon compact, ten inch tall plants. (See color plate 7.) It is often mistaken for the iron cross begonia, *Begonia masoniana*.

P. microphylla, artillery plant, has a low and spreading habit with extremely small, succulent medium green leaves growing closely along the stem. The common name comes from the fact that a puff of pollen is released from mature staminate (male) flowers.

Plectranthus australis
Swedish Ivy
Lamiaceae or Mint Family
A native of Australia and the Pacific Islands
Light: Medium
Soil: Moderately moist

As the common name suggests, this is a very popular plant in Sweden. The round foliage is glossy, bright green with leaves with rounded, serrated margins. This is not an ivy but a mint. Two characteristics of this family are that the leaves grow opposite each other in pairs and the stems are square.

Swedish ivy is a fast grower and is easy to maintain. The soft, green stems of the Swedish ivy plants become woody with age.

Temperature: Cool to intermediate, from 55 to 75° F., but tolerates those as low as 35° F.

Humidity: Moderate to dry.

Overall shape: Full and gracefully vining.

Texture: Medium.

Availability: In 6 to 12-inch diameter containers, usually as a hanging basket size.

Placement: Hanging baskets, shelf planters or as groundcovers.

Be aware that: Mealybugs are an occasional pest.

Helpful hint: When pruning, an orange sap may stain whatever it touches.

Related plants:

P. coleoides 'Marginatus,' white-edged Swedish ivy, has fuzzy green foliage with irregular, wide, white leaf margins. The leaf is larger, to three inches long. It offers great contrast to green foliage plants. (See color plate 7.)

P. oerendahlii, also called Swedish ivy, has green foliage with prominent white veins and a purple underside.

Podocarpus macrophyllus
**Podocarpus, Buddhist Pine, South-
ern Yew**
**Podocarpaceae or Podocarpus
Family**
A native of China and Japan
Light: Medium
Soil: Moderately moist

This elegant coniferous tree is not a pine and not a yew. It grows upright with very narrow, linear foliage—four inches long and one-half inch wide. The medium to deep green foliage with lighter undersides resembles willow leaves. Those flat needles are arranged in dense, spirals in an upright manner along the trunk. This is a slow growing plant that stays within its bounds. It also is a tough and durable plant, well suited for a harsh interior plantscape.

Temperature: Intermediate, from 65 to 75° F. but tolerates cold drafts and temperatures as low as 40° F. High temperatures are not tolerated.

Humidity: It tolerates low humidity.

Overall shape: A standard tree or shrub form; a pyramidal form is available. (See *P. gracilior* 'Pyramid' below.)

Texture: Fine.

Availability: In 8 to 21-inch diameter containers. The 17-inch container has 3 ppp. (plants per pot) and is six to seven feet tall and is three feet wide. Tree forms are also available.

Placement: Use it in a special place, such as an executives office or in a lobby close to an important piece of artwork. Or as a specimen tree in an atrium or in an Asian design.

Be aware that: This is a relatively pest-free plant. The foliage is toxic to cats.

Helpful hints: The best way to clean leaves is to gently shake the plant to dislodge dust and any dried foliage. Overwatering causes the needles near the trunk to turn yellow.

Cultivars include:

'Maki,' southern yew, has branches that grow nearly vertical with a dense and compact growth habit. It has smaller foliage and grows no larger than shrub size. Keep an eye out for the Podocarpus aphid, *Neophyllaphis podocarpi*, especially on this cultivar. It is a small, blue to reddish-blue insect usually found on the underside of new growing tips. Try to catch the problem early. If the infestation becomes severe colonization occurs on all growing parts. Symptoms include a general yellowing of the foliage, a "dirty" overall appearance, and/or curled, stunted new growth. A shiny, sticky substance called honeydew appears on the foliage. An early method of eradication is to wash off the aphids with a soapy water cleaning solution. If severe, trim the leaf tips or use a foliar spray[12].

Related species:

P. gracilior, weeping podocarpus, has branches held in a more horizontal manner creating a wider plant with a softer effect. (See color plate 6.) It will do well under slightly lower light levels. The 17-inch diameter container has 3 ppp. and is six to seven feet tall and four feet wide. Plants to fifteen feet may be special ordered.

'Pyramid' is trained on a pyramidal bamboo teepee and used for the holiday season. In the 10-inch diameter containers, plants are about four feet tall; in the 14-inch containers, plants are five and one-half feet tall.

---

[12]   Endeavor produced by Novartis Crop Protection Inc., Greensboro, NC, disrupts the feeding activity of the aphids a few hours after spraying and has a residual effect which controls future generations.

Polyscias balfouriana
Balfour Aralia
Araliaceae or Aralia Family
A native of India through Polynesia
Light: Medium
Soil: Moist

All the aralias are elegant plants presenting challenges. (See "Be aware that:" below.) This straight species plant is commonly available and less expensive than others, yet is quite elegant, and is the easiest to maintain. The trifoliate foliage is round, scalloped, and dark green with some lighter variegation. The mature foliage is heavily puckered. Look for the juvenile foliage that is smaller and grows as a single leaf.

These three to four foot upright plants often have straight trunks with naturally branching stems. Many plants per pot are usually grown, although single trunks are also seen. The new growth of the stems is dark green speckled with gray. The older stems are entirely gray and contorted which makes them architecturally interesting.

Temperatures: Intermediate, from 65 to 75° F. Can tolerate as low as 40° F.

Humidity: Moderate.

Overall shape: Treelike or full to the base but still tall and slightly narrow. Or shrublike.

Texture: Medium.

Availability: In 6 to 14-inch diameter containers. Table top size, also.

Placement: As a specimen plant in a formal lobby or executive office.

Be aware that: Plants in the *Polyscias* genus have a reputation for being a challenge to maintain. They are susceptible to many problems. The most common one is leaf drop caused by uneven watering. Soluble salt sensitivity, low air temperatures or low humidity are other causes. So, if you have a false aralia that is doing well, keep it in that location and continue the same care that you've established. False aralia is also susceptible to spider mites and occasionally to brown scale and mealybugs. If you have a prized specimen, you may consider applying a systemic insecticide/miticide prophylactically. Stem and root rot may occur if overwatered. Subirrigation systems work well.

Helpful hint: There are many unusual aralias that become available from time to time. They are all beautiful.

Cultivars include:

'Dinner Plate' has large, rounded foliage resembling its name. The thick and leathery foliage is three inches in diameter. There is a variegated type available, too.

'Lacy Lady' resembles the chicken gizzard aralia. (See "Related species:" below.)

'Marginata' or 'Variegata' has wide leaf margins variegated white. (See color plate 7.) This cultivar requires more light to maintain the variegation. Keep the foliage dry to avoid *Alternaria*, a fungal leaf spot, appearing as small red spots and *Xanthomonas campestris* pv. *hererae*, a bacterial leaf spot.

'Pennockii' has yellow colored areas that extend on either side of the midrib and veins surrounded by a wide green leaf margin.

'Roseleaf' has the trifoliate arrangement resembling a rose leaf with the center leaf much larger than the others. The green leaves have very narrow white margins.

Related species:

P. crispa 'Chicken Gizzard,' 'Geranium' or 'Gigi' is similar to the balfour aralia, but with the central leaflet being the smallest. The leaf then turns upright and is cupped at the serrated margins. The foliage appears in layers staggered along the stems which are more contorted towards the base. This is considered to be an easier aralia to grow. Does it look like a chicken gizzard? Not really. It looks more like a shiny geranium leaf.

P. guilfoylei, black aralia, is considered the most elegant of all the aralias. The black-green foliage is so very puckered then curly towards the leaf margins that it's hard to tell the exact leaf shape. (See color plate 7.) This plant is beautiful, unusual, exotic, very expensive and hard to maintain.

P. scutellaria, fabian or plum aralia, has large, heart-shaped, smooth and glossy foliage. (See color plate 7.) The midrib and other veins are light green, whereas the undersides of the foliage have purple coloration. The foliage margins tend to cup upward.

Polyscias fruticosa
Ming Aralia
Araliaceae or Aralia Family
A native of India through
 Polynesia, and tropical Asia
Light: From medium to high
Soil: Moist

This upright, but full tree resembles the Chinese ming tree that we recognize from paintings. It has lacy, bright green foliage that is light and airy. (See color plate 7.) When viewed up close, the foliage resembles flat-leaf parsley. The foliage is evenly distributed from the base to the top of the plant.

The wonderfully contorted, naturally branching, pale beige trunks offer great counterpoint to the drooping foliage. Many plants are in each container.

Temperature: Warm, from 75 to 85° F. Chilling injury occurs if lower than 55° F.

Humidity: Moderate.

Overall shape: Upright and narrow.

Availability: In 10 to 21-inch diameter containers; in the 14-inch size, they are five to seven feet tall, in the 21-inch size, they are twelve feet. Heavy stump specimens in larger sizes. Table top sizes, too.

Placement: As a specimen plant in a formal lobby or executive office.

Be aware that: Plants in the *Polyscias* genus have a reputation for being a challenge to maintain, as well as being expensive. The ming aralia is very slow growing, growing ten feet in ten years. But, once it is established in an ideal location, then it is good for many a year. The most common problem is leaf drop caused by uneven watering. Soluble salt sensitivity, low air temperatures or low humidity are other causes. So, if you have a false aralia that is doing well, keep it in that location and continue the same care that you've established. False aralia is also susceptible to spider mites and occasionally to brown scale and mealybugs. If you have a prized specimen, you may consider applying a systemic insecticide/miticide prophylactically. Stem and root rot may occur if overwatered. Subirrigation systems work well.

Alternaria, a fungal leaf spot, causes small yellow spots and defoliation. Keep foliage dry when watering to prevent any fungal diseases from occurring.

Helpful hint: Instead of dusting the leaves, grab the trunk and shake it. The dust and dry leaves are easily dislodged.

Cultivars include:

'Elegans,' parsley aralia, has smaller foliage that is more curled, such as in extra curly parsley. The overall plant is slightly more compact and dense. Smell these leaves—I think back to those years when I received my first box of sixty-four crayons. The smell of the metallic colors, especially copper, had the same smell

Primula vulgaris
English Primrose
Primulaceae or Primrose Family
A native of England
Light: From medium to high
Soil: Moist

This harbinger of spring is another chance to bring the outdoors in. The large, fragrant flowers come in all the bright colors plus blue and orange. Pastels, bicolors and white most often have yellow centers surrounded by five flat petals with notched tips.

The light green foliage is elliptical and rough textured and forms a flat ring around the colorful, low-growing flowers.

Length of bloom time: From one week to six depending upon the temperature.

Temperature: Cool, from 55 to 65° F.

Humidity: Moderate.

Overall shape: Low and wide.

Texture: Delicate in flower, medium in foliage.

Availability: From late fall through late spring in 4 to 8-inch diameter containers.

Placement: In planter boxes in breezeways. Close to an open doorway. For a short term, en masse for a groundcover, or tucked here and there. As a specimen flower on a table.

Helpful hint: Primrose has the same cultural conditions as the cinneraria, *Senecio cruentus*.

Cultivars include:

'Dana Mix' in a variety of bright colors, some bicolored with yellow centers. (See color plate 7.)

'Supreme Mix' with extra large flowers in a variety of bright colors.

Danova Series:

Many colors, including a cherry with yellow edge, are featured in this compactly growing plant.

Related species:

P. malacoides, fairy primrose, has clusters of flowers one foot tall. The heart shaped foliage has serrated margins and grows upright upon long leaf petioles.

P. obconica, German primrose, has numerous flowers in upright umbels (clusters) rather than on individual flowerstalks. The Twilly Series includes many colors and standard and miniature sizes. A special Twilly Touch Me Series is primin-free[13]. Eight single colors and three bicolors are available.

---

[13]   Primin is usually present in the hairs of the foliage. Some people are allergic to it and develop skin rashes with contact. These plants are primin-free, consequently their name is 'Touch Me'.

Radermachera sinica
Radermachera, China Doll
Bignoniaceae or Bignonia Family
A native of tropical China
Light: Medium
Soil: Moderately moist

This plant has only been in wide use since the 1980s. It fell out of favor in the '90s and then became popular again. It's interesting how style and trends filter into our work.

These pyramidal treelike plants are lovely with their glossy green and lacy, pinnately compound foliage. This foliage extends horizontally for a formal look. The glossy, rich green leaflets droop which adds much to its character. Many plants are in each container for a full look. (See color plate 7.)

Temperature: Intermediate to warm, from 65 to 90° F. but tolerates as low as 50° F. and as high as 95° F.

Humidity: Moderate.

Overall shape: Pyramidal.

Texture: Fine.

Availability: The 8-inch diameter container has two ppp. (plants per pot), The 10-inch size has three ppp. and is three feet tall. The 12 and 14-inch diameter containers are larger yet. Plants are available to nine feet tall in larger containers. Table top sizes, too.

Placement: As a specimen plant, as a background screen. In an Asian design.

Be aware that: Mealybugs and scale insects may occur.

Helpful hints: Watering is most critical. If the soil is kept too moist, then the lower leaves turn yellow. If kept too dry, then the leaves turn crispy. Try subirrigation.

The best way to clean leaves is to gently shake the plant to dislodge dust and dried foliage.

Rhapis excelsa
Lady Palm
Arecaceae or Palm Family
A native of southern China and Japan
Light: Medium, but acclimates to low levels
Soil: Moist

If a client is looking for an elegant plant of medium size, consider lady palm. It's also very durable and slow growing. The dark green, glossy and pleated leaflets—from five to eight— form a fan-shape (palmately compound) and are attached to slender leaf petioles. The green stems are attractively covered with stringy brown fibers. This palm forms dense clumps of foliage from the soil surface to the top. (See color plate 8.)

Temperature: Tolerates a wide range, from 45 to 95° F., but prefer the 50 to 72° F. range.

Humidity: Moderate but adapts to low humidity.

Overall shape: Upright and full.

Texture: Medium.

Availability: In 6 to 17-inch diameter containers. The 10-inch size is approximately three feet tall and as wide.

Placement: As a specimen plant or near an entryway. Any area near drafty areas.

Be aware that: Rarely is this plant bothered by pests, although scale insects may appear.

Helpful hint: If tipburn develops, gather all the leaflets on one frond and either cutting them on an angle or gently tearing across the tips.

Cultivars include:

'Variegata' with an attractive white leaf margin.

Rhododendron simsii, R. indicum[14]
Azalea
Ericaceae or Heath Family
The former species is from Japan and the latter is from southern China and Southeast Asia
Light: Medium, but acclimates to low levels
Soil: Moist

Azeleas are the third most popular blooming plant used in the interior plantscape. They were traditionally used as gift plants in the spring. Indica hybrids were developed in Belgium in the 1850s and quickly became popular in the United States. Most varieties are grown in Canada and Ohio.

These aristocratic shrubs are covered with trumpet-shaped flowers. The colors range from delicate to vibrant—white, pink, lavender, salmon, peach, red, magenta and bicolors. The light colors often have contrasting colored throat blotches or spots. The flowers with a white picotee (margin) are some of the all-time favorites. Flowers may be single, double or semi-double. Full-size plants covered with miniature flowers are lovely.

The foliage is small, oval, shiny and deep green, contrasting nicely with the flowers. The woody stems are multibranched and light tan. (See color plate 8.)

Length of bloom time: Purchase when most buds are showing color and one-quarter are open. Then, these relatively expensive plants last a long time—at least four weeks. If planted with a subirrigation system, I have seen them remain looking presentable for nearly three months.

Temperature: Cool, from 60 to 70° F.

Humidity: Moderate.

Overall shape: Shrublike.

Texture: Medium.

Availability: In 4 to 10-inch diameter contain-

---

[14]   *R. simsii* is a single or double large flowered plant and the main parent of the Indica hybrids. *R. indicum* is a single small flowered plant.

ers where they are available year-round. Azaleas are grown in azalea or three-quarter pots which are more shallow with the height being three-fourths of the top diameter.

Placement: These are rather large flowering plants so few in number cover a large area. Take advantage of this fact.

Be aware that: Azaleas are planted in peat moss as these plants are acid loving. It is important to keep the peat moist so that the flowers do not wilt. Once peat dries, it is difficult to remoisten. But, all is not lost. Remove the azalea from its location and submerge the growing container complete with plant in a bucket of warm water. A wetting agent may be added. Within a couple of hours, the azalea revives. So, this flower may be saved.

Helpful hints: Azaleas are high maintenance plants not only because of frequent watering, but also because the dead flowers must be removed. The brown scales (sepals) surrounding the flowers are constantly dropping and must be cleaned up.

Cultivars include:

'Bliss' has four inch, single, fragrant bright pink flowers.

'Inga' has a single, dark pink flower with a white picotee (margin.) Each flower is two inches in diameter.

'Ornament' has a dark coral-rose flower with a ruffled margin.

'Party Favor' has a dark pink flower.

'Prize' has a large, single, magenta flower.

'Remembrance' has a dark pink flower.

'Vogel Helmut' has a large, double fluorescent magenta flower.

Rosa chinensis* var. *minima
Miniature Rose
Rosaceae or Rose Family
**Roses are believed to have been
    first cultivated in Greece**
Light: Medium
Soil: Moderately moist

Miniature roses bring some of the outdoors inside and well tolerate interior conditions.

The fragrant flowers come in many shades of pink, red, yellow, orange and white. They are small, often only an inch across, but many petalled. The small, familiar foliage is abundant. (See color plate 8.) They grow on their own rootstocks. Improvements include: larger flowers with fewer branches.

Length of bloom time: Several months, if spent blooms are removed.

Temperature: A wide range, from 50 to 90° F.

Humidity: Moderate.

Overall shape: Shrublike.

Texture: Delicate.

Availability: In 4 to 6-inch diameter containers in the spring, summer and fall. Miniature roses are often sold for winter holidays, too.

Placement: In a cool, harsh location, maybe close to a drafty area. Singly, on a table or desk.

Helpful hint: Roses are heavy feeders and require monthly fertilization if kept on a long-term basis.

Hit Series: In 5-inch diameter containers.

'Pure Hit' has white flowers.

'Isabel' with red flowers.

'Ramona' with pink flowers

Palace Series: In 6-inch diameter containers.
'Peace' with large yellow flowers.

Parade Series: In 4-inch diameter containers.
'Charming Parade' with orange-red flowers.

'Denise' with large cream colored flowers.

'New Heidi' with large salmon-coral flowers.

Saintpaulia ionantha
African Violet
Gesneriacaeae or Gesneriad Family
A native of Tanzania in coastal
**   areas**
Light: Medium
Soil: Moist

Everyone knows a little old grandmother who raises African violets under grow lights, and that's often how we think of them. True, the African violet is the most popular houseplant but it also is used in the interior plantscape. The native purple violets were discovered in 1926 by Baron von Saint Paul. He sent seeds back home to Germany and since then, hybridization has created thousands of variations.

Flowers may be single or double, large to miniature, bicolored, spotted and striped, or with picotee or ruffled margins. Colors range through all the lavenders, blues and violets, pinks, reds, fuschias and white. The familiar, velvety leaves are a perfect backdrop to the flowers. Some have white variegation or ruffled margins. These leaves are attached to fleshy leaf petioles that arise from a central crown. (See color plate 2.)

Length of bloom time: The African violet is floriferous several times a year. Poor flowering occurs because of low light, low humidity or too cool temperatures.

Temperature: Consistent, from 65 to 85° F.

Humidity: From 60-80% is preferred but 40-50% is tolerated.

Overall shape: Low with horizontal foliage.

Texture: Medium.

Availability: All year-round in the 4-inch diameter container where the plant is four to six inches high and eight or more inches wide. Miniatures are sold in 2 to 3-inch diameter sizes.

Placement: Placed among groundcover or in table top gardens. They provide a nice touch to an executive office.

Be aware that: When watering, use tepid water to avoid getting the crown and foliage wet. This will prevent *Botrytis* blight to the crown and leaf spotting caused by soluble salts.

Fertilizing with a high phosphorous number, such as 10-20-10, is necessary if African violets are kept after blooming. Soluble salts may also collect on the rim of containers causing damage to any fleshy leaf petiole that may touch.

Mealybugs are a rare pest as are cyclamen mites which cause brittle and curled leaves. Discard the plant if mites are the cause.

Helpful hint: African violets are often used as a temporary plant until after the first flush of flowers.

Related plant:

Episcia cupreata, flame violet, is very attractive for underplantings or hanging baskets. The large leaves have a quilted look with light green centers and veins. The tubular, orange-red flowers bloom all year long and are a great focal point. This plant spreads by stolons (horizontal stems at or below the soil surface) bearing new plantlets.

Sansevieria trifasciata 'Laurentii'
**Snake Plant, Mother-in-Law's
  Tongue
Agavaceae or Agave Family
A cultivated variety from native
  plants of Nigeria
Light: From medium to very low.
  Tolerates as low as 25 foot-
  candles. Nearly in the dark!
Soil: Dry**

What an awful name, especially the latter one. If you know of anyone that has a black thumb, this is the plant for them. The snake plant grows just about anywhere—except full sun—and requires minimal care. 'Laurentii' is one of the oldest and most common cultivars. (See color plate 8.)

The stiff, sword shaped leaves have alternate bands of dark and light green with yellow leaf margins and grow vertically right out of the soil. Actually, they are attached to an underground rhizome (thickened storage stem.) And this explains why the plant should be allowed to dry out after watering—the rhizomes store water. The straight species, without the yellow banding is also available.

Temperature: Very tolerant of a wide range, from 50 to 90° F. but 65 to 85° F. is ideal. Chilling injury occurs below 45°F.

Humidity: Very tolerant of low humidity.

Overall shape: Vertical.

Texture: Bold.

Availability: In 6 to 17-inch diameter containers where the larger sizes are four feet tall.

Placement: Groupings emphasize the wonderful verticality. Great for any high trafficked, low light, drafty areas. Or good for any hard to reach areas. Often used in modern and art deco interiors.

Be aware that: Overwatering is lethal. *Erwinia,* a bacterial rot, occurs. If this happens, throw the plant out. Rarely are insects ever a problem, although mealybugs may occur.

Helpful hint: This plant does well if potbound; the rhizomes have been known to crack a clay pot.

Other cultivars include:

'Bandel's Sensation' has bands of white and green running the full length of the leaf, emphasizing its verticality.

'Black Coral' has a nearly black leaf with few and far between irregularly horizontal golden to silver bands—depending upon light exposure—increasing towards the base. It is three feet tall.

'Black Gold' is black-green with wide bands of yellow gold along the leaf margins, emphasizing its verticality. It is three feet tall.

'Hahnii' and 'Golden Hahnii' often called the bird's nest sansevieria, has been around since the 1940s. It looks less representative of the genus because it forms a low rosette, looking similar to a bird's nest. Each leaf is wide and short. Upon closer inspection the pattern on the foliage is similar to 'Laurentii'. 'Golden Hahnii' has foliage with wide bright yellow leaf margins. Both are great for interior groundcovers.

'Moonshine' is a very light green cultivar that has wider, shorter leaves—six inches wide and twenty inches long—that grow upright and every which way.

'Silver Laurentii' is an improved version of 'Laurentii' with solid medium green centers and wide yellow leaf margins.

'Silver Queen' has nearly solid silvery-pewter leaves with only a few thin bands of green towards the base. A great art deco plant. (See color plate 8.)

'Zeylanica,' an older cultivar, is a pewter color with closely spaced dark green narrow bands.

Schefflera actinophylla 'Amate'
Schefflera or Austrialian Umbrella Plant
Araliaceae or Aralia Family
A cultivated variety from native plants of Australia, New Guinea and Java
Light: Medium, but acclimates to low levels
Soil: Moderately moist

This plant used to be called the "Scheff" but now, is simply referred to as 'Amate' as in "I need an 'Amate'". The leaves form an umbrella shape, thus, its other common name.

The large and naturally glossy palmately compound leaves may be up to one foot across and consist of six to eight glossy, dark green leaflets. But near the top, the constantly emerging new foliage has the same, ever so tiny, arrangement. The wide leaves combined with many plants per pot make this a very full, dense plant, uniform from the base to the top. (See color plate 8.)

'Amate' offers such a magnitude of improvement over the species. It has thicker, glossier, healthier looking, darker green foliage which is more resistant to spider mite infestation, leaf spots—*Alternaria* fungus is most common—and physical damage. Its compact growth habit and shorter leaf petioles, tinged with dark red, make it very uniform and upright. It also becomes easy to place because it is adaptable to less light and watering without lower leaf drop. It just looks better and is better.

Temperature: Adaptable to a wide range of temperatures from 35 to 105° F. but those from 60 to 90° F. are preferred.

Humidity: Moderate.

Overall shape: Treelike and full with foliage to the base. 'Amate' is also available as a single stem standard or as many stemmed, short, full plants called tips.

Texture: Bold.

Availability: In 8-inch diameter container where 2 ppp. (plants per pot) are two feet tall, in 10-inch sizes where 3 ppp. are three and one-half feet tall, in 12-inch sizes which is four feet tall, in 14-inch sizes where 4 ppp. are five or six feet tall, in 17-inch sizes which are six or seven feet tall, in 21-inch sizes which are eight or ten feet tall, and 29 to 32-inch diameters which are ten to fourteen feet tall. Standards are as tall as the multistemmed plants while the tips are three feet tall.

Placement: Specimen plants which provide formal symmetry, massed as a screening or background plant. A large area is required for proper proportion.

Be aware that: Occasional fertilizing helps maintain a rich, green color. 'Amate' is quite tolerant of soluble salt buildup.

Helpful hints: The foliage is very shiny naturally. Leaf shine is not necessary. Pruning is required during periods of active growth. Using a subirrigation system is a good choice.

Other cultivars include:

'Nova' with deeply lobed leaflets resemble the leaf of a pin oak, although they are longer and narrower. Five or six leaflets are palmately arranged. It grows upright to six feet and about three feet wide. Spider mites may develop in hot, dry areas.

'Renegade' is a sport (a naturally occurring mutation) of 'Amate' that grows as a tall, columnar pillar. The entire plant is no more than two feet in diameter, often less and usually about four feet tall. Full-sized leaves grow upon shortened leaf petioles attached to one main stem with shortened internodes. (See color plate 8.) This is a successful solution for narrow areas.

Schefflera arboricola
Hawaiian Schefflera, Arbs
Araliaceae or Aralia Family
A native of Taiwan
Light: Medium, but acclimates to low levels
Soil: Moderately moist

Just read about the *Schefflera* above and reduce it to about one-quarter the size. There you have the Hawaiian (why isn't it called the Taiwanese?) scheff. In essence, it does look and perform similarly. It is a very durable in a manageable size with great versatility in the interior plantscape.

The palmate leaves grow to six inches in diameter with many stems in a container giving this plant a dense appearance. This is a "cheerful" and "cute" plant and is always welcome. (See color plate 8.)

Temperature: Adaptable to a wide range, from 35 to 105° F. but those from 60-90° F. are preferred.

Humidity: Moderate.

Overall shape: Shrublike.

Various forms:

Tree or standard with either a single, braided, or corkscrew stem; columnar and pyramidal shapes are available. There is a mini-arboricola perfect for table top gardens, specimen plants or groundcover.

Texture: Medium.

Availability: In 8 to 10-inch diameter containers as shrubs, in 14 and 17-inch diameter containers as standards. In 3-inch diameter containers for bonsai arrangements, in 4 to 6-inch sizes for table top gardens.

Placement: As a bridge between tall plants and a groundcover layer in atriums. As a free standing shrub flanking taller plants. Often used in a row as an indoor hedge. The columnar and pyramidal shapes are great as free standing plants in offices or small areas.

Be aware that: Occasional fertilizing helps maintain a rich, green color. Luckily, the dwarf scheff is quite tolerant of soluble salt buildup.

Helpful hint: Pruning to maintain the bushy appearance may be necessary.

Cultivars include:

'Compacta' is a slower growing, compact plant.

'Covette' is a cross between the Australian and the Hawaiian schefflera. The dark green foliage with wavy leaf margins is halfway between the two leaf sizes.

'Gold Capella' has green leaves variegated with bright yellow.

'Gold Finger' has narrow green leaflets variegated with bright yellow.

'Henrietta' is a solid green mini-arboricola.

'Jacqueline' is similar to 'Gold Capella' but with more and brighter variegation at the leaf margin.

'Luseane Bush' is a mini-arboricola that is available in 3 to 4-inch containers used for table top gardens, in 6-inch containers that are fourteen to sixteen inches tall and 8-inch containers that are twenty-eight inches tall.

'Renate' has shallow lobes at the leaf tip, resembling a footprint.

'Trinette' has mostly cream colored foliage with minimal green. Often grown as a columnar plant. (See color plate 8.)

'Worthii' has green leaves variegated with creamy white. But, it also has shorter internodes and leaf petioles, keeping it compact and full. It is slower growing and maintains its variegation under lower light. Available in 10 and 14-inch columns.

Schlumbergera spp.[15]
Holiday Cactus, Zygocactus
Cactaceae or Cactus Family
Hybridized from native plants of
the Brazilian rain forests
Light: Medium
Soil: Moderately moist when bloom-
ing, moderately dry at other times

Here's a cactus plant that originated in the rain forest which is rather unusual. They grow in moderate shade and humid conditions. The spines have been reduced to a few soft brown hairs at the stem[16] junctions. Being epiphytes that naturally grow without soil—they grow in trees with aerial roots absorbing nutrients from water, air and dust particles.

The entire plant has many green stems arching gracefully downward. Each of the stems is divided into segments about two inches long. If the margins are scalloped, the parent plant was the Christmas cactus; if pointed, it was derived from the Thanksgiving or crab cactus. (See color plate 8.) In actuality, most hybrids are bred from *S. truncata*.

Numerous delicate but large blossoms appear at the ends of the many stems. The traditional color has been fuchsia, but many shades of red and pink are available as well as more unusual colors of orange, peach, lavender, purple, white and yellow and bicolors. The blossoms vary in shades as they mature.

Length of bloom time: Extended bloom times of several weeks is common.

Temperature: Intermediate, from 65 to 75° F., but tolerates brief periods of temperatures as low as 38° F. and as high as 90° F.

Humidity: Tolerates low humidity only when not in bloom.

Overall shape: Upright, arching and pendant.

Texture: Medium.

Availability: Mostly in the fall to winter; spring and summer on a limited basis in 6 to 10-inch diameter containers. Hanging basket and table top sizes, too.

Placement: As a specimen plant where people can see but are not close enough to accidentally knock off the fragile buds. In a hanging basket.

Be aware that: Spider mites and mealybugs occur on rare occasions.

Helpful hints: The flower buds fall if the soil gets dry or if the plant is moved. Keep the roots potbound for best flowering.

---

[15] *S. bridgesii*, Christmas cactus; *S. truncata*, Thanksgiving cactus and *Rhipsalidopsis* spp., Easter cactus natuarally bloom at those times but are forced for other seasons.

[16] Botanically speaking, what appear as leaves are actually flattened stems that photosynthesize. *Schlumbergera* has no true leaves.

Sedum morganianum
Burro's or Donkey's Tail
Crassulaceae or Stonecrop Family
A native of Mexico
Light: High
Soil: Dry

It's nice to add a succulent to the list of hanging basket plants. If the proper light is available, do try this one. The short and fat, glaucous[17] light green leaves are tightly packed and directly attached to a thick, fleshy light green stem. These stems become woody with age. Pink or magenta blossoms are a nice contrast to the foliage.

Temperature: A wide range, from 50 to 95° F.

Humidity: Moderate.

Overall shape: Low and trailing.

Texture: Bold.

Availability: Hanging basket sizes, or table top garden sizes.

Placement: In a sunny atrium.

Be aware that: The leaves fall off very easily when bumped.

Helpful hint: This is another plant with easy maintenance.

Cultivars include:

'Buretti' has shorter rounded leaves that grow on short strong stems.

Related species:

S. pachyphyllum, jelly beans, has gray-green foliage in a jelly bean-shape with red leaf tips at maturity. The stem tips curve upward. (See color plate 8.)

S. sieboldii, October plant, has flat but fleshy round red margined leaves arranged in whorls of three and attached to slender, green stems. 'Variegatum' is attractive with an irregular yellow center and a light green leaf margin.

---

[17]   White or blue-gray coloring. This coating, called the "bloom" is composed of waxy substances which help the leaf retain water.

Senecio cruentus, S. x *hybridus*
Cineraria
Asteraceae or Aster Family
Bred from native plants of South
Africa
Light: High
Soil: Moist

Cineraria is a virtual mound of daisy-like flowers often in fluorescent and electric shades of red, fuchsia, purple and blue—yes, blue! The darker colors such as maroon and brick red are intense and vivid, also. The pale pastels of pink and lavender are easy on the eyes. Being in the aster family, the inflorescence is composed of outer ray and central disk flowers. (See *Chrysanthemum.*) Sometimes the vivid ray flowers are white near the base creating a striking ring around the center.

The dark green foliage is large and thin with ruffled margins. It is densely packed surrounding the flowers. This vibrant flowering plant always attracts attention. (See color plate 8.)

Length of bloom time: Cool locations are the secret to keeping cinnerarias for the longest time period—up to six weeks. In warm locations, the flowers last a week to ten days.

Temperature: Very cool temperatures, from 40 to 65° F.

Humidity: Moderate.

Overall shape: Mounded.

Texture: Medium.

Availability: Cinerarias are sold as a seasonal plant in the spring in 6 to 8-inch diameter containers.

Placement: Where can you find these low temperatures? One example is in planting urns near the outside entrance to a restaurant during the spring. Otherwise, use them as a short-lived but gorgeous flowering plant, perhaps grouped at a holiday buffet table.

Be aware that: These show-stopping flowers require high maintenance. Cinerarias wilt if the soil becomes the least bit dry. In most locations (warm temperatures, low light), the foliage quickly yellows and must be removed (This is not all that bad.) *Primula* or primrose have similar cultural requirements.

Helpful hints: This is a flower that may be purchased with nearly all mature buds. They quickly open when placed indoors. Since the inside and outside of the ray flowers may be different shades, buy a plant with at least one open flower to insure a proper color choice.

Related species: The following are foliage plants:

S. mikanioides, German ivy, is an attractive vining plant used as an alternative to English ivy since they both prefer cool temperatures. The leaf is similar in shape but larger and wider. It is very soft to the touch and on the eye. The three inch long leaves have five to seven lobes. The leaf petioles may be six inches long where they attach to the main stem. Medium light levels are best. Mealybug may appear in the leaf axils (the junction between the leaf petiole and stem.) It is a fast grower so pruning the vines may be necessary. Use German ivy on a totem for tall and narrow locations. Try this ivy for a different look.

S. rowleyanus, string of beads, is a succulent with leaves that are modified as round, pea shaped forms —three-eighths of an inch in diameter— and are attached to thin stems that resemble a string of pearls. The gray-green "beads" are glaucous (See footnote #17, p. 139.) and hang over the edge of the container and are best suited for use in hanging baskets. It also is a different looking plant suitable for a succulent or cactus garden. (See color plate 9.) It tolerates a wide range of temperatures from 65 to 80° F., low humidity and dry soil.

Sinningia speciosa
Gloxinia
Gesneriaceae or Gesneriad Family
Bred from native plants of Brazil
Light: Medium
Soil: Moist

This showy relative of the African violet was discovered first in 1817—seventy-five years before the African violet—and it became a popular gift plant in Europe and the United States.

The trumpet-shaped velvety flowers are vibrant colors of red, purple, blue, lavender and pink They may be solid, or bicolored with a white throat or spattered with a contrasting color and have a white picotee or a ruffled margin. In the 1970s, the flowers were bred for large size (double its previous size) while the entire plant became compact. The velvety leaves are huge and held horizontally in a rosette framing the flowers.

Length of bloom time: Two to three weeks.

Temperature: Intermediate-warm, from 68 to 80° F. are preferred.

Humidity: From 60-80% is preferred but 40-50% is tolerated.

Overall shape: Upright flowers with horizontal foliage.

Texture: Bold.

Availability: In 6 to 8-inch diameter containers all year-round. Miniatures are available, too.

Placement: Great in a board room or location where the beauty can be appreciated by all.

Be aware that: The foliage tends to be brittle and breaks easily.

Helpful hint: Some cultivars have more flexible foliage. But, still be careful when handling. Gloxinia is often grown locally and then transported only short distances.

Cultivars include:

'Plum' has deep purple flowers with a white throat. (See color plate 9.)

Avanti Series:

This series has flexible foliage. The brightly colored red, magenta, or purple flowers are extra-large and stand well above the foliage.

Glo Series:

'Gloxy Stars' has semi-double, frilly white petals with prominent deep red-purple centers. Other colors are available.

Spathiphyllum spp.
Peace Lily or Spathiphyllum
Araceae or Arum Family
Bred from native plants of tropical America especially Venezuela and Colombia
Light: From low to medium
Soil: Moist

The peace lily is not only one of the top sellers in the United States, but also throughout the world. It has been popular since Victorian days when it was known as the tail flower. It is a flowering plant to use in those low light interior plantscapes. It not only thrives in minimal light, but blooms.

The inflorescence, usually four to five inch high, stand like sails high above the foliage. Naturally, the peace lily blooms from late winter through early summer, but flowers are forced year-round. Many cultivars are known for their very long lasting bloom times. When the inflorescence is past its prime, it begins to turn green at which time it should be removed.

The bright to dark green foliage are elongated ovals with prominently indented midribs and veins forming a pattern. They are attached to short leaf petioles that attach to an underground rhizome (thickened storage stem.) New leaves are always emerging from the soil surface.

Temperature: Intermediate to warm, from 65 to 90° F. are preferred, but 'Sensation' tolerates as low as 40° F. and as high as 100° F.

Humidity: Moderate.

Overall shape: Rounded, as tall as it is wide.

Texture: Medium.

Availability: The 10 to14-inch diameter containers are the most widely-used sizes, smaller sizes are available, too. Some of the large-sized peace lilies are available in 17 to 21-inch diameter containers.

Placement: As specimen plants in hallways, corridors and well trafficked areas. En masse, as background plants. As table top gardens.

Be aware that: *Cylindrocladium*, a bacterial rot, is characterized by dark brown spots surrounded by yellow halos on the foliage with lower leaf yellowing and wilting. The roots rot and the plant dies. There is no treatment for this disease. Sterilize all containers before plant replacement. Pests seldom are a problem. Likely causes of tipburn are fluoride toxicity as well as a sensitivity to soluble salts.

Helpful hints: Keep this plant on the drier side to induce flowering. Be careful, because the entire plant may wilt but is easily revived when watered. And, who knows, maybe it'll produce blooms.

Cultivars include:

Miniatures: These plants are one foot tall. (In 4 to 8-inch diameter containers.) 'Annette,' 'Claudia,' 'Cupido,' 'Ministar,' 'Orion,' 'Princess' and 'Tasson'.

'Patrice' is an upright grower, great for small spaces. The inflorescence is held upon strong stalks.

'Piccolino' is wide and full with large white inflorescence.

'Sensation Mini' is precisely what it says it is—a miniature version of the giant size 'Sensation' cultivar. It has a very columnar and upright growth habit with wide foliage. The 6-inch diameter container is ten to twelve inches tall.

'Silver Streak' has foliage with a silvery-white midrib and veins. It is sixteen inches tall.

'Sonya' has a twisted spathe tip. The leaves are smooth.

'Symphony' has very attractive wavy leaf margins.

Intermediate: Roughly one and one-half to two and one-half feet tall and as wide. These are available in 8 to 10-inch diameter containers, sometimes up to 14 inches. Improved cultivars in this intermediate size are the fastest growing segment of the market. Many are upright growers, great for narrow areas.

'Alpha,' 'Calypso,' 'Connie,' 'Pallas,' 'Polaris,' 'Sparkle,' 'Tasson' and 'Taylor's Green'.

'Ceres' is twenty to twenty-two inches tall.

'Domino' is different with irregular, white splotched foliage. The colorful foliage is an important decorative feature since this cultivar has fewer blooms. (See color plate 9.) It is very resistant to chilling and heat injury.

'Emerald Swirl' has very attractive wavy leaf margins.

'Figaro' has a very wide look with dark green horizontally held foliage. It is a prolific bloomer with large, white inflorescence.

'Flower Power' holds its inflorescence high above the lance-shaped foliage. The large size, profusion of inflorescence and long-lasting quality are great assets.

'Hi Ho Silver' is a colorful variant of 'Ceres' with gray-green foliage.

'Kallisto' has large inflorescence held erect and high above the compact foliage.

'Lynise' is twenty-six to twenty-eight inches tall.

'Starlight' is a prolific bloomer with tough and durable, dark green foliage. It is on the smaller side of the intermediate growers. (See color plate 9.)

'Sunlight' is a prolic bloomer with the inflorescence held just above the tough and durable, dark green foliage. It is slightly larger than 'Starlight'.

'Textura' has an interesting leaf texture crinkled and resembling crepe paper—with strongly rippled leaf margins.

'Viscount Prima' is very floriferous with deep green foliage.

Sweet Series: All cultivars are multiple flowering.

'Sweet Chico' is a narrow form with full foliage. The spathes are held high above the foliage.

'Sweet Pablo' has the same upright shape as 'Sweet Chico' with large spathes. The foliage has a light colored midrib.

'Sweet Beniho,' 'Sweet Claudio' and 'Sweet Dario' are others in the series.

Large size: Roughly, three feet to four feet tall and as wide. Available in 10 to 14-inch diameter containers.

'Galaxy' 'Jetty' and 'Macho' are common cultivars.

'Grand Dad' has large ivory-colored spathes with large dark green horizontally-held foliage. The overall width of the plant is over four feet.

'Knockout' looks similar to 'Supreme' with more prominent leaf venation upon a very full plant.

'Maxey' has upright growing foliage. A good choice for narrow areas.

'Stephanie' has large inflorescence appearing slightly above the large and full foliage.

'Supreme' is a tissue cultured improvement of the old 'Mauna Loa' which has been a standard of the industry since its introduction in 1980. 'Supreme' has long and broad dark green leaves with prominent venation. This durable plant is wide and upright. The seven-inch wide, pure white inflorescence are held above the foliage on compact, strong stalks. (See color plate 9.) It is available in 8 to 14-inch diameter containers.

Extra-large size: These are over five feet tall and as wide.

'Sensation' sometimes even grows to the sensational size of seven feet and nearly as wide. This tissue cultured spath introduced in 1989 is known more for its large-size, leathery, very dark green foliage than its infrequent blooms. The foliage has very prominent depressed parallel venation along the midrib. (See color plate 9.) Wonderful for covering large atrium areas with enormous plants. It is the most heat and cold tolerant peace lily and is available in 14 to 21-inch diameter containers.

'Sensation Jr.' is columnar and upright, great for those narrow areas. The foliage is slightly rounder than 'Sensation' It is available in 8 to 14-inch diameter containers.

Strelitzia nicolai
White Bird-of-Paradise
Musaceae or Banana Family
A native of South Africa
Light: From high to medium
Soil: Moist

The white bird-of-paradise plant is related to the banana and is a lush, tropical looking plant. The entire inflorescence resembles its named bird sitting upon a perch. Each inflorescence has three white petals and a blue center protruding up to fifteen inches all emerging from a red-brown bract. The inflorescence appears near the top of the plant from spring to summer on mature plants that are four to six years old.

The enormously large—four feet long and two feet wide—lance shaped, glossy foliage grows on thick and fibrous leaf petioles. These long petioles overlap and form a flattened, woody stem resembling a palm trunk. Two plants grow opposite each other in a growing container in order to achieve a three dimensional shape. (See color plate 9.)

Length of bloom time: The inflorescence lasts for several weeks. But grow this plant for its lush tropical foliage, too.

Temperature: A wide range, from 60 to 90° F.

Humidity: From low to moderate.

Overall shape: Tall and arching, fan-shaped.

Texture: Bold.

Availability: In 10 to 14-inch and larger diameter containers where it is from ten to twenty feet tall.

Placement: In a large area where its true shape can be enjoyed by all. Alongside a pool.

Be aware that: Often, the foliage splits along the veins. Some clients like the way it looks, and others don't. Also, this plant sends up new shoots from the base. Keep these facts in mind when considering using this plant. Mealybugs and spider mites may occur.

Helpful hints: When placed in a high light area, lightly fertilize regularly. But be careful; this plant is sensitive to excessive soluble salt buildup.

Related species:

S. reginae, bird-of-paradise, is more versatile and smaller—up to five feet tall—with foliage one and one-half feet long and six inches wide. Mature foliage has a distinctive white midrib while the immature foliage has a red midrib. The orange-yellow and royal blue flowers resembling the bird's topknot of feathers, emerge from a beaklike red and green bract (modified leaf.) The inflorescence is six inches wide; smaller than its white counterpart. But these flowers are very conspicuous as they are borne upon a separate long stalk. (See color plate 9.) 'Mandela's Gold' has yellow flowers.

Streptocarpus saxorum
Streptocarpus, False African Violet
Gesneriaceae or Gesneriad Family
A native of eastern Africa
Light: Medium
Soil: Moist

This close relative of the African violet has similarly-shaped flowers. Colors range from white, bicolored, through dark purple, with the darker colors having smaller flowers. They extend beyond the foliage on thin stalks in a delicate manner.

The velvety foliage is smaller—one to two inches long—than that of the African violet but is very attractive with prominent depressions along the midrib and veins. The lush plants fill and gently spill over the sides of a hanging basket or container. (See color plate 9.)

Length of bloom time: Continual flowering occurs for several months

Temperature: Intermediate, from 60 to 75° F. If too warm, the foliage may yellow and flowers may droop. But also keep streptocarpus out of chilly drafts.

Humidity: From 60-80% is preferred but 40-50% is tolerated.

Overall shape: Mounded and trailing.

Texture: Medium.

Availability: In 4 to 6-inch diameter containers and hanging basket sizes.

Placement: As a hanging basket near a water feature. Added to a table top garden.

Helpful hints: Treat this as an African violet. Water with tepid water from below to avoid getting the crown and foliage wet. This will prevent *Botrytis* blight and leaf spotting.

Bavarian Belle Series:

‘Suzie’ has magenta-purple flowers with deep yellow throats and is a larger plant than others.

Olympus Series :

‘Sirius’ has velvety deep purple flowers with a delicate white netted pattern and picotee (margin.) Cultivars in this series have a more delicate and compact habit.

Related plants:

S. x *hybridus*, cape primrose, has flowers resembling streptocarpus and long, textured foliage resembling that of a primrose.

Syngonium podophyllum
Nephthytis, Arrowhead Vine
Araceae or Arum Family
A native of Mexico through
Panama
Light: From medium to low
Soil: Moderately moist

These plants have come a long way in recent years. The cultivars are mostly self-heading meaning that they are basal branching, do not climb and do not require pruning. The subtle colors of the foliage are soft and always a pleasure to look at.

These compact plants have all stages of arrowhead-shaped leaves growing, from the tightly curled brighter colored new leaves to the fully opened subtly colored leaves. Each leaf is attached to a long, strong petiole attached to the stem. The leaves are arranged in such a manner that they form a full plant from top to bottom.

The vining types, led by 'White Butterfly,' are also available on totems.

Temperature: Warm, from 70 to 95° F. Extremely heat tolerant as they do well in temperatures of 105° F. At the low end, 63° F. is the limit before chilling injury occurs.

Humidity: They do well in low humidity.

Overall shape: Upright, with leaves ascending outward.

Texture: Medium.

Availability: In 6 to 8-inch diameter containers.

Placement: As a colorful foliage plant on a desk or table. In a table top garden. As a taller underplanting for trees growing in a large diameter container. Growing on totems.

Be aware that: Mealybugs and spider mites are occasional pests.

Helpful hints: Water with tepid water. Cold water causes leaf spots.

Cultivars include:

'Glo-Go' has strong white venation on compact plants.

'Lemon Lime' has both light and medium green markings.

'Neon' has hot pink coloration.

'Pixie' has small leaves is a non-vining miniature that branches freely but remains compact. The green foliage has a central area of white.

Allusion Series: This series is prized for its disease resistance and a compact growth habit. They do best in the brighter side of medium lighting.

'Berry' has nearly pink leaves with pink venation.

'Bold' has a lighter green leaf with pink venation on larger, rounder leaves.

'Exotic' has a very pale green leaf with more pronounced pink venation on larger leaves.

'Exotic Cream' has red-wine colored leaf petioles and new foliage. As the leaf matures, the red blends with the olive green color to form a somewhat coppery color, so many different leaf colors appear on the same plant. (See color plate 9.)

'Maria' has pink leaves that fade to burgundy-green.

Butterfly Series:

'Pink Butterfly' is a compact grower with overall dusty pink colored foliage with a vining habit.

'Robusta' is a selection of 'White Butterfly' with dense, low growth that is reluctant to vine. The green foliage has a central area of white.

'White Butterfly' is the traditional vining cultivar. The midrib and veins are a very light cream color in the new leaves. Mature leaves have white centers with a thin margin of green.

Tolmiea menziesii
Piggyback Plant
Saxifragaceae or Saxifrage Family
**A native of west-coastal North
    America from northern Califor-
    nia to Alaska**
**Light: Medium, but acclimates to
    low levels**
Soil: Dry

This is a curious plant with new plantlets arising at the base of the leaf—looking like its name. The mature leaves are lobed, and light green with stiff hairs on the surface. The leaves grow to three inches across. The leaf petioles are flexible giving a soft, draping effect. Many plants are placed in each container. (See color plate 9.)

Temperatures: Cool to intermediate, from 55 to 70° F., but tolerates temperatures as low as 40° F. without chilling injury.

Humidity: Moderate.

Overall shape: Densely mounded.

Texture: Medium.

Availability: Hanging basket sizes, in 4 to 6-inch diameter containers.

Placement: In cool, dark areas. in a drafty location or close to an entryway. Hanging basets and shelf plantings in such areas.

Be aware that: This is a pest and disease-free plant.

Helpful hint: This is a durable plant with easy maintenance. Do not use leaf-shine products.

Veitchia merrillii, Adonidia merrillii
Adonidia Palm, Manila Palm
Arcaceae or Palm Family
Native plants of the Philippines
Light: From high to medium
Soil: Moderately moist

When looking for a tall palm, look no farther. These related palms are the ones people most often think of as typical island palms. The large pinnately compound leaves, up to six feet long, are bright green and leathery. Attractive green fibers hang down from the leaflet tips. The foliage reaches high above and slightly arch over.

The tall tan trunks have decorative "rings" which are the remnants of the fallen leaf petioles. Towards the top, the trunks are green. Since the foliage is large but not plentiful, these palms are often double and triple trunks. (See color plate 9.)

Temperatures: Warm, from 70 to 95° F.

Humidity: Moderate but tolerates low humidity.

Overall shape: Typical palm tree shape.

Texture: Bold.

Availablity: In the 17-inch diameter container, this palm is seven and one-half to eight foot tall plant. Larger specimen plants may be 15 feet tall.

Placement: The adonidia is used as a specimen plant often placed in large planters in atriums. Adonidias are also planted on either side of an indoor pathway giving a sense of enclosure to those who walk there.

Be aware that: The two-spotted spider mite is endemic to this plant. Apply a miticide prophylactically.

Helpful hint: When looking for large palms, there are many from which to choose.

Other tall palms include:

Hyophorbe verschaffeltii, spindle palm, has very long feather type foliage attached to orange colored leaf petioles. The narrow leaflets turn downward and give a weeping appearance. The gray trunk is architecturally interesting with its spindle shape, narrow at both ends and wider in the middle, and overlapping dried dark brown leaf petioles providing decoration. This palm is often found in the twelve to fifteen foot size.

Neodypsis decaryi, triangle palm, is so named for the prominent three-sided trunk. The long feather type leaves are also arranged in three rows creating a distinctive shape. Long fibers extend from the leaflet tips often to the ground. The trunk has a whitish cast due to a waxy coating. This palm is available as specimen plants usually in the twelve to fifteen foot range. It tolerates low light levels, rather unusual for taller palms.

Ravenala madagascariensis or *R. robustior*, traveler's palm, may be thirty feet tall with interesting leaf petioles that overlap and form a solid flat plane near the base. They consist of two rows growing opposite each other. They separate halfway up and then terminate into large leaves that form a matching fan shape overhead. These leaves grow to ten feet. This plant has another archtecturally interesting shape.

Roystonea elata, Florida royal palm, was named after General Roy Stone. How interestingly names come about. This tall palm has a slender trunk topped by a crown of dense, pinnately compound dark green leaves and may be thirty feet tall.

Trachycarpus fortunei, windmill palm, is tall growing—to thirty feet— with fused fan-shaped leaves and a slender trunk covered by many loosely arranged, dark brown fibers. The lower, older leaves turn brown and droop becoming part of the ornamentation. This palm is very tolerant of cool temperatures.

Washingtonia robusta, Washington palm, often twenty feet or taller, is used in large atriums. The palmately compound leaves are fused at the base and separate halfway up. Curly tan fibers dangle from all the leaflet margins in a decorative manner. The trunk gets progressively smaller in diameter near the top with brown remnants of overlapping leaves forming an interesting pattern. (See color plate 9.)

Wodyetia bifurcata, foxtail palm, is aptly named—the long feathery leaves arch and resemble a fox tail. The trunk is horizontally banded, smooth, pale green and flared at the base. The 21-inch diameter container contains a plant eight feet tall.

Vriesea **spp.**
Flaming Sword Plant
Bromeliaceae or Pineapple Family
A native of the Americas from
Mexico to Argentina, especially
Brazil and Guyana
Light: From medium to slighly
lower levels
Soil: Moderately dry

The *Vriesea* has been greatly hybridized with spectacular results making them widely used in the interior plantscape. When seeking out an eye-catching plant, choose one of these.

A brightly vibrant inflorescence (See footnote #2, p. 25) composed of colorful bracts arises from the center of the plant This single spike stays tightly closed and resembles a sword. The small and insignificant flowers arise from between the bracts.

This bromeliad has attractive straplike medium green foliage banded sideways with dark green gradually darkening to dark purple or black towards the base. These wide leaves are soft yet hold their shape well. The foliage gracefully arches from the base. What brilliantly colored, long lasting, easy maintenance plants.

Length of bloom time: Usually about three months of color is provided. When placed in low light, the color slowly fades.

Temperature: A wide range from 55 to 85° F., and can tolerate short periods of cooler and warmer temperatures.

Humidity: Adapts to low humidity although moderate is preferred.

Overall shape: Narrow and vertical with a wide base of foliage.

Texture: Medium.

Availability: In 4 to 6-inch diameter containers. 'Splenriet' is twenty-eight inches tall including the inflorescence. Others are ten inches tall. The foliage extends fifteen inches across.

Placement: Anywhere attention and drama is desired—at a reception desk, on a glass table, or in a restaurant. As a substitute for flowering plants. Although these plants may be more expensive initially, in the long run they are economical because of the long lasting color, durability and minimal upkeep.

Be aware that: These epiphytic plants—they have aerial roots absorbing nutrients from water, air and dust particles—may become top heavy and need to be weighted down to avoid toppling over.

Helpful hint: The *Vriesias* retain their color better than other bromeliads when placed in lower light.

Cultivars include: Most of the following are derived from *V. splendens*:

'Annic' has yellow branched inflorescence.

'Asahii,' painted feathers, has a large central inflorescence consisting of many red bracts blending with bright yellow at the tips. These bracts are pinnately ranked like a feather. Several smaller inflorescence surround the prominently centered one. (See color plate 9.)

'Barbara' has a bright red branched inflorescence.

'Charlotte' has yellow branched inflorescence with red centers upon red stalks. It is eighteen inches tall.

'Christine' has red inflorescence that is very wide and flat.

'Ella,' painted feathers, has prominent red bracts pinnately ranked like a feather. Small yellow flowers emerge from the margins. The wide and low growing lighter green foliage offers a restful pause. (See color plate 9)

'Poelmanii' has a bright red branched inflorescence.

'Solo' has a bright red inflorescence.

'Splenriet' has a bright red inflorescence. The foliage is banded with light and dark green. (See color plate 9.)

Related species:

V. rodigasiana is very similar to the red flaming sword plant but it is yellow.

Closely related to:

Tillandsia cyanea, a native of the Americas from Florida to Argentina, is small—growing less than a foot tall. The inflorescence consists of colorful bright pink bracts joined together forming a flat surface of color. Small but spectacular, electric blue true flowers arise from the bract margins. The silvery green and grasslike foliage gracefully arches from the base. (See color plate 2.) Tillandsias are notorious for losing all color when placed in low light levels. 'Anita' and 'Paradise' have three-dimensional inflorescence. 'Creation' has pink branched bracts with bright pink flowers. 'Fancy' is different looking with a most interesting bright, lavender pink inflorescence with numerous long and thin branches at nearly right angles towards the bottom advancing to sharper angles with the terminal one vertical. This is a larger cultivar with broad and prominent foliage.

Interesting fact: This aerial bromeliad is closely related to *T. usneoides*, Spanish moss.

Yucca elephantipes
Spineless Yucca
Agavaceae or Agave Family
A native of Mexico
Light: From high to medium
Soil: Moderately dry

The spineless yucca is an absolute favorite for its easy maintenance, wide range of tolerances and rugged and clean appearance. The woody, thick and rough barked canes support whorls of leathery, stiff and sharp sage green foliage. Each leaf is about two inches wide and three to four feet long. (See color plate 9.) Many forms of this plant are available.

This is a slow growing plant, so when ordering, request the height that properly fills its intended location.

Temperature: A wide range, from 65 to 95° F., although even warmer temperatures are tolerated. Chilling injury occurs at 40° F.

Humidity: Adaptable to low humidity.

Overall shape: Most commonly, as upright staggered thick canes with full heads of foliage. They create a full plant from base to top.

Other forms: Single plants grown as standards, some being cut back to allow multiple heads; low growing thick stumps with tufts of foliage; and a bush form consisting of multiple tip cuttings. Small tips are sometimes seen in table top gardens.

Texture: Bold.

Availability: In 6 to 21-inch diameter containers. The 10-inch diameter container contains 3 ppp. (plants per pot) with staggered heights of 5-4-3 (feet.) The 14-inch container contains 4 ppp. and may be eight feet tall and six feet wide.

Placement: A formidable presentation as a specimen plant or structural component in a large interiorscape. Among cacti and other succulents for a southwestern accent. Out of the mainstream of foot traffic.

Be aware that: Spineless yucca has sharp leaf tips and edges. Fertilize only those plants situated in high light areas. It also is somewhat tolerant of soluble salt build up but intolerant to fluoride expressed as tipburn. Usually, a pest and disease-free plant.

Helpful hints: The yucca plant is the high light level counterpart to the *Dracaena* and should be used as such.

Use a feather duster to clean the foliage. The glaucous (See footnote #17, p. 139) nature of the foliage is not compatible with the use of leaf shine products.

Cultivars include:

'Variegata' with a cream colored leaf margin. Contrary to most variegated cultivars, this is a more vigorous grower than the species. If water is splashed on the foliage, yucca leaf spot, which is fungal, may occur. It affects the variegated area first. The circular spots have raised fruiting bodies in the center. Often the spots merge. Remove those leaves and apply a fungicide.

Zamia furfuracea
Cardboard Palm, Jamaican Sago Tree
Zamiaceae or Coontie Family
A native of eastern Mexico
Light: From high to medium
Soil: Moderately dry

This is another easy maintenance plant with a wide range of tolerances. It is related to the ancient cycads with the same distinctive sculptural look. The large—five inches long and one inch wide—thick, waxy, elliptical, dark green leaflets are ranked along a two or three foot long leaf. It's interesting to note that the leaflets lack a midrib. They also feel like corrugated cardboard when rubbed; they have short brown hairs on the leaf surface. The foliage forms a rosette on a short, thick, fibrous trunk attached to an underground tuber. (See color plate 9.)

Temperature: Tolerates a wide range from close to freezing to 95° F.

Humidity: Tolerates low humidity.

Overall shape: Stiff and arching.

Texture: Bold.

Availability: In 6 to17-inch diameter containers. The 10-inch plant is two and one-half feet tall and the 17-inch plant is three and one-half feet tall.

Placement: As a specimen plant, a spot where it will be noticed. This is a hard plant to place among others due to its coarseness. Try it in harsh locations.

Be aware that: This is a pest and disease-free plant. It is very tolerant of excessive soluble salt build-up.

Helpful hint: Large attractive cones form in the center of even young plants. Remove them when they are past their prime.

Related plants:

Hybrids of *Z. furfuracea* and *Z. loddigesii* which has palm-like foliage are often sold as cardboard palms.

Zamioculcas zamiifolia
ZZ or Easy ZZ Plant
Araceae or Arum Family
A native of Zanzibar and other parts of tropical Africa
Light: Medium but acclimates to low levels
Soil: Dry

With a scientific name like this, it's easy to see why the common name is an anagram. And it is a durable plant with easy maintenance and a wide range of tolerances.

The leaves resemble the *Zamia* plant listed to the left, deriving its scientific name thusly. The thick, elliptical, dark green leaflets are only three inches long and one inch wide and many are smaller. The entire leaf is up to two feet long. The new foliage is attractively rolled up before its opens. All leaves grow upon very short, green, fleshy leaf petioles that become bulbous close to the soil surface. Many plants per container are used for a full specimen. (See color plate 9.)

Temperature: Tolerates a wide range from close to freezing to 95° F.

Humidity: Tolerates low humidity.

Overall shape: Stiff and upright.

Texture: Bold.

Availability: From 6 to 10-inch diameter containers; the10-inch plant is two feet tall. The ZZ plant is less frequently offered in the 12 to 14-inch sizes.

Placement: As a specimen plant. A great plant for harsh locations. Among desert-like plants. This is a hard plant to place among others due to its coarseness.

Be aware that: On rare occassions, soft brown scale may occur.

Helpful hint: If a leaf needs to be removed, just wiggle it back and forth at the soil surface. It just comes right off. This separation is where the underground rhizomes (thickened storage stems) and thick leaf petioles are attached. This plant tolerates overwatering.

Cultivar:

'Emerald Frond' is that shade of green.

Zantedeschia **spp.**[18]
Calla Lily
Araceae or Arum Family
Bred from native plants of African
**   rainforests**
Light: Medium
Soil: Moist

In the United States, calla lilies were originally grown as cut flowers or garden plants, and then moved indoors. The calla lily is both simple and elegant and is the classic art deco flower. However, it is not a true lily but has inflorescence that consists of a spathe and spadix. The tubular spathe opens at the top to become nearly funnel-shaped. It surrounds the short yellow spadix. The inflorescence has a light scent. Colors include white, pink, yellow, orange, red, red-orange, bronze and some bicolors. (See color plate 9.)

The elongated heart-shaped foliage may be spotted or mottled white and arches gracefully on thick and long leaf petioles which arise from an underground rhizome (thickened storage stem.)

Length of bloom time: The inflorescence lasts for several weeks.

Temperature: Cool, from 55 to 65° F.

Humidity: Moderate to high.

Overall shape: Tall and upright.

Texture: Bold.

Availability: They are available in bloom during the spring and at various seasonal holidays in 4 to10-inch diameter containers where they are from eighteen inches to two feet tall.

Placement: En masse in a container, or as a seasonal underplanting surrounding a containerized tree.

Helpful hint: In warmer temperatures, the foliage tends to turn yellow even before the inflorescence fades. Discard this plant when spent.

Interesting fact: In South Africa, where callas grow wild, pigs dig up and eat the rhizomes. Thus the plant is called "pig lily".

Cultivars include:

'Calla Stars' has an elegant white inflorescence with a prominent, pink-peach throat.

'Red Sox' is a true red color.

---

[18]   *Z. aethiopica* is the white calla lily and is a native of the Transvaal of South Africa; *Z. elliottiana* is the yellow calla lily with eye-catching foliage speckled white; *Z. rehmannii* is the pink calla lily. Numerous hybrids abound.

Zebrina pendula
Wandering Jew, Silvery Inch Plant
Commelinaceae or Spiderwort Family
A native of South America and Mexico
Light: Medium, but acclimates to low levels (variegation is lost)
Soil: Moderately moist

This is a colorful plant that goes in and out of fashion. It is very easy to maintain, and has many tolerances.

The pointy, oval leaves have two wide silver stripes that extend lengthwise. The underside of the foliage is dark green to purple. The leaves are directly attached to flexible and succulent stems creating a cascading effect. (See color plate 9.)

Temperature: Tolerates a wide range of temperatures, from 55 to 95° F. Chilling injury occurs with temperatures lower than 55° F.

Humidity: Tolerates a wide range.

Overall shape: Upright then trailing.

Texture: Medium.

Availability: Hanging basket sizes as well as smaller diameter containers.

Placement: Most often in hanging baskets or in shelf planters. Also as a groundcover or in table top gardens.

Be aware that: Rarely are pests a problem, although spider mites may occur. Older plants may exhibit fluoride tipburn.

Helpful hint: This durable and fast growing plant requires occasional pruning.

Cultivars include:

'Quadricolor' has metallic green foliage striped with red, light green and white.

Related species:

Z. purpusii has solid red-green to dark red foliage.

Other closely related plants (Sometimes listed as *Zebrina*):

Tradescantia albiflora 'Albovittata,' giant white inch-plant, is just that. 'Laekenensis Rainbow' has leaves that are predominantly white with a center streak of dark red-green. The undersides are dark red as are the stems.

T. fluminensis 'Quicksilver' with the majority of the leaf consisting of white variegation.

Index